PLACE IN RETURN BOX to remove this ~~item from your~~ record.
TO AVOID FINES return on or before date due.

DATE DUE	DATE DUE	DATE DUE

WATERSHED REDEMPTION

A JOURNEY IN TIME ON FIVE U.S. WATERSHEDS

DIANA HARTEL

Watershed Redemption, A Journey in Time on Five US Watersheds
Library of Congress Control Number: 2018911268
Copyright © 2018 Diana Hartel
Published by Madrona Arts Press

ISBN: 978-1-7327890-0-5 (pbk)
ISBN: 978-1-7327890-1-2 (eBook)

Cover and author photo: David Lorenz Winston,
https://www.davidlorenzwinston.com

Back cover photo: Lower Hudson River estuary and watershed; NYDEC,
https://www.dec.ny.gov/lands/5098.html

For more information, please visit http://www.madronaarts.org
To book Diana Hartel for a speaking engagement or workshop,
inquire at diana.hartel@gmail.com

Printed in the United States of America

To all who devote their lives to protecting and regenerating healthy river and watershed ecosystems and to the growing numbers who join in every day.

CONTENTS

Diana Hartel is at once a scientist, an activist, and an artist. She brings her deep compassion and sense of social justice to this story of five of our major rivers and the lives, including flora and fauna, that are a part the rivers' watershed. *Watershed Redemption* is a fascinating major feat of environmental writing from a unique person.

I first met Diana when she was a graduate student in environmental epidemiology at Columbia University. She was hired to analyze data collected by a fledgling HIV research program at Montefiore Hospital in Bronx, NY. It was 1985 and HIV was a new disease with no treatment, almost uniformly fatal at the time. The Bronx was an epicenter of HIV and the Centers for Disease Control funded us to study this disease devastating drug users, hemophiliacs, pregnant women and their babies, and sexually active people in places, like the Bronx, where HIV was common. I was a research fellow in Infectious Diseases at Montefiore Medical Center. Diana Hartel and I began a long partnership studying HIV.

Diana is still a scientist with a doctorate in epidemiology, and that perspective is one thread coursing through this book. Early on she taught me how to let the data show what was important and not to squeeze details that go beyond what the data can responsibly do. Her approach to analysis was tempered by the realities of the community we were studying, HIV and drug users. But with her facility for biostatistical analysis and data interpretation, she could find the major messages from our studies. Diana was always respectful of the data and she represented it with statistical honesty which made our studies more meaningful. Her book has this same respectful big picture approach with her stories of the rivers and the activists working on preservation and restoration.

After Diana left her faculty position, a renewed focus on the environment was in evidence. She expanded her perspective, especially through direct on-site painting of rivers and wetlands and by meeting environmental experts and activists. She also defended the Klamath River near her west coast home as she initiated a nonprofit group of environmentally committed artists to express the river's natural beauty midst its human-caused conflicts. The paintings themselves tell stories about the Klamath River. I began to hear stories from her about the Yurok Tribe and the salmon. The story went back thousands of years. It's clear that Diana understood, as she learned about the Klamath, that what was happening to this river and people who depended on it, was probably happening to other rivers, differing in specifics but with a common story of heartbreaking abuse and stalwart, intelligent defense. This was likely the beginning of a major new investigation that underlies the essays in this book.

Each river has many stories to tell. They are old. The Mississippi River sediment has been carbon-dated by 35,000 years. With each chapter we learn more about rivers and watersheds, each with a different emphasis and unfolding stories. When the American settlers staked their claim in the Upper Mississippi watershed, it led to the displacement of the Dakotas and other indigenous nations, who were forced onto reservations and decimated in staggering numbers. The Mississippi watershed drains two-thirds of the U.S., a major thoroughfare, and in many areas the river has been cemented over to accommodate locks and levees and dams. In other places branches of the river have been moved. Floods, toxic leaks and dumping have affected the health of the communities living on the river, fish and animals.

A thread of Diana's own family story unfolds in the Upper Mississippi watershed. Her forebears were among early settlers seeking a better life. The reality is a painful juxtaposition of the lives of the settlers and indigenous people in Minnesota where her great-grandfather had a homestead. The entwined tales add dimension and heartbreak, introspection, forgiveness, and honoring all who have died in the conflicts created by colonization. This particular essay also looks to hopeful multi-nation alliances to protect the waters, including the actions at Standing Rock to stop the Dakota Access Pipeline.

In Georgia, Diana kayaks a stretch of the Chattahoochee River's rapids amid tangled second growth forest. She has an adventurer's spirit and as readers we too experience the river as she does. It's here too, where the Center for Disease Control is located, that we are given a view of the historical foundations of epidemiology and how one investigates waterborne disease such as cholera, and water-related mosquito-borne disease such as malaria. Diana's discussion of the environmental issues of the Chattahoochee is inextricably linked to civil rights. She doesn't need statistical models to see the patterns. The river provides water to city of Atlanta, which then dumps its waste back into the river. Since the Civil War inadequate sewers overflowed with each storm spewing waste into river communities. In the 1980s the black neighborhoods of West Atlanta were inundated with fecal waste. Residents related how they had to close their windows at meal times to keep out the stench. Sewage protests in the 1980s led to a growing movement for the river in this southeastern watershed.

Throughout the book you hear about people working to stem the damage to the river and their land. They are all very different, brought to life in each *Watershed Redemption* essay. In the Rio Grande watershed, naturally occurring minerals include uranium, lead, and molybdenum all of which become hazardous when mined, milled, and used in manufacturing. There has been background radiation and heavy metal exposure for 1000s of years here, but recent and extensive uranium mining has increased the toxicity to the river, drinking water, soil, food ... it seems to be everywhere. This is where the Los Alamos laboratories developed and tested the atomic bombs before they were dropped on Japan in 1945. An important citizen action group, Amigos Bravos, brings together a strong coalition of environmental and social justice groups, including indigenous people of the pueblos. In a long-standing fight, they sued the Molycorp Mine in Questa, a major polluter, using the Clean Water Act, got the area designated a superfund site, and closed the mine. They have also taken action against radioactive waste from Los Alamos and many other polluters of the land and water.

Through the people we meet in these watershed essays, we find inspiration. Many spent decades of dedicated study and activism and fostered successes for the lives of all connected to the water flowing through watershed basins, into rivers, and sinking into groundwater. Though the dumping and leaching of toxic chemicals into the rivers and contamination of the land continues, the successes are worth remembering as we continue with our own sense of justice and even optimism for our collective actions. It is about the power of each one of us, working together, to right environmental wrongs.

Diana Hartel is a master story teller. In places the story is about the land or the animals and often about the intrusion of toxic dumping and the people who fight to stop the toxic dumping. It is about fighting unnecessary dams and faulty engineering of waterways, or how we stop abuses of the river to better it and the lives dependent on it. Other stories are about her family and her own work as an epidemiologist. The book is well written. The information flows effortlessly, in places building suspense, in other places providing reflection. The various strands are artfully woven together. *Watershed Redemption* is a book about action, the natural action of the river and the unnatural action of harming it. It is a call to action. Diana Hartel's book provides hope that there can be redemption.

Ellie E Schoenbaum, MD
Professor of Epidemiology and Population Health
Albert Einstein College of Medicine, NY

CHAPTER ONE

WE BEGIN IN WATER

DRESSED FOR A DAY ON the river, a group of 20 people follow behind an ebullient, long-limbed woman with greying hair pulled back into a spray of tendrils to her mid-back. Wearing a cobalt blue tank top and rolled-up putty-colored pants, Basia Irland leads us down winding, uneven stone steps to the river at the bottom of the Rio Grande Gorge 800 feet below. Some of us carry heavy blocks of ice molded into the shapes of books. Native riparian seeds, once common on the river, form the texts embedded in the ice books. Basia Irland calls her project "Receding/Reseeding," to turn back the receding, degraded riverbanks, to literally re-seed them. We watch the ice books, gleaming in their wobbly float downriver, slowly melting and releasing their seed messages of Rio Grande cottonwood, sheep fescue, and desert willow. Reddish-brown seeds on one book spell out "350" for the global average parts per million of carbon dioxide to which we need to return to abate global climate disruption. In 2016, even the Antarctic shot past 400 ppm, the first time in four million years. A Bighorn Sheep with her young, part of the thriving herds reintroduced to the Rio Grande, watches us unconcerned from a rocky outcropping.

Like Basia's ice books of native riparian seeds, the intention of this book is to plant seeds of inspiration to grow into watershed environmental actions. These stories of watershed protection and restoration gathered from around the country act as passage of a baton from one generation to the next. Embedded in these geological and ecological river histories are stories of people dedicating their lives to riparian wildlife, to clean rivers and wetlands, safe drinking water, and healthy ecosystems. The stories have beginnings but no endings; their continuance depends on who takes up the work next.

In this book, we hear voices of scientists and activists, of ordinary people doing extraordinary work. My own voice is present as well, for these watershed stories are personal, places through which I thread my own life as a biomedical scientist, artist, and environmental activist. My wish is to befriend, inform, and engage you, to bring you on this journey that matters so deeply to us all. The long-form narrative nonfiction essays in this book weave many threads in which the actions of watershed protectors shine like river pearls in a basket of harvested native river willow.

The Yurok Tribe of the far northern coast of California sees the earth as one circle with a river flowing through. That circle is the watershed. We live in the embrace of the watershed, that elongated ruffled bowl-like expanse of earth defined by the course of water moving from high ground to low, recharging groundwater, running down above and below ground, and returning to the sky in a vast cycle. Water is older than the earth itself, most of it created beyond the earth's current orbit before the earth was formed. The physicist Brian Greene tells us the story of water stretches back 12.8 billion years to about one billion years after the Big Bang, when the stars fused a great number of chemicals, including water molecules, in their fiery chemistry labs. While the embryonic planet earth coalesced from debris in what would become our solar system, its high temperatures and lack of atmosphere could not hold oceans of water. As things cooled down, and the atmosphere developed, comet and asteroid collisions deposited their far more ancient water and ice to become earth's oceans so that the young earth became covered in shallow seas. About 3.5 billion years ago, or 9.5 billion years after the Big Bang, oxygen formed by the earliest photosynthetic organism, cyanobacteria, bubbled to the surface of the water to form most of the 21 percent oxygen of our atmosphere. As terrestrial animals we breathe oxygen given to us by ancient ocean dwellers in a hydrosphere delivered to us from space on a small rocky planet we call home.

Water is far greater than us, ultimately unstoppable, yet we act as if it were otherwise. We dam it, divert it, tunnel under rivers, restrict it with concrete, run it into multi-branching, uncountable pipes and faucets. Our water constructions do not last without repair and replacement.

They break down especially when the economy fails as it does with increasing frequency. Our great dams and reservoirs are already filling with silt and may one day become unnatural waterfalls. Aging dams will burst, as they have so many times before, leaving bodies, debris, and ruin behind. As clean water scarcity grows, epidemics increase, food security drops, and poisons already in the watershed concentrate.

In conflict regions, such as some parts of the US-Mexico borderlands, the water infrastructure and all dependent on it suffer by its division and partitioning. Divided and fragmented wildlife critical habitat threatens the close to 7000 species of plants and animals of the Sky Islands ecology, an intersection of desert and mountain extending from northern Mexico through the US southwest. Nearly half the bird species in North America can be found in the Sonoran and Chihuahuan Desert mountains.

Water reflects what we do to it, carrying the consequences of our actions in the hydrologic cycle of the watershed around and beyond anything we construct. And water reflects the beauty of what we do. In some places, rivers flow clean, and the land around is vibrant with life. Things were far worse in the United States of America after the 1850s and prior to environmental laws such as the Clean Water Act. Over the decades since the act's passage in 1971, the movement of watershed environmental defense and restoration, wielding environmental laws, has blossomed and spread even into unlikely partnerships between environmentalists and religious fundamentalists, liberals and conservatives, Native nations and ranchers, hunters and back-to-the-land bohemians and hipsters. The stories of this book come from this resurgent collective action.

Winona LaDuke, an Ojibwe member of White Earth Reservation and activist in many spheres, speaks of a prophecy of her people regarding this time of environmental crises in which we live. In the prophecy, there are two paths, one well worn but scorched and one that is green. It seems obvious to choose the green path over the scorched earth, but it is not as familiar to us. We travel the green path almost as strangers, the green movement just a few decades old. Many of us have not experienced a fully healthy watershed, and dedicated research scientists struggle with defining it. Things are better in many places since the environmental movement and laws came into being, but much remains lost and destruction continues as well. We proceed through our love of the land and water, pained by its damage, testing the ground, correcting course with what knowledge we gain. It can be a slow process when we work to generate a new earth in which human needs do not dominate but have a place in the web of all living beings.

Without substantial change, we likely face massive global water and food shortages. Without change, we have only 60 harvests left to sustain the current global human population, given shrinking water supplies, loss of arable land, poor soil health, unstable weather, reductions in pollinators, and increasing toxins in water, sky, and land. Sixty harvests, or three 20-year birth generations, mean so many children, grandchildren, and great grandchildren may starve or die from lack of resource support. The effects of systems collapse, which unroll piecemeal at first, hit some groups before others. The impoverished of the world, those already living with prolonged drought, severe storms, and flooded coastal areas show the effects already.

Our die-off, partial or full extinction, would give habitat and restoration to other species that survive us. In Alan Weisman's thought experiment, *The World Without Us*, it would not take long, about a period of 200 years, for our structures to fall, for vegetation and forests to take over, and many animal species to rebound. Some change would happen relatively quickly, such as we have seen in the Chernobyl Exclusion Zone, over thirty years on from that nuclear plant meltdown. There the disappearance of human activity has led to resurgence of wildlife, including wolves, brown bears, foxes, boars, lynx, Eurasian bison, and an introduced rare species of horse. In spite of its long-lived radioactivity, wildlife researchers describe the exclusion zone as an unplanned nature preserve. Scientists who work on wildlife issues there say that we humans are worse than radiation for other species on earth.

The global dry biomass of humans, our collective weight after desiccation into a giant theoretical brick, comes to about 125 million metric tons for the year 2000. Biologists use dry biomass to make comparisons between species due to highly variable between species water content. In that same year, domesticated animal dry biomass roughly outweighed total wild vertebrate mass by 25 times, an increase of domesticated to wild of 3.5 times over the past 100 years, according to Vaclav Smil's extensive and cautious analyses. In mid-2018, the global human population exceeded 7.4 billion, and with it our collective biomass rose in sheer numbers and average individual body weight, along with domesticated animals, wildlife harvests especially aquatic, and ecosystem destruction to serve human ends. Our outsized boot heel on wildlife shows in the Living Planet Report of 2016: a primarily human-caused loss of a mean estimated 49 percent of all terrestrial and aquatic wildlife (total estimated individuals rather than species extinction counts) of the wildlife population living at the time of the first Earth Day in 1970. The numbers are rough as most total species counts can be slippery, but the overall message is not wrong. Some would call it a mark of successful evolution that our current collective biomass is greater than any single past extinct terrestrial vertebrate species. But we are a debtor species with our environmental debt going beyond the capacity of the earth to carry us every year. World Overshoot Day, a model-based inflection point at which we exceed our yearly resources, came on August 2 in 2017, earlier than any previous year. Being overdrawn at the global ecology bank every year means increasing ecosystem destruction and tragic losses of non-human life. It also means our "bank" shrinks every year while our demand for resources grows.

To understand what business-as-usual means in the future, the key factor is our population size and its attendant use of the planet's biosphere. A great number of studies make point estimates of over nine billion people by 2050 for peak population, possibly followed by declines or long-term growth rate stabilization. But multiple systems collapse and their interactions can be a multiplicative disaster. We could be gone forever, by our own hand, to join so many species of animals and plants we have driven to extinction. Or our species could go down to a few small groups in what are called population bottlenecks as is now occurring for wildlife species on what is called the red list or international endangered species list. Evidence exists for one such bottleneck for *Australopithecus africanus* as they transitioned into *Homo erectus* about two million years ago. Another more recent bottleneck, a long-term bottleneck of limited genetic variability, may have occurred in sub-Saharan Africa with population numbers as low as 2000 for as long as 100,000 years until expansion in the Late Stone Age. These numbers are rough, more based on calculation than hard evidence. But to go from what were undoubtedly limited early human populations to what we are now took adaptability, sufficient food and water resources, and relatively hospitable long-term climate conditions to bring us to our current 7.4 billion people. As I write this last sentence, the online World Population Clock rises by 100 (births minus deaths) in less than two minutes. It keeps ticking. We are already short on water and fertile land resources, and we definitely cannot count on hospitable long-term climate conditions. What remains is intelligent adaptability; may we use that for the good of all life.

Watershed health is completely entwined with our food web. Agriculture uses more river, stream, and groundwater than any other sector, 70 percent in global statistics. For California, 80 percent of that state's increasingly scarce surface and depleted groundwater goes to agriculture. Fertilizer and pesticide and animal waste runoff from agriculture also top the nation's list of water pollutants that enter water in all its forms, including wells. Food-related emissions from livestock to farming, deforestation, and food waste, constitute what Project Drawdown authors show as "the number one cause of global greenhouse emissions."

"Why bother?" asks Michael Pollan rhetorically in a 2008 *New York Times* article. He's speaking to apathy in the face of dire predictions for climate crises when "terrifying feedback loops threaten to boost the rate of change exponentially." In the face of the problem of too little and too late, Pollan urges us to plant gardens. There is more we can do, however, besides plant our hope gardens. The ever-optimistic Paul Hawken, editor of *Drawdown: the Most Comprehensive Plan Ever Proposed to Reverse Global Warming*, shows multi-authored action plans in every sector. We do not know if the nations of the world will enact these plans, but we do know that people throughout the world are already doing so much of it, and it's growing into a much larger movement. Plant a garden and join the movement for non-polluting energy and food systems along with clean water. Enter anywhere you feel passionate, caring, willing to defend what you love. Surely there is a river or stream nearby that you treasure, wildlife in forests and meadows you love, even the birds in your yard or at your windowsill.

We would like to see our descendants thrive in balanced and healthy ecosystems, with other animals that also thrive, in a land with diverse vegetation, abundant watersheds, and restored ocean life. We can let it all go to hell, not enact change as we take anything and everything we want, but that would soon mean human population decline. After that, it could be Weisman's world without us.

Before we carried Ice Books to reseed the Rio Grande, Basia Irland found communities all along the Rio Grande who agreed to pass a container of river water from the Rio Grande headwaters in Colorado to the Gulf of Mexico. Taking five years to complete, it brought attention to the plight of the river after it first failed to reach the gulf in 2001. These communities met one another, learned about the river that connects them, and still work for the health of their watershed. Each watershed story in this book places the work of water activists in the complex settings of their watershed, including problems of social justice, polluting industries, and powerful opposing forces. It is my belief that grassroots coalitions can be the most powerful force for the good of our watershed lives. Grassroots actions informed by history and utilizing the environmental laws and agencies for which we fought so hard.

Five distinct watershed regions were chosen for this book: the Pacific Northwest, the Southwest, upper to middle Midwest, Northwest, and Southeast. The selected watersheds are the Klamath from near Crater Lake to the Pacific Ocean, the Upper Mississippi from Minnesota headwaters to the tip of Illinois, the Lower Hudson from the Troy Dam, NY to the river mouth and harbor on the Atlantic, the Apalachicola-Chattahoochee-Flint from the southern Blue Ridge to the Gulf of Mexico, and the Rio Grande/Rio Bravo from Colorado to the Gulf of Mexico. Travel from one to the other comprises a circumambulatory circle around the Lower Forty-Eight and roughly the order in which I collected stories of watershed defenders and scientist.

As an epidemiologist, I have witnessed striking changes in human health and its inter-relationship within our watershed ecosystems over my lifetime. It is in the trends since the time of my maternal and paternal grandmothers, born at the end of the nineteenth century, and forward to the present that the changes are most vivid for me. In my life, from 1950 to the first model-predicted tipping points of 2030, the greatest potential threats to our species come as what some may call karmic payment for our hubristic, aggressive collective greed. It is a time for change, one way or another. Our lives are but moments strung together, like water flowing, merging into greater bodies of water, to the ocean, in endless cycles. Our time is both brief and long. It is our responsibility to remediate environmental destruction and bring vitality and harmony to the watershed and all its inhabitants.

Water defines the places we live, supporting our bloodlines and the uncounted brother and sister beings here with us through our profound interconnections. This book is our story, the one I have the honor to witness and co-create with all its difficulties, painful changes, joys and beauty. This shared story brought me to sit one night on a stone bench in Mount Tremper near my current home in Phoenicia, NY. The sky was clear and the stars felt near enough to touch. I was missing my father with a love edged in tears effortless as rain. My father worked as a meteorologist most of his life. He especially cherished the night sky just as his favorite hymn declares: "I see the stars, I hear the rolling thunder, thy hand in the universe displayed." It is all of us and greater than us, powerful and awe inspiring in its ongoing creation, even as we live in a biosphere heavily damaged by our unsustainable ways, our relentless burning of fossil fuels changing the global climate, potentially bringing a future of scarcity and strain. It is already a time of human-caused mass wildlife extinction with dozens of species going extinct each day. But we do not have to let the gathering forces of destruction determine the future of our species and all the species that remain. It is a time to reflect, and it is a time to act.

CHAPTER TWO

UNDAM THE KLAMATH

The Klamath

IN THE SPRING OF 2003, after a gap of nearly 30 years, I returned to Northern California in the Klamath watershed. My father had been diagnosed with a form of dementia that progressively blocks communication between his cerebellum and his muscles, starting in the extremities. Our relationship also had a form of dementia, full of disconnections with the past. To help my parents, I moved nearby, just over Siskiyou Pass from their home in Weed, California. Each visit to family was a journey from dense conifers and madrones in the Oregon Siskiyou Mountains, over the highest pass of Interstate 5, to the scruffy low hills dotted with juniper, Manzanita and sagebrush of my parents' home near Mount Shasta. Every trip there held a full view of the Klamath River, carrying the reflected sky on its way to the ocean.

Each trip over the river and along its banks, I felt a nearly subliminal scent of home, perhaps the way the salmon smell the minerals of their home rivers. Perhaps the dust carries microscopic remnants of junipers and scrub oaks to match my memories. In this familiarity, I found solace. When I returned to the Klamath watershed, the losses in my life were piling up: my mother-in-law died in the Bay Area, and, shortly after, my ex-husband's died in Japan. My sister's ex-husband burned down her home near our parents' place in Weed, after which he set fire to three other structures before he was arrested. My store of family trauma and heartbreak found resonance and kinship in the river, in its losses of old growth forests, indigenous homelands, the endangered lamprey and green sturgeon, short-nosed suckers, and the vanishing salmon. All 263 river miles of the mainstem Klamath, from its source in Upper Klamath Lake to the Pacific Ocean, called out to me. In time, the river moved into my life and I became one of the many voices to speak for the river.

In 2005, I became acutely aware of the battle over re-licensing of four dams on the Klamath River, the lowermost of which is the 173 foot Iron Gate dam near Hornbrook that I passed on travels to family. It filled me with hope that dam removal could bring salmon to reaches of the river that had not seen a spawning salmon for nearly a century.

Some of my relatives and many of their neighbors were against dam removal. Their arguments had a lot to do with settler pride of place, how we took this wild river and made it useful—building cheap hydropower, irrigating onions, growing potatoes for Frito-Lay, watering livestock. The arrival of my maternal grandmother's family in California in 1870 was an oft-told tale that was thought to give us our rightful place in the West. But the land had changed since then. The Sierras where they first lived now see decreasing snow packs. In summer, the rivers of the Klamath watershed where they later lived are too warm, its color neon yellow-green. In some years, stretches of the Shasta and Scott tributaries of the Klamath dry up.

It was at a California Water Board public hearing in September 2008, just two months before the Klamath settlement that included dam removal was signed, that I got a good look at settler pride in action. At the highway turnoff into Yreka in Siskiyou County, the moon cast long shadows from the statue of a bearded miner panning for gold beside his mule. Inside the meeting room, fluorescent tubes lit the stained walls of the conference room and its restless inhabitants. "Coho, Chinook, steelhead, Pacific lamprey, and green sturgeon could disappear from the watershed," a voice lamented through the microphone. Speakers defended the Klamath dams as "improving the river" and "fish like algae" and other inaccurate and simplistic forms of denial. Farmers and ranchers who spoke did not address the collapse of Native fisheries, or the deepening poverty and loss of Native diet of the river's indigenous people. For farmers and ranchers, higher water releases from the reservoirs for fish rather than farms brought nightmare images of empty fields and abandoned ranches. There were angry voices on all sides. But the speakers I found most difficult to hear were those with settler backgrounds like my own, proud of their place in the West and sadly ignorant of the plight of the Native people on the river.

Diabetes, an important indicator for the problems of Native people, began ravaging the people of the Klamath well after the Gold Rush ended. But the nineteenth century laid the foundation for the fisheries collapse—and that in turn caused the most important shift in the Native diet. There were, and are, many causes of collapse: stream-bank degradation from mining and livestock, deforestation and erosion, commercial overfishing, dams blocking river flow and access to spawning habitat, heavy water withdrawals and diversions, pollutants from agricultural runoff, drought and now global climate change.

But there is a larger story behind it all, involving Native displacement from ancestral lands and the breaks in cultural knowledge created when generations were forcibly removed to Indian boarding schools. Most important of all is the loss of the salmon at the heart of the culture. In pre-contact times, the Salmon Nation diet consisted of an estimated 450 pounds of salmon per person per year. Today, it's less than five pounds per person per year.

Ron Reed of the mid-Klamath Karuk Tribe remembers that his family could still fish and feed everyone as recently as the 1960s, when Iron Gate, the last Klamath dam, was completed. By the mid-1980s the Karuk found it difficult to catch enough salmon, lamprey, steelhead, freshwater mussels, and sturgeon to sustain their families. Acorns, game, and dozens of other foods were also scarce in the logged-out areas of the land. By the 1990s, Klamath coho were listed as threatened and spring Chinook runs were dangerously small. As fisheries declined, Native families increasingly filled their bellies with store-bought and government commodity foods—cheap starches, fats, and sugar. Chronic unemployment, despair, and addictions rose in the gap left by the vanishing life in the river.

By the 1870s, when my great-grandmother came to California, the indigenous population on the Klamath had already declined by 75 percent overall with some Native communities hit harder than others. The 6000 Shastas inhabiting the lands of the middle Klamath from Mount Shasta up to the Rogue Valley in Oregon numbered 100 by 1910. Infectious diseases arriving with early 1800s fur trappers and traders cut the Native populations in half; then the frenzy for gold in the 1850s brought the rest down to ¼ of pre-contact numbers. A century after the trappers, speculators, missionaries, settlers, and gold miners, diabetes, once virtually unknown to the watershed's indigenous people, stalked the descendants of the survivors.

Among the settlers, diabetes was known long before the Gold Rush. My own family has known diabetes for many generations that include my great-grandfather, my grandmothers, several uncles and aunts, and my father. Most recently, my sister was diagnosed with metabolic syndrome and insulin resistance—strong precursors of diabetes. One of my earliest childhood memories is of Grandma Nellie standing at the dining room table as she tested her urine over a flame. I watched as she pulled up her floral print skirt to a few inches above her knee and drew down beige woolen stockings to slide a needle into her thin thigh. Her chin was set, mouth firmly shut. "Your grandma has sugar diabetes," my mother told me. But I could not possibly link the word "sugar" to what I had just witnessed. That day, my grandmother's life seemed as forbidding as the mineshaft with fallen crossed timbers next to her mountain home.

Insulin injections kept Nellie alive in her tarpaper-shingled home in the mountains, far from medical offices, long enough to briefly know her grandchildren. These days, I cannot recall my grandmother's voice, but I remember her death. As I drew pictures on the linoleum floor of hospital hallway, Nellie DeWolf died of kidney failure and a diabetic coma in 1956. She was 65.

I believe that we—the settlers and their descendants—effectively introduced the spike in Native American diabetes rates in the watershed through disruption of Native culture, forcible colonization, and cruel assimilation programs. By far the most common form of diabetes for Native people is Type 2, which progresses from insulin resistance to full-blown disease. This is the form that is most strongly related to too much fat and sugar, processed foods, sedentary living, and prolonged stress. Diabetes is like the Japanese knotweed, fish infections, and algal blooms that proliferate unchecked in our disrupted watershed and its blocked waterways. Our bodies, designed to handle alternating periods of natural abundance and scarcity, cannot cope with the unrelenting, invasive plenty.

The pathways between insulin and the mitochondria, the energy organelles of the body, become overwhelmed and damaged. Endocrine disrupting chemical and reactive nitrogen compounds from agricultural runoff, industrial waste, and consumer products add to the internal chaos. There is no doubt that Type 2 diabetes is fostered by our way of life—poor eating habits and a sedentary car-centered culture, shackled by electronic media. Even the less common autoimmune Type I diabetes is increasing—not due to genetic shifts but to environmental triggers and cofactors. For the descendants of white settlers, the loss of food natural to our bodies is tangled up in centuries of migration and dislocation. We barely know what we have lost. But we know that as we gain weight with metabolic disorders and diabetes, fish species go extinct.

It is through the Native people on the Klamath that the deep roots of the diabetes epidemic are most clearly seen. Karuk Tribe medical records reveal a 21% occurrence in 2005, compared to 7% in the general population in the same age group. And all age groups, Native and non-Native, are still showing increases in Type 2 diabetes, especially among the most impoverished. Also, among similar Native nations, 55% of those aged 45 and older show pre-diabetes or metabolic syndrome—double that of the US population. Metabolic syndrome is a combination of medical disorders that increases the risk of diabetes along with kidney, stroke, and heart disease. While all the tribes on the river now have diabetes risk reduction and medical care embedded in their health services, the issues extend far beyond these sorely needed clinics. We also need sustainable local foods—thriving fish and farms in a healthy, restored watershed.

Melodie George-Moore, a member of the Hoopa Valley Tribe on the Trinity tributary of the lower Klamath, told me of a time when white soldiers had killed a great number of Natives in retaliation for a small number of soldier deaths. One tribal elder walked out to meet the soldiers carrying a notched stick—one side marked with the soldier deaths and the other with the much higher number of Indian deaths. He displayed it silently. The soldiers asked him to sign a piece of paper, so he made his mark, believing justice would be done. Instead, he was told he had signed away the people's land. It was an incomprehensible idea for him that was later violently enforced.

Violence is at the root of every broken place in the land, in the wanton extraction of metals, timber, and wildlife for short-run gain. It is at the root of the breakdown of communities and of dynamic natural cycles. In the Klamath River watershed, it left a land in which diabetes and its related cardiovascular diseases could flourish as Native food ecology collapsed.

Much as all Westerners, Native and non-Native, might wish this history away, we must face it together. We live in one watershed. In these times, we are easily disconnected from ancient life rhythms, our species evolving midst far older species of plants, insects, and animals that sustain us. Once disconnected, we can wreak havoc on everything around us. The diabetes epidemic that robs us of vitality, making us crave hollow substitutes for the true sweetness of life, is an indiscriminate killer. On the tribal elder's scored war staff, we need to include the uncounted lives lost to diseases of malnutrition in our disrupted landscape.

WHO WE ARE IS CHANGING

"You need to come to lunch with us; you need to learn about Tribal Trust rights" Troy Fletcher, the Yurok fisheries expert, said to Alice Kilham, a fourth-generation rancher from near Klamath Falls, Oregon. They came from opposite ends of the river, Alice Kilham from irrigators near the headwaters, and Troy Fletcher from 10,000 years of Yurok ancestors at the river mouth on the Pacific in California. At the time Alice was a Clinton appointee to the Klamath River Compact Commission, an Oregon-California interstate water apportionment organization acting at the behest of Congress for the Klamath Basin water issues since 1957. The Compact's original aim was to protect upper Klamath River interests, but in time those interests involved the entire watershed. Before the Compact Commission under Alice Kilham, Troy Fletcher had been working hard to create the sound science and meticulous records of Yurok Tribal fisheries. Later he was to become the Yurok's negotiator in the Klamath Settlement talks, fighting to remove dams and restore the river's in-stream flows to support the life in the river, especially the salmon. He was not the first to cross the divide from the river's salmon Native nations to the farmers and ranchers, but he was one of the most visible and respected at a time of extreme water crisis.

It was a conversation long overdue. In Alice Kilham's Klamath Falls, a city of over 21,000 without a waterfall due to the impoundment of the Link River, the federal government recognizes The Klamath Tribes—an amalgamation of Modoc, Yahooskin of the Snake, and Klamaths who inhabited the land of the Upper Klamath watershed for thousands of years. Their history remains deeply embedded in the Klamath River water struggle. Forced into ceding over 23 million acres to the US government in 1864, the tribal homelands were later distributed to settlers, the US Forest Service, the Bureau of Land Management, the Bureau of Reclamations, and the Klamath Basin National Wildlife Complex. The last members of the Klamath Tribes, after the Modoc conflict ended in 1873, were forced to take up residence on the reservation near Chiloquin Oregon.

In the beginning of reservation life, The Klamath Tribes built up successful businesses to become one of the wealthiest Native nations. Then, Congress revoked The Klamath Tribes' nation status in 1954, condemning a further 1.8 million acres of the tribe's land in the process. Not only did this nation lose sources of livelihood, but they also lost potential government supplemental health, education, and housing services that would be needed in the wake of The Klamath Tribes' termination. The loss of land-based livelihood from forestry and ranching brought deepening poverty, addictions, suicides, high infant mortality, and shortened lifespans. Reinstatement of the The Klamath Tribes came in 1986, but without the land base, Native foods, and forestry businesses that had once sustained them. Reservation land now exists in small non-contiguous patches totaling 308 acres for the 4,500 enrolled members, most of whom live off-reservation in Klamath County. Fishing and hunting rights, however, were retained with seniority water rights reserved for The Klamath Tribes, referred to as Tribal Trust rights.

In addition to The Klamath Tribes, there are five federally recognized Native nations downstream in the Klamath River watershed as well as the unrecognized Shasta Nation, all placing Native subsistence fisheries at the heart of their cultures. The Yurok and Hoopa Valley Tribes, in the lower river, also have federally reserved fishing rights. All of these fisheries would benefit from restored runs of Chinook salmon from historical habitat upstream from dams on the Klamath River. But agreements to share the water for farms, towns, industry, wildlife refuges, and aquatic life, especially endangered or threatened species, could not be made until the key settler descendants learned the untaught and erased Native history.

What brought everyone face-to-face in the past decade and a half were two signal events on the river. The first was a government-ordered shutoff of irrigation water to protect endangered fish runs in 2001 during an intense drought period. The second event occurred in the wake of water releases to irrigators still in drought that resulted in a massive salmon kill downriver.

The 2001 water shutoff to protect three endangered fish species of salmon and suckers brought angry irrigators to illegally turn the water project head gates back on. They cut the head gates with chainsaws, and thousands rallied in support. In a series of actions called *The Bucket Brigade,* farmers and ranchers from as far away as the Midwest brought buckets of water as tokens of their support. In one event over 200 men on horseback carrying flags accompanied an 11 foot metal water bucket to the front of the Klamath Falls courthouse where it remained until 2014.

The following year, with the Klamath still in drought conditions, high-profile federal political appointees turned on the irrigation head gates as a demonstration of faith to their conservative voting base. The result was a massive die-off of over 34,000 mature salmon in the estuary below the Trinity River. The fish crowded into the estuary waiting for conditions that signal their move upriver, but it never came. The low water flows and rising temperatures along with crowding in the estuary led to an epidemic of "Ich,"for *Ichthyophthirius multifiliis,* and related diseases causing the massive die-off and terminating the upriver spawn that would affect salmon runs for years to come.

Just when feelings against in-stream flows for fish, identified with the Endangered Species Act and Native rights, were at their peak in the wake of the 2001 water shut-off to irrigators, a Modoc named Jeff Mitchell went door to door to speak with his neighbors. He reached out then as he still does to bring about community dialogue. These days more neighbors are listening than at any previous time. Mitchell describes the time to which he was born, that of the tribes' termination and later restoration with hunting and fishing rights but the land gone. "We had a generation or two with tremendous guilt [for failing their descendants], using alcohol and drugs to try to forget, to cover pain and sadness of all our losses. But it was more important that we make something out of all this tragedy, this mess, to pull community back together." He felt that during the period of the 2001 irrigation water shutoff followed by the 2002 fish die-off, the irrigator and Native communities were on the brink of open warfare. Mitchell said their experiences of one another were mostly in court at the time, but he did not know the whole community, and he set out to change that.

The Tribal Trust and Native rights knowledge were crucial to Alice Kilham's leadership role on the Klamath Compact Commission. From Troy Fletcher (Yurok), Ron Reed (Karuk), Leaf Hillman (Karuk), Merv George Jr (Hupa), Ronnie Pierce (Non-Native Intertribal Representative), Jeff Mitchell (Modoc) and other Native leaders, Alice Kilham began to learn that rights derived from Native nation treaties collectively referred to as the Tribal Trust, take precedence over all other water rights in order to ensure in-stream flow for Native fisheries. Through court decisions and interpretations of treaty law, fishing rights guaranteed "in perpetuity" translate into in-stream flows and water quality for fish populations, especially those listed threatened or endangered under the Endangered Species Act. Since federally recognized Native nations are sovereign but dependent (that is, enclosed within the United States) nations in US laws, the decisions are based on nation-to-nation agreements, not local or state governments. For all her education and unique position as a liberal among conservatives, Alice confesses she was ignorant of Tribal Trust and much of the long litigious history of the Native people throughout the watershed. Her education began that day at lunch with Troy Fletcher.

Klamath River watershed with sub-basins from headwaters to Pacific Ocean.

And there was another force at work. Alice recalls a series of meetings she set up led by Bob Chadwick, a consensus-building mediator, who facilitated a shift in the people of the Klamath watershed. This was one of the greatest gifts of Alice Kilham's sincere dedication to peace on the Klamath. Chadwick asked everyone to drop their opinions and speak about who they really are and what they love. He carried out listening sessions, asking for what they saw as failures and as successes of the meetings, what consensus means on the Klamath, to envision accord. As they talked and listened, they grew to know one another. They cried together for the brutal treatment of Native families in which grandparents had been taken from family homes and forced into Indian school as children, for the loss of Native culture so entwined with the ancestral lands, for troubled children on both sides. And they wept for farm families scratching a living from the dirt, navigating countless harbingers of crop failure and personal financial ruin. They rejoiced with the births, graduations, and weddings, sympathized over illnesses and grieved over deaths in one another's families. They cried when two of the opposing leaders hugged, saying they were tired of suing each other. They listened and found their common watershed ground in one another.

Speaking of his changes through the Settlement process, Greg Addington said, "My friends accuse me of turning liberal." Greg is a dark-haired man of compact build in his forties. He comes from a multi-generation ranching family, hired by the rancher/farmer irrigators in the Klamath River talks. At the time of the first negotiations in the wake of the water cut-off, he headed the Klamath Water Users Association, representing 1200 farms and ranches. He speaks passionately of the life of a farmer who gets paid just once when his crop comes in. When there is a drought or the water gets cut off, there is no crop and no income. He spoke for irrigators and listened closely to all perspectives in the meetings. Even Greg Addington, for all his predisposition to listen and learn, admitted he grew up without knowing the history of Native nations. He says the problem for him was finding out our perceptions of each other were too black and white, but worst of all, not based in fact. He went on to sign the later Klamath Settlement agreement in the name of the irrigators he represented.

Another Upper Klamath farmer who completely changed his original position was Steve Kandra. As he neared retirement as owner-operator of his 100 year-old family farm, he spoke of his spiritual revolution, from hard attitudes to cooperation especially with Native people. He went from being a plaintiff in a lawsuit against Endangered Species Act designation of the short-nosed sucker and other fish to collaboration with Native nations and understanding of the importance of the Native traditional fisheries. The suit was later dismissed, although Steve had dropped out of the suit long before.

The third generation in his family to farm in the Klamath Basin, Kandra described how his grandfather was lured west a century ago by the promise of good soil and a reliable water supply, courtesy of the Klamath's federal irrigation project. But that water supply hasn't been as reliable as Kandra needs it to be in order to grow alfalfa and vegetables on his 800-acre farm. His kids came of age during the water wars of a decade ago and decided to take their chances elsewhere. This will make Kandra the last of his family to farm in the Klamath basin. Still he hopes others in the area benefit from this new direction of cooperation. "We're going to try to work things out together instead of trying to work things out by suing each other to death." And now Mexican-Americans are entering the picture as they progress from farmworkers to managers and eventually to owners. Kandra envisions future local fairs with salmon-potato-taco celebrations.

These cracks in self-images and beliefs, although painful, were necessary to creation of what would become the Klamath Basin Restoration Agreement (KBRA), the first ground-breaking agreement between 28 major groups in the watershed. It would be the first of many agreements and attempted agreements to come. It is not something one seeks without cause but through necessity. It takes courage to step past the history of genocide, broken and twisted treaties to create a new agreement with descendants of the settlers whose ancestors took part in Native dispossession. It takes emotional strength to feel deep remorse for atrocities against Native people. It is simpler just to say it wasn't me and it could not have been my kin who murdered or stole. Settlers and their descendants felt entitled to the land as sanctioned by the government. But bringing herds of cattle, setting up commercial fisheries and canneries at the mouth of the river, dredging the rivers for gold, logging off the forests, and homesteading lands acquired at gunpoint by the government proved in the end more lethal than armed soldiers.

Who we the descendants of the settlers and the Native nations are is changing. Lucy Moore, a mediator involved in early Klamath

River negotiations and Chadwick sessions says, "Battles of lawyers and scientists can dominate environmental water agreements leaving locals out unless they are given a chance to reach their own positions. At times mediation does not produce agreement, but it produces people who see one another as humans, as having a legitimate say. Then the next steps can bring resolution with this grounding as happened on the Klamath."

Steven Jay Gould and Niles Eldridge have a theory of evolution they call punctuated equilibrium. They say that species stay the same throughout long periods of time, until major events disrupt patterns. Then sharp turns in evolution can occur in a short amount of time. On a human spiritual level, I recall asking John Daido Loori, founder of Zen Mountain Monastery in New York, if it takes just as long to clear delusions as it takes to build them. He replied, "I knew a stone carver who could hit the exact spot in a rough stone to open it rather than slowly chipping away." Evolutionary pressure of the Klamath conflict and finding the right spot to break open to consensus and peace has occurred here and can occur again.

Jeff Mitchell believes we are now at a broader turning point, where everyone needs to look each other in the eye and speak, to establish basic relationships and understanding of one another. How much of that has happened? He says, "For the leadership it has happened, but the whole community, while moving in that direction, has not yet embraced it. . . . The latter takes time, and the turning point hinges on recognition that nobody is going anywhere, so how are we going to get along?"

OREGOS

At the mouth of the Klamath stand two unique rock formations called Oregos or Sister Rock. Depending on the location of the break in the sandbar at the river's mouth, one or the other guardian rock is awake. Legend holds that the Spirit Oregos liked people so she decided to be a huge rock at the mouth of the Klamath River. Her job each year was to tell the fish when they should leave the ocean and head upriver. And so, each year, Oregos guides the smelt and candlefish upriver where the people net them. They are so oil-rich that they can be burnt as a candle for light. Then in the spring she sends up the cutthroat trout, followed by the giant green sturgeon, and in summer she calls in the first salmon runs, then the steelhead run, followed by the silver salmon, and in winter the Pacific lamprey. Or so the legend goes.

Will the future leave Oregos with no fish to guide? In 2017, only 11,000 Chinook were estimated to be on their way to the Klamath and its tributary the Trinity, the lowest run on record. The severe decline results from two consecutive juvenile fish disease outbreaks, ongoing water diversions, dams still in place, drought, and poor feeding conditions in the ocean. Subsequently, the 2017 fall and winter Chinook fishing seasons were closed. Dan Bacher of Fish Sniffer Magazine points out another factor—misappropriation of $32 million in Bureau of Reclamation funds given to Klamath irrigators rather than to system improvement to benefit fish and wildlife, including screens to prevent fish deaths. The Bureau has no mechanism to address this theft, and the alternative may be lawsuits—again. Things continue toward the cliff edge, and time is running out to enact our hard-won written agreements.

Petey Brucker, an attendee of the Kilham-Chadwick Klamath Compact sessions, carries a long thread of Klamath environmental history in his life. He had been working for environmental issues from the beginning of his time in the watershed in the early 1970s, later to become the first designated Klamath Riverkeeper, a position created through the national organization of the Waterkeeper Alliance. Hundreds of rivers throughout North America have sustained protection through Waterkeepers, citizens who monitor water and watershed wildlife violations, and who pursue enforcement when needed.

Peter Brucker and his partner Geba Greenberg once lived at Black Bear Ranch, an 80-acre intentional community founded in 1968 in Siskiyou County about 25 miles from the Forks of the Salmon. The back-to-the-land idealist hippies, many coming from the East Coast, were a new brand of settler, not interested in pursuit of personal wealth and power. But they were naïve, impoverished in local knowledge and survival skills. Their undisguised admiration for the local Karuks brought a few Native friendships in the beginning, although not all Karuk saw it that way. At least the Black Bear young people seemed harmless and thus tolerated. Their relationship grew and matured over time to become one of the most important activist teams of Klamath Riverkeeper and the Karuk Tribe.

Geba tells a story to illustrate that unique early time at Black Bear. One icy winter night there were visitors at the door, local Karuk who were friends of the residents of Black Bear. They brought Geba and some others out to Ishi-Pishi Falls. It was and still is a sacred place for the Karuk—the outside public not permitted to enter. Geba took her turn on the icy rocks hearing only the roaring falls as she felt for the presence of the Pacific lamprey, somewhere in the dark waters below. She pulled in one, then two, until she had 30 in her basket. Each man took a turn. They returned through the forest with heavy baskets on their backs. After the salmon feed the Karuk people in the fall, the smoked salmon and the lamprey kept them alive in the coldest months. It was in this way Geba came to know the gift of the winter river, and the importance of local Native fisheries she and Petey endeavored to protect ever afterwards.

Standing outside in bare feet, temperatures in the 30s, Petey spoke to me in non-stop detail about his activist life, beginning with the Klamath Forest Alliance. He credits Felice Pace, founder of that group, as his life-long mentor. At this time, Brucker's focus is on the declining wild spring Chinook and the cooperative effort to restore them. He is angry with the EPA for its refusal to list the spring Chinook as endangered even though their numbers could be less than 2000 in some years. The spring Chinook are now under consideration for endangered species listing, joining their listing on other west coast rivers. He is tireless in the neighbor-to-neighbor effort to unite Native people, loggers, ranchers, and federal employees outside of their official roles. Together they have voluntarily stopped 80% of spring Chinook takes to save this local species.

Petey is so tall I have to tilt my head to watch his bearded mouth open in broad laughter. He composes activist music like the Iron Gate Dam song, and stages salmon fishery dramas. One year he rode a Redwood log around the whole country to let people know the plight of these deep, forested river canyons. Never deterred, he has endured more than one forest fire while dug in below a fire tent. These days younger people are taking his place at the helm of local environmental groups; some of them children of Black Bear, including a Klamath Riverkeeper successor, Erica Kate Terrence. And they work with the Karuk Tribe in a powerful alliance.

Petey brought me to the bridge at Forks of the Salmon in the Klamath watershed where a female Chinook was slowly finning, angled to the current. Here the river spread over gravel shoals before curving into steep canyons covered in firs, pines, madrones, and alder. It picks up speed past water-carved rocks, crashing down Class VI rapids at Ishi-Pishi

Falls to the estuary 90 miles away. Weeks ago, this salmon waited in the estuary for the right water temperature and flow. Then she swam over rapids and riffles, shot up Ike's Falls below the confluence of the Klamath and the Salmon Rivers, resting at times in pools beneath fallen snags to arrive at this bridge, the place of her birth and final spawn. Her tail white-spotted, injured in digging a gravel nest to just the right depth, slowly fans in the clear water. Though exhausted, this effort to remain by the nest is her last gift to the future young fry. With luck she would become food for the insects that would later feed her young. Time could be shortening for her species unless we take strong, intelligent action.

PEACE WITH MY OWN SETTLER LINEAGE

As my father came to have increasing bouts of illness, non-linear struggles with limited mobility, we stopped re-opening the old wounds. It did not mean pretending the unpredictable rages of a young father never happened. But we came to see one another in a new light, that of the present through our mutual love. It took a lot longer for me to make peace with the shame I felt in my settler lineage. The opportunity for new insight into that heritage came when my mother brought me three small black notebooks. There was a hint of dry rot in the binding from where they had been lodged undisturbed in the attic for many years. "These are your Grandma Nellie's from when she was young," said my mother and added, "This is a side of my mother I never knew."

Nellie Shifley Dewolf's 1906 Northern California diary entries bore no resemblance to the woman near the end of her life I knew as my grandmother. The markings of her pen were round and free, lacking pretense. Below each date she inscribed a list—rain in the morning, grade for algebra, jump over a picket fence, walk to town. It took 2 ½ pages to take a train trip from Northern California to Bucyrus, Ohio to visit relatives, an uninterrupted succession of mountain and river views, names of uncles, aunts and cousins, apple pie, taters, turkey and biscuits, then more window views back to California.

In the diaries I met a young woman filled with love for the mountains and rivers of the West. She noted moonlit picnics, walks to the tops of hills to meet the sunrise, hikes in mountains, camping beside mountain streams. Life was harder then in their drafty mountain cabin, but it was filled with joy, beauty, and wonder, love of friends and family. This sudden rift in the story of my ancestral line was more than disconcerting. It threw into question all my dog-eared family stories and oft-fingered explanations of who I am. My grandmother's love of the mountains, the fog she called "the grey lady," and all the wild creatures of the land resonated with my own deep love of this land. And I realized this is what we share and what we love best whatever our path, profession, and lineage, disagreements, or difficult history.

And like my grandmother, I have explored the watershed. Once I arrived in Weed to help my parents, I walked and rode all through the Klamath watershed from headwaters up by Crater Lake to the mouth at Requa. I have gloried in the diverse colors and textures of boulders, and knots of volcanic stone, veins of serpentine, rocks of pink and bluish-purple, light grey fossils, and red-brown stone. Like my grandmother, I see how the fog that rolls through the canyons and valleys graces the land. And reaching out toward the river from the rocky soils, I am nourished by the sight of the orange-to-pink curving limbs of the broadleaf evergreen madrones that feed winter wildlife, their red berries atop yellow-green to deep olive green leaves.

Most of all I love the living river. As the river moves from high desert of its headwater lakes, it cuts into canyons on its way to the sea, oak and juniper, followed by conifer and broadleaf evergreen forests changing to inter-montane meadows, then becoming the redwood and Doug fir forests and cypresses of the coast. All through this land, from high desert to ocean, the river races past water-carved boulders, leaps gravel piles, and flies down semi to totally un-navigable waterfalls. In the estuary there is the ever-changing sandspit, flanked on both sides by Oregos, the sister rocks that direct the movement of salmon into the estuary. On the ocean side, grey whale cow and calf pairs can be spotted migrating after the larger whale pods.

This love of the watershed is our lifeline that inspires us to make the difficult changes we need to make to find accord, consensus and peace on the river.

KLAMATH SETTLEMENT AND ITS AFTERMATH

In January 2008, the Klamath Settlement Group, which included representatives of tribes, irrigators, ranchers, fishing associations, government agencies, environmental and conservation groups, offered a proposal for public review—a comprehensive plan to restore the watershed. During the years of Settlement meetings, and after the Chadwick sessions, more people joined and continued to create lasting friendships across the disparate groups. They sat in motel meeting rooms learning of births of grandchildren, divorces, graduations, river ceremonies, festivals, the deaths of parents and friends. And in their new relationships they found a way to restore the Klamath. As Roger Smith, a biologist with Klamath Falls Fish and Wildlife, put it: "It is beyond my wildest dreams."

Well into the Settlement negotiations, one important signature was missing—PacificCorp, the company that owns the dams. It is a subsidiary of Mid-American Energy Holding Company, itself an affiliate of Berkshire-Hathaway Inc., which is run by one of the world's richest men, Warren Buffett. PacifiCorp removed itself from Settlement talks because it was seeking 50-year renewals on dam licenses that expired in 2006, a key issue in the restoration.

Native nation members and environmental activists traveled together to protest at Berkshire-Hathaway public meetings. Merv George, Jr. brought his Brush Dance regalia and hitched up a trailer to carry his family's antique redwood canoe to Buffett's headquarters in Omaha, Neb. Few were allowed to address Buffett. Merv George's wife, Wendy, spoke to an image of Buffett's face on theater-sized conference screens. She sobbed as she asked him to remove the dams. "Sir, I have heard you are kind. The dams are killing the fish and destroying my people's way of life." The enormous Buffett lips asked if she had finished, then explained utility company politics as if to a child. Even *Forbes Magazine* wondered how he could be so heartless. Surely this monetary Great Oz presiding in the Midwest could do something.

But nothing was done until the dams became too expensive to renew. One of the oldest forms of life on earth held a key. Farmers, ranchers, fishermen, and reed gatherers call it an algal bloom, but its real name is cyanobacteria—a photosynthesizing single-cell organism over three billion years old. Over the past few decades, cyanobacteria has shown up with increasing frequency in livestock watering holds and irrigation ditches. It forms thick mats in the reservoirs. And along the river, in the summer months of dusty pine scents, the acid-green mats pile up below the willow-covered riverbanks. With its seasonal appearance, hazard signs are planted along the river. Its decay byproducts poison dogs and wildlife that drink the water or swim in it, and injure human skin, liver, and brain tissue.

Cyanobacteria thrive in the warm artificial lakes, low-flow waters, and agricultural run-off of the dammed and diverted river. Klamath Riverkeeper and Native ceremony leaders sued PacifiCorp for fostering the toxic blooms—and won. The process of re-licensing the dams was terminated in 2009. Even if the dams could have been re-engineered for fish passage as required by law, it would not have stopped cyanobacteria. In the end, PacifiCorp joined the Settlement, saying the dams were too expensive to fix. Cyanobacteria was not named in the final PacifiCorp documents but it certainly lurked there, hidden in the torpid, stagnant language of the relicensing paperwork.

On Feb. 19, 2010, the then Interior Secretary Ken Salazar, PacifiCorp, the governors of Oregon and California and the Settlement representatives signed the Klamath Basin Restoration Agreement (KBRA). It pledges to restore and sustain natural fish species throughout the Klamath, maintain water for the National Wildlife Refuge, establish reliable water and power supplies for agricultural and community use, and develop the sustainability of all Klamath Basin communities. On May 5, the California Public Utilities Commission added its voice, recommending removal of the Klamath dams to help restore salmon and other fish species at risk.

The greatest impediment at the moment takes shape in the form of a strongly anti-environment, pro-elite business US Congress. As in so many places in the United States now, action is in the hands of locals and local organizations. For the Klamath, it all moves forward with the states of California and Oregon, along with county and city local governments, agencies, environmental groups, and all the voices and stakeholders of the Klamath who have worked and continue to work so hard for agreement.

Immediate help comes from the alliance of the Karuk Tribe and Klamath Riverkeeper on the Shasta River watershed sub-basin, where my parents once lived at Lake Shastina reservoir. A lawsuit settled out of court by Klamath Riverkeeper and the Karuk Tribe ended in a 2013 agreement for higher flows and better water quality on the river. The agreement includes changes to the operation of Dwinell Dam and Lake Shastina to curtail the illegal "take" as decimation of Southern

Oregon/Northern California Coast Coho salmon, a species unit listed under the Endangered Species Act. The agreement lays out the required allocations of water coming from Lake Shastina into the Shasta River system. Improvement to this historically important salmon spawning habitat is one of many needed for salmon critical habitat. According to Karuk Tribe spokesman Craig Tucker. "We're happy it's worked out the way it has; we believe we'll see an immediate benefit to fisheries and ensure irrigators have water." This agreement bears the stamp of the many consensus and agreement sessions preceding it in its consideration of both fisheries and farms.

Felice Pace, ever at the leading edge of environmental activism whether others agree with him or not—and many do not, outlines some of what remains. While all agree the four mainstem river dams, Iron Gate, Copco I and II and JC Boyle, will be removed beginning in 2020, Felice Pace offers an idea that has been neglected:

> *"Completely lost in the conflict is a potential win-win. Farmlands within the bed of the former Lower Klamath Lake, once even larger than Upper Klamath Lake, were created by draining and shrinking the lake in the early twentieth century. But the land is salty and so it can only be used to grow grain or for pasture, two agricultural activities that do not produce the high yields and income row crop growers in the bed of the former Tule Lake obtain.*
>
> *"Restoring Lower Klamath Lake would provide wildlife benefits, including expanding scarce stopover for Pacific Flyway birds, and would clean the Klamath Irrigation Project's highly polluted agricultural wastewater before that water reaches the Klamath River. Restoring the lake would also provide additional winter water storage and help eliminate deficits in water supply that have plagued the Klamath River Basin for decades."*

Can we do this? Expect either continued neglect or a storm of opinions, a few lawsuits, and consensus meetings to come. The groundwork is already in place.

WE RENEW THE WORLD

There are among us those who speak against ecosystem destruction, natural resource poverty, and diseases brought on by the history of violence, who cry out for their people, moved forward by the waters of truth and compassionate justice. In 10,000 years and 500 generations of Native grandmothers on the Klamath, there is one named Geneva Mattz. She was born in 1903 in the town of Requa/Requoi at the mouth of the Klamath not long after my maternal grandmother was born in 1891. My grandmother loved the land and rivers but had no awareness of the Native struggles of the watershed, and surely never heard of Geneva Mattz. My grandmother notes in her diary that her mother gave socks to "Indian Mary" but she wrote little else about Native people still living nearby.

In the 1970s, Geneva's sons took a case for tribal fishing rights to the US Supreme Court and won. The ruling was ignored by the US Fish and Wildlife Service, which issued a ban on fishing in the Klamath estuary. Native fishermen, the Mattz family among them, dipped hooks capped with corks into the river in protest, not taking any fish. Emery Mattz, Geneva's husband, was arrested. On hearing this, Geneva and her daughter went out in a rowboat. It was autumn, peak of the Fall Chinook run. The estuary that ordinarily would be filled with cormorants, pelicans, ocean-fattened salmon, and fishermen was instead populated with federal agents in riot gear and powerboats. The agents tried to grab the fishing net of Geneva's daughter and Geneva became frightened. According to her granddaughter, "She stood up in the boat and held her arms up and sang," As she sang out her prayer, a great flock of birds came flying very close all around her. Carried by the water, her powerful prayer pierced the federal agents' hearing, striking fear in their hearts. The men in riot gear fled.

Geneva's great song has never been stilled. Her great faith in crisis carries into the work on the Klamath dam removal and restoration. The entire decades-long process in its multiple hues of opinion, debate, negotiation, legal actions, and consensus—interim and longterm—moves forward on her endless prayer.

At the age of 53, Troy Fletcher died in 2015 without seeing the dam removal and restoration he fought so hard to obtain for his Yurok nation and others on the river. He died a few months after Bob Chadwick, who believed all people at heart have a deep wish for consensus. The spirits of Troy Fletcher and Bob Chadwick join Geneva's spirit to inspire all those who work for the harmony and health of the Klamath watershed, regardless of ancestry or past ignorance. Joined with them is the spirit of Ronnie Pierce, a non-Native environmental engineer, who died in 2005. According to Merv George, Jr. of the Hoopa Valley Tribe, Ronnie taught everyone on the river the intricacies of fisheries biology and Native fishing rights. Let us join together in gratitude to all who have worked together here, the living and those who have died. And we honor those we do not yet know who will take up this honorable work and sacred trust.

As the work on Klamath and its living species continues, no timeline can ever be complete, but this one covers 1849 through the end of 2017.

∼

KLAMATH RIVER CHRONOLOGY

Excerpted from Water Education Foundation on December 22, 2017, http://www.watereducation.org/aquapedia/klamath-river-basin-chronology.

1849-50 Gold discovered in the Lower Klamath Basin. Farms and ranches established in the Scott and Shasta valleys.

1855 Klamath River Reservation established on the Lower Klamath River.

1864 Hoopa Valley Tribe and Klamath Tribes cede most of their lands for settlement but retain large reservations.

1868 Two farmers dig first irrigation ditch in the Upper Klamath Basin.

1888 California state court rules Klamath River Reservation abandoned, opening the lower river to non-Indian commercial fishing overseen by the state of California.

1891 Determination that the Yurok Tribe had abandoned its reservation is reversed and the old Klamath River Reservation is attached to the Hoopa Valley Reservation.

1905 Klamath Project authorized.

1907 First deliveries of water through Klamath Project "A" Canal.

1908 President Theodore Roosevelt creates nation's first wildlife refuge for waterfowl, the Klamath Lake Reservation—now called Lower Klamath National Wildlife Refuge.

1917	First opening to homesteaders of land in Klamath Project.
1918	The first dam in the Klamath Hydroelectric Project, Copco 1, becomes operational, ending salmon runs in the Upper Klamath Basin.
1921	Link River Dam completed, allowing control of water releases from Upper Klamath Lake.
1925	Copco 2 Dam becomes operational.
1928	Dwinell Dam constructed on the Shasta River, cutting off most spawning habitat to the largest Klamath Basin salmon run.
1928	Tule Lake Bird Refuge (now Tule Lake National Wildlife Refuge) created.
1933	Commercial salmon fishing on Klamath River is banned; tribal gill-net fishing is prohibited.
1954	Congress terminates the Klamath Tribes' federally recognized tribal status and liquidates its reservation lands.
1956	Klamath Project irrigators' electricity rate contract is renewed for 50 years at the 1918 rate of 0.6 cents per kilowatt-hour; Oregon "off-Project" irrigators sign a contract for power at 0.72 cents per kilowatt-hour.
1957	Klamath River Basin Compact is approved by California and Oregon legislatures and ratified by Congress.
1958	Big Bend Dam—later J. C. Boyle Dam—is completed upstream of the Copco dams.
1962	Iron Gate Dam completed.
1963	Lewiston Dam on the Trinity River completed.
1964	Large flood on Klamath River and tributaries causes debris to block channels—a problem that persists today.
1964	Kuchel Act precludes future homesteading on refuge land; provides for continued leasing of refuge land for farming to the extent it is consistent with refuge purposes.
1965	Keno Dam constructed to replace Needle Dam on the Klamath River.
1971	Lost River and shortnose sucker identified as species of concern under California law.
1972	California designates Klamath River from Iron Gate to the ocean a Wild and Scenic River, Federal designation follows in 1981.

1973	US Supreme Court rules that stretches of the Trinity and Klamath River flowing through the Hoopa and Yurok reservations are "Indian Country," effectively restoring tribal salmon fishing rights.
1976	Oregon Water Resources Department begins Klamath water rights adjudication process.
1977-78	Tribal salmon fishing resumes on Lower Klamath River, but is quickly stopped by the federal government on conservation grounds.
1983	United States v. Adair upholds Klamath Tribes' right to enough instream water to support fishing and hunting on former reservation lands, but does not establish an amount.
1985	California state court confirms limited tribal fishing rights for Karuk Tribe at Ishi Pishi Falls.
1986	Congress passes Klamath River Basin Fishery Resources Restoration Act; the program is funded at $1 million per year.
1986	Klamath Tribes restored to federal recognition as an Indian tribal government, but former reservation lands are not returned. Karuk Tribe receives federal recognition.
1986	Klamath Tribes close their sucker fishery on Upper Klamath Lake and its tributaries.
1987	Indian salmon harvest on Klamath River reopened for five years.
1988	Lost River and shortnose suckers listed as endangered under the federal Endangered Species Act.
1988	Oregon Scenic Waterways Act designates the Klamath Scenic Waterway from J. C. Boyle Dam to the state line. Federal designation follows in 1994.
1988	Hoopa-Yurok Settlement Act establishes the Yurok tribal government as independent from the Hoopa tribal government; the Yurok Reservation is split from the Hoopa Valley Reservation.
1990-92	Severe decline in Klamath River salmon runs nearly closes commercial ocean salmon fishery.
1993	Federal government sets Klamath River tribal salmon fishing limit at half the total available harvest.
1996-98	The Lost, Klamath, Salmon, Scott and Shasta rivers are listed

as impaired under the federal Clean Water Act, launching regulatory steps to improve water quality.

1997   Coho salmon in Southern Oregon and Northern California Coastal region listed as threatened under the Endangered Species Act.

1998   First of several unsuccessful negotiations undertaken among some Klamath Basin water interests.

2000   PacifiCorp begins federal relicensing process for the Klamath Hydroelectric Project dams.

2001   Klamath Project irrigation water crisis.

2002   At least 34,000 salmon die near the mouth of the Klamath River in September.

2005   Multi-party negotiations that ultimately lead to the Klamath Basin Restoration Agreement and the Klamath Hydroelectric Settlement Agreement begin in earnest.

2006   PacifiCorp's license for Klamath Hydroelectric Project expires. The relicensing process continues; the company faces major costs to meet environmental standards required by federal regulators.

2006   Projected weak runs of Klamath River Chinook salmon force closure of the ocean salmon harvest from Monterey, California, to Southern Oregon.

2008   In January, Draft Klamath Basin Restoration Agreement released; provides for settlement of key water conflicts and calls for a major salmon restoration effort; also calls for separate agreement concerning the removal of the Klamath Hydroelectric Project dams.

     In November, the United States, California, Oregon and PacifiCorp announce an agreement regarding dam removal; it is the first time the dam owner commits publicly to such a scenario.

2009   Draft Klamath Hydroelectric Settlement Agreement released.

2010   Final Klamath Basin Restoration Agreement and Klamath Hydroelectric Settlement Agreement signed. Implementation contingent on authorizing legislation, funding and environmental review.

2012   Final Klamath Dam removal EIS/EIR issued

2013   Klamath Project Biological Opinion issued

2013 With the region in drought conditions, Klamath tribes and federal government exercise water rights in the Upper Klamath Basin for the first time. This cuts off irrigation water to agricultural growers in the upper basin.

2016 Department of the Interior, US Department of Commerce, PacificCorp, and Oregon and California sign agreement to remove four dams on the Klamath River by 2020 following a process administered by the Federal Energy Regulatory Commission.

2020 Earliest year in which dam removal would begin under the Klamath Hydroelectric Settlement Agreement.

CHAPTER THREE

IMMORTAL RIVER, MORTAL SOIL

Upper Mississippi

THE UPPER MISSISSIPPI RIVER USED to have a natural waterfall. It still exists in paintings, Albert Bierstadt's and George Catlin's romanticized brushstrokes of a captured moment, but it can no longer be found on the river itself. St. Anthony Falls in Minneapolis ceased to be a natural falls under a series of botched engineering hydropower feats for lumber, textile, and flour mills, among them Pillsbury flour operating from 1881 to 2003. Below the falls, meeting grounds for trade between indigenous nations, nesting places of eagles on Spirit Island, and the Dakota nation councils at Carver's Cave no longer exist. Saint Anthony, the intercessor for lost things and the patron saint of Father Hennepin, the first European visitor in 1679 to the falls and to the now vanished town in the center of the Dakotas' traditional lands, has much work to do.

St. Anthony Falls lost its natural form between 1850 and 1869 in less than a single generation. First it filled with industrial wastes. Then waterpower shafts for mills drilled through limestone into the underlying sandstone accelerated erosion; tunnels underneath made things worse. Dams then diverted water, exposing the sandstone to cycles of freezing to weaken it further. Partial tunnels between two of its river islands collapsed on October 5, 1869, when the limestone cap of Hennepin Island was breached and torrents of water poured through the tunnel. Tradesmen, lawyers, and store clerks rushed to throw logs into the breach to no avail. Until a wooden apron could be constructed, water raced from the tunnel scouring the waterway and tearing at the sandstone.

A concrete apron now ushers the water downstream in broad sheets. Islands in the river disappeared in the onslaught of industrial engineering and a navigational lock, a closed box of water filled to raise vessels for passage up or down river. The lock no longer functions, closed in 2015 to stop the movement of invasive Asian carp. Losses continue to the present, the most recent on August 2007 with the collapse of the eight-lane bridge of Interstate 35 built across the river. In a tangle of broken concrete and debris, 111 vehicles and 13 lives were lost into the Mississippi River below.

The Upper Mississippi and her vast webs of water above and below ground from the Rockies to the Alleghenies, from Lake Itasca in Northern Minnesota to the confluence of the Ohio River at Cairo, Illinois, witnessed losses for the indigenous people there. European infectious diseases, decimation of native foods, and dispossession from homelands changed their world. If they survived, most were forced into poverty-stricken internment camps the government calls Indian reservations. The Upper Mississippi received increasing tonnages of soil from erosion, and toxic wastes from farms, cities, and industry coursing down its watery veins to all the interconnected communities of fish, animals, plants, insects, birds, and people once European settlers took over the land.

The story of the Upper Mississippi watershed culminates in an important movement for indigenous rights to clean water and undisturbed homeland. In parallel to indigenous rights, the environmental movement to halt destruction and restore the land grows with every year. We bear witness to the most recent turn of this centuries-long struggle as an action to block an environmentally destructive crude oil pipeline, the Dakota Access Pipeline (DAPL), on the banks of the Missouri, a major tributary of the Upper Mississippi. This story, 338 years after Father Hennepin's voyage to what was then named Kaposia, now called South St Paul, has complex roots including my own family history entwined in the telling.

WATERSHED OF THE GRANDFATHERS

Crazy Horse
We hear what you say
One earth one mother

One does not sell the earth
The people walk upon
We are the land
How do we sell our mother

—John Trudell, Santee Dakota

In the bottomlands of the Mississippi watershed can be found the historically richest soil in North America, supporting vast and diverse biological ecosystems. Before the river was bound in concrete by the Army Corps of Engineers and separated from so much of its floodplain, the Mississippi River floodwaters gathered natural nutrients from the land to mix with suspended river sediments as the river overflowed its banks. The waters roared and churned, settled and receded. It changed course, leaving plant and animal organic matter throughout the floodplain in wetlands, ponds and lakes appearing for variable lengths of time. We call these ancient cycles of flooding, naturally disrupted species habitat, and nutrient renewal spread over millennia the river's *flood pulses*. They underlie the region's historical fertility and species diversity, renewing the watershed ecosystem by taking life and giving back even more life.

The Mississippi River bears as many names are there are nations who have lived in its watershed. Some names translate as mother of waters, big river, or great river, although those are names also given to other very powerful rivers. The unique name for the Mississippi translates as "the river outside of time," for it is outside of human time, going back 10,000 years in its present form after the retreat of the great ice sheets. We glimpse its earlier history in its carbon-dated sediments from 55,000 years ago, with its earlier history invisible to our scientific instruments. Some call it the immortal river as we cannot see its beginning or its end. In the river's headwaters, the river shapes itself into a long question mark visible from space, before it heads down to the Gulf of Mexico, 2,320 miles away. The name for its headwater lake, Itasca, comes from "truth" or "head" in Latin. But Elk Lake or Omashkoozo-zaaga'igan in the language of the Anishinaabe is its name for the people who first lived here in the upper part of Minnesota. These people and the Dakotas to their south and west inhabited the land before Europeans arrived and gave the people the names Chippewa and Sioux respectively.

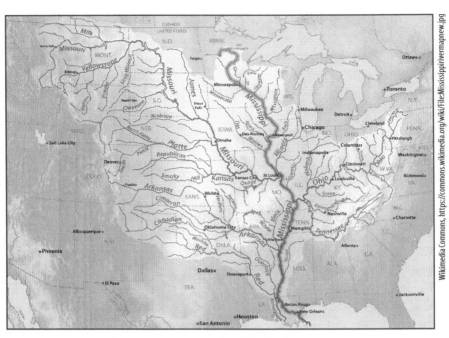

Mississippi River Drainage

For the Anishinaabe still living in the river's headwaters, there are six names for the river based on each river segment. The one from Crow Wing River to the Gulf is the name we use: *Misi ziibi*. While the river may be called immortal, the soil proved mortal once settlers busted the deep sod that had been forming for centuries. Through all eras, the Mississippi River flows, reshaping the surface geology. The map below shows its vast drainage, shaped like great wings over two-thirds of the continental United States. The Upper Mississippi from headwaters and tributaries to Cairo at the tip of Illinois accounts for most of the entire Mississippi River watershed.

How did so much of the river become corseted in concrete and the land degraded, the waters poisoned? And what of its restoration? The first step was to dispossess indigenous tribes, survey it into rectilinear sections of 640 acres each, establish townships and county lines along the gridded surveys, and sell parcels of those sections to homesteaders who knew little or nothing of sustainable farming in the Upper Mississippi watershed. As the land changed under environmentally damaging clearing and cultivation, engineers attempted to control the flood pulses of the river for navigation and bottomland development. It is a well-worn story that needs retelling in multiple perspectives as we can lose the history over successive generations.

Like a rapid succession of unexpected hundred-year floods, European-descended settlers radically reshaped the lives of the occupants of the land and retold the story of the watershed. My maternal grandfather's line followed a common settler path from Europe to Minnesota, then on to the Rockies and Sierras in the west. My family was unaware that the original geographic center of the Dakota Nation could be found at the confluence of the Mississippi and the Minnesota Rivers. We still use the Dakota word for Minnesota—*Mni Sota Makoce,* land where the waters reflect the clouds. This place includes what is now Mankato, where my maternal grandfather was born in 1883 shortly after the Dakota Nation's dispossession after 1862.

Mankato, MN. The US Census records show my grandfather, Bert Ludington DeWolf, was born in Mankato, Blue Earth County, Minnesota. His birth came 21 years after the US Army executed 38 Dakota men in Mankato the day after Christmas 1862. Lincoln commuted the death sentences of all but 38 of the original 303 condemned Dakotas. Mankato will never lose its association with the Mankato 38 that ended what was then called the Dakota-US war, in the second year of the American Civil War. In a little over four months, 77 soldiers and some 450 settlers were killed. For the Dakota, there were 150 deaths in skirmishes with soldiers, and uncounted thousands of Dakota lives lost to European diseases and forced starvation. Deliberate withholding of promised government food stores owed to the Dakotas became the inciting action, spurred by US government Agent Andrew Myrick who famously said, "Let them eat grass or their own dung." At the same time, the Union and the Confederate armies clashed in the east and south with deaths mounting into the hundreds of thousands. How did this relatively small Dakota "war" merit the unparalleled mass execution? Military records at the time show explicit intentions to starve out the Dakota just four years after Minnesota was declared a state. Land greed combined with federal fund shortfalls due to the Civil War crippled the lives of the Dakotas. Even Mary Todd Lincoln had a part with her profligate spending on redecorating the White House that required two special fund reallocations in Lincoln's first year in office. The cuts fell heavily on the Office of Indian Affairs, harming people the Great Emancipator never freed and who would not be permitted to vote until 1924.

The New York Times reporter who witnessed the hanging in Mankato wrote that the condemned men were singing prayers to *Wakan Tanka*, the Great Mystery, when they walked to the gallows:

> *". . . a scene has been here enacted the like of which, those of us who witnessed it, desire to see again nevermore. . . . the poor wretches made such frantic efforts to grasp each other's hands, that it was agony to behold them . . . Thirty-eight human beings suspended in the air, on the bank of the beautiful Minnesota."*

The land in Minnesota suddenly ceased to be home to the Dakota Nation, and nearly all of the Dakotas were force-marched out to the short grass prairies and high plains to the west. Exceptions were made only for valued household servants, those married to whites, and friends of whites who hid them. In 1871, not quite a decade after the hangings in Mankato, my second great grandfather Moses DeWolf moved to homestead land that had been Dakota homeland in southern Minnesota. He likely knew what the papers called the savage Indian massacres of whites in Minnesota while he served the Union Army in Virginia. No hero, Moses DeWolf was discharged from the Union Army once for crashing a wagon while inebriated, and, after re-enlisting, discharged a second time for debilitating and intractable dysentery. He also did not do well as a farmer, just like so many others new to this land.

The events from first European contact to settler displacement of the watershed lands can be traced in pictorial and oral histories of the people the US government called the Sioux, using the French and Anishinaabe name for the Dakotas. The word Dakota designates a language group that is closely related to the Lakota, the latter migrating to the Great Plains as far west as the Tetons prior to imposition of the reservation system. We now have Dakotas classed into Eastern (Santee) and Western (Yankton and Yanktoni) Dakota. Lakota also have sub-group and band names although the federal government still calls them Sioux. For simplicity in the plethora of names self-given and government-given, scholars use Dakota to designate all these language-related tribes including the Lakota.

Because of my own family history in the lands of the Dakota, I focus on them, although there were many nations and cultures here before the United States came to be. Indigenous homelands pre-contact could be defined but were not mapped, with somewhat fluid boundaries. To map the changes in Native nations, we would need hundreds of maps with each change in conquest, treaties, and displacement once Europeans arrived. Nations in general were pushed into one another's territories generally westward, piling up people on people as if pushed by a berserk conveyor belt.

Many Dakota bands, like other Native cultures, kept records called Winter Counts or Ledger Narratives. Typically a new pictograph was added to preceding years, drawn on hides and passed down through a lineage of Winter Count keepers. The counts can be dated to western calendar years given an event known as "The Year the Stars Fell"—a great Leonid meteor shower of 1833-34 found on nearly all Winter Counts covering that time. Originally the counts or ledgers were tribe or band histories, though with changes due to diaspora post-contact, counts began to follow a more narrow family narrative and were drawn on ledger paper.

One of the longest extant counts comes from a Winter Count keeper named Battiste Good (Brown Hat) covering the years 1700 to 1879. Good was born in 1821, the year a comet streaked across the sky "making a loud noise" as noted in his lineage's Winter Count of that year. He was Brule (Sichangu), and lived on the Rosebud Reservation in South Dakota in the 1880s until he died in 1907. The dates of his life span closely match my maternal second great grandfather, Moses DeWolf, who died at the end of 1902, four years before Good died.

Rivers figure throughout the Winter Count, mainly as floods or ice or winter camp locations. Fights with other tribes, deaths of important chiefs or prominent band members, dances, and ceremonies find their place in pictographs before the first whites appear. The dates of my maternal grandfather's line midst selected Battiste Good's Winter Count narratives related to the arrival of whites are listed below.

BATTISTE GOOD SELECTED WINTER COUNTS

1707   Many Kettle Winter (got 3 guns and many pots from an English trader)

1708	Brought Home Omaha Horses (horses in multiple winters after this date)
1734	Used Them Up with Belly Ache (1st Euro-derived epidemic for this band)
1739	Found Many Horses (wild horse herds developing)
1757	Went on Warpath on Horseback (1st horseback war for this band)
1779	Smallpox Used Them Up Winter (also in the following winter)
1784	**My third great grandfather John born France or Poland, fought with Napoleon at battle for Moscow in 1812, then moved to Canada**
1791	Saw a White Woman Winter (first time for this band)
1801	The Good White Man Came Winter (trader people liked)
1802	Smallpox Used Them Up Again Winter
1803	Brought Home Pawnee Horses with Iron Shoes (first horseshoes)
1810	Little Beaver's (log) House Burned (log houses begin to appear in winter counts)
1812	First Hunted Horses Winter (using lariats adapted from whites)
1819	Smallpox Used Them Up Again Winter
1822	Star Passed By With Loud Noise (year of Battiste's birth)
1824	White Soldiers Came Winter (band sees white soldiers for first time)
1826	**My second great grandfather Moses born Oswego NY, then family moved to MN**
1845	Broke Out on Faces and Sore Throat (unknown disease outbreak)
1851	The Big Smallpox (year of 1st Fort Laramie Treaty creating mapped Great Sioux Reservation but not noted by Battiste Good)
1852	First Issue of Goods Winter (loss of indigenous resources, dependence on US government supplies)
1854	**My great grandfather George born NY, later moved to MN**
1856	Battiste Good Taken Prisoner (130 Dakota killed, prisoners taken by US Army)
1857	Trades with Battiste for Furs (white trader Ft Robinson,

	pictographs become more personal as bands and family groups are broken up)
1858	Hunted Bulls Only Winter (no cows, increasing demise of great herds)
1861	Broke Out With Rash Stomach Pains and Died Winter— another unknown epidemic
1862	Killed Spotted Horse Winter (A Crow man killed by Dakotas, no mention of hanging of 38 Dakotas in Mankato)
1868	Battiste Good Made Peace with Gen Harney (2nd Fort Laramie Treaty of 1868 many chiefs and generals involved including Battiste Good)
1873	Measles and Sickness Used Up People Year
1877	Crazy Horse Came To Make Peace And Was Killed With His Hands Outstretched (aftermath of Custer death of 1876— also Custer not in Battiste Good account)
1879	Sent the Boys and Girls to School Winter (final entry for Battiste Good)
1883	**My grandfather Bert born Mankato MN**

~

What I remember: My grandpa Bert never told me he was born in the Upper Mississippi watershed. In fact, we rarely spoke as he was always immersed in some kind of work in the garden and woodshop. Grandpa Bert wore blue bib overalls with lots of pockets and loops for tools. On Sundays he wore his best clothes for prayer service in the small church he helped build. I can still see him checking the water level in the yellow well house with a pole as tall as a young tree. In my memory he burns trash in the stone circle of the shared backyards of his home and the homes of two aunts. The houses stand together like a semi-permanent ring of settler wagons in their last stop from Minnesota. I see him on the last day of life, his long frame skeletal, sunken into the tan living room sofa with my mother, Aunt Sis, and Aunt Peggy like a bower of tree limbs above him.

    What I Learned: The most oft-told family story was that my third maternal great grandfather was French and deserted Napoleon's army in the Battle of Moscow although another record shows birth in Poland.

The family somehow got to Canada, then into NY. They moved to Minnesota, then North Dakota, followed by living in a cabin above Leadville, Colorado. They moved west by rail, taking their few possessions and farm animals from one hardscrabble living to another. During the First World War, Bert's three-year-old son drowned in a creek and his wife died in the flu pandemic. Heart-broken, my grandfather boarded a night train to California, taking his one-year-old daughter against the wishes of the family matriarchs. He remarried, had two more children, and lived as an unpaid caretaker on a pear ranch in the mountains of Northern California.

My grandfather's lineage in the Upper Mississippi watershed in Minnesota comes shrouded in a sparse and confusing history from an unknown French or Polish birth to the Dutch DeWolf surname after crossing what was then the porous border from French Canada into the United States. My family stories rarely carry historical context although my aunt exclaims in her family history notes: "How short the bridge between us and those who were part of the founding of our country." True the period of settlement is short, but the family does not go back to the founding of the country for my maternal grandfather's line. They were, however, among the hundreds of thousands who poured into the newly divided land in the Upper Mississippi watershed in the mid to late 1800s to move west within two generations.

For the settlers, most of them impoverished in Europe or the Eastern United States, "the land of beginning again," as they called it, held a mighty pull. Just as river flows increase to overflow its banks, immigration flow grew to flood the land due to US government genocidal actions toward indigenous people, broken treaties, and sales and giveaways of lands seized from the Dakotas and other Native nations. Perhaps settlers including my ancestors knew this; perhaps they chose to erase it from their minds. It rarely entered family stories. When I raise the issue with my mother, she counters, "I've heard that a family member was scalped by Indians." That would be a horrifying and tragic event. It could be true, although there is no evidence. Scalping arose in many cultures, evidenced in writings of Herodotus and in archeological remains of a Crow Creek, SD massacre in the mid-fourteenth century. In wars against Native people in the US, both sides took scalps, but a bounty was paid for Native Americans, noncombatant men, women and children included. The history of population decimation of indigenous people at the time of the rapid settlement by whites, gives firm evidence that death rates for Native people were extreme and highly disproportionate to whites.

When I find my grandfather's birthplace of Mankato on digital maps, brown grids, networks of streets, and nearby farms appear, filling in the twice-told tales in our family history. Zooming out, Mankato shrinks to a brown spot encircled by rectangular farm fields. As the map zooms out further, the gridded patches of yellow-green to dark green become smaller mosaics to cover the whole of Minnesota, Wisconsin, Iowa, and beyond. Zooming out is like a fast-forward of settlers arriving, with homesteads replacing the prairie. The Boreal Forest that spreads across Canada, now with but a toehold in Northern Minnesota, also shrank with the relentless march of farms, roads, and towns. The settlers, however, did not arrive to a land untouched by humans. Indigenous people periodically set fires to the prairie, aiding the reign of grass over woodlands to sustain herds of bison, elk, and deer and to plant fields of maize and squash in the prairie margins.

The Minnesota River, like a reverse checkmark across the state when viewed from above, reaches its southernmost point and its ethical nadir in Mankato with broken treaties and expulsion of the Dakota the year after the Mankato 38 hanging. The population numbers alone bear testimony. Just 6,077 white people were counted at the time of its 1858 statehood (officially just the eastern half of what is now Minnesota). It jumped to 172,023 in 1860, then to 780,773 by 1880 shortly before the time of my grandfather Bert's birth. By 1900, there were over 1.75 million people residing in Minnesota. Indians "not subject to taxes" were not counted. However, the small number of "half-breeds" living with whites could be enumerated.

No one knows precisely how many people lived in the Americas before Europeans arrived. For the Upper Mississippi Dakotas as a whole, estimates based on explorer and soldier records count 22,500. In 1655, Dakota nation life centered on the confluence of the Mississippi River and the Minnesota Rivers where Pilot Knob formed the center of the Dakota world. Traditional homelands spread in all directions from there, including many ricing lakes to the north, overlapping with the Anishinaabe nations. Upon contact with whites, the numbers of Dakotas plummeted from diseases, wars, poverty and famine to an estimated

8,500 by 1900, a 62 percent drop. But the people proved to be resilient, adaptable, and mobile, especially those moving to the western prairies through which the Missouri runs in western Montana and Wyoming as well as North and South Dakota. The population tops 170,000 in the US 2010 census at present, including mixed race, far greater than pre-contact numbers.

Originally the Dakota people lived not in the prairies though they hunted there, but in woodlands, or mixed woodland-savannah. Westward movement brought them first to the tallgrass prairies. The historic range of tallgrass prairie falls south and east of the Minnesota River angling up to Canada, covering much of what is now Southern and Eastern Minnesota, Iowa, Illinois, and Northern Missouri. These prairies coincide with the historic range of bison, although the bison could be found far beyond the borders of the prairie in pre-contact America.

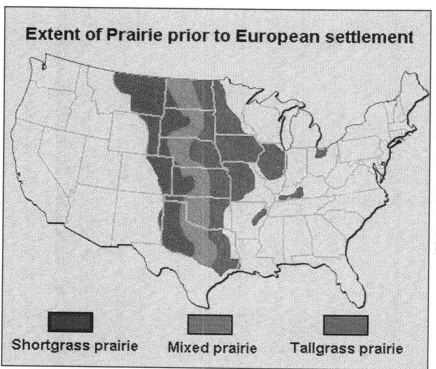

Shortgrass, mixed, and tall grass prairie prior to European settlement

WATER DEFINES THE PRAIRIE

Watershed landforms take shape from dynamic interactions of the rivers and streams, along with rainfall and run-off, against the strength of soil or rock and resistance from vegetation. Short, mixed, and tallgrass prairies depend on water, or, more precisely, on water evaporation rates. Pre-contact fires, wild and those once set by indigenous people to foster grasslands or flush game, have a place but do not fully define the range of the prairies. The ecologist John Madson writes in *Where the Sky Begins*, "Tallgrass prairie is found in a great array of situations, glaciated and unglaciated, well-drained and wet, level and hilly, and over a variety of parent soil materials—loess, glacial till, clay, sand, and rock. The one factor that dictates the presence of prairie and relative absence of trees is a critical degree of evaporation." Where evaporation exceeds inches of rainfall, grasses dominate over trees. Prairie trees such as the Bur Oak evolved to survive in prairie as they drive down a deep taproot with little above ground in its first two years. In its third summer the circle of Bur Oak roots can be four feet in diameter and six deep with just a three-foot sapling above ground. Bur oak sits quietly amongst the tall grasses of big bluestem and perennial bunchgrass, capable of growing to over nine feet. There are few relict areas with elderly bur oak and original prairie grasses.

Settlers coming into the Upper Mississippi believed it was an untouched farming paradise. But cultivating soil below the dense, deeply rooted grasses, especially those in glacial till clay soil, was not as easy as felling trees and plowing the land of the Eastern woodlands. It took up to 20 oxen to break the prairie sod, with new homesteading farmers renting a team and massive plows costing 600 mid-nineteenth century dollars. Planting accelerated after 1837 when John Deere, a blacksmith living in Northern Illinois, invented what he called the self-cleaning polished steel plow blade. It came to be known as "the plow that broke the plains." In the 1930s Dust Bowl, wheat-depleted soils of the High Plains to the south and west of the Upper Mississippi watershed rose up into killing black and red and yellow dust blizzards, blowing as far away as Washington DC where farm bureau officials began to realize something had to be done.

The rich black soil forming for centuries, thought to be inexhaustibly fertile, gave out in two generations of farming wheat in the Upper Mississippi. Geological surveys as early as 1867 noted formerly clear streams ran muddy due to erosion. When wheat moved out to the high plains, corn moved into the prairies, further depleting the soils and increasing erosion. Today corn grows in what had been tallgrass prairies, wheat in the shortgrass prairies, with cattle and hogs replacing the great wild bison and elk herds.

One of the greatest errors of farmstead settlement was misapplication of European crop cultivation methods. Unfamiliar storm patterns, two to three times greater than for western Europe, could carry six to seven times greater erosional force. Soggy tree-shorn hillsides began to make their way into the rivers carrying topsoil, undercutting homes, barns, and paddocks. Thick mudflats stranded animals and ensnared vehicles where once the land had been held by big and little bluestem, *helianthus*, needle grass, milkweed, coneflower, and countless other grasses and wildflowers, along with Bur Oaks, and other prairie adapted trees. Despite the obvious failures, farmers continued to plow along original rectilinear survey lines, ignoring streams to plant straight rows. Roads also ran along survey lines and washed out repeatedly.

Contour plowing, terracing, cover crops, and crop rotation became widely advocated in the 1930s in response to the Dust Bowl. Agricultural demonstration projects eventually changed farming methods, especially in the hilly regions of the Upper Mississippi. By the 1980s, in quiet decades of change, farmers began to adopt no-till farming, injecting seeds into the soil to minimize disruption of the natural living soil communities that foster fertility. John Madson's work on prairie ecology also brought a quiet movement among farmers who began to set aside portions of the land for prairie restoration. With this came noticeable increases in wildlife numbers and diversity. Over time a few organic farm pioneers like Farmer John of Angelic Organics outside of Chicago and star of the film "The Real Dirt on Farmer John" appeared. Growing consumer demand now brings natural and organic farming to the Midwest though the overall percentage of land still remains small. At present, a total of 4.1 million acres have been planted as organic pesticide-free crops, most of it corn and soy. Sustainable land management and chemical-free farming, while increasing, still only accounts for 0.31 percent of all corn planted.

In order of acreage planted, corn, soy, hay, alfalfa, wheat, sugar beets, sugar cane, potatoes, sorghum, and rice dominate US crops. Corn, the most common crop, would be unrecognizable to those who first cultivated *teosinte*, its natural parent species. In southern Mexico close to

9,000 years ago, indigenous horticulturalists created the first corn, *Zea Maize,* with one-inch ears resembling rice grains on spindly spreading grasses. As it was cultivated and bred over time, it began to resemble contemporary corn though colors and types were still diverse when it came into North America about 1000 years ago. It is still a crop of the Americas and remains the dominant crop of the Upper Mississippi throughout Iowa, Illinois, Indiana, Nebraska, Minnesota, the eastern Dakotas, Kansas, Wisconsin, and Ohio. These states contribute 77% of nearly 97 million acres of corn planted each year in the United States. No longer hand cultivated and bred, corn is big business, 85% of it genetically modified and 40% going to produce ethanol.

Corn, declared King in the Midwest since the mid-1880s, leads the post-settler story of the Upper Mississippi watershed in land use, river barge traffic, pesticide pollution and fertilizer runoff, along with corporate controlled seeds. Just as the decline of mayfly populations, so important to aquatic food webs, indicates the poor health of the river, we can think of corn as the indicator species for what we can now term the corn-soy-cattle-hog chemical fertilizer and pesticide drenched biome that altered the land and waterways of the Upper Mississippi.

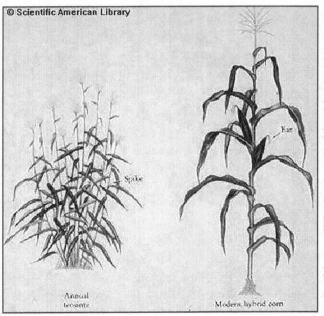

© Scientific American Library

Annual teosinte

Spike

Ear

Modern hybrid corn

Scientific American and UC Davis, https://www.sciencedaily.com/releases/2004/12/041201085546.htm

Teosinte and modern hybrid corn

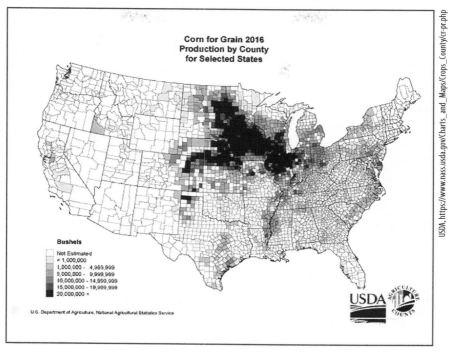

Corn for Grain 2016
Production by County
for Selected States

Bushels

Not Estimated
< 1,000,000
1,000,000 - 4,999,999
5,000,000 - 9,999,999
10,000,000 - 14,999,999
15,000,000 - 19,999,999
20,000,000 +

U.S. Department of Agriculture, National Agricultural Statistics Service

USDA

USDA, https://www.nass.usda.gov/Charts_and_Maps/Crops_County/cr-pr.php

Bushels of Corn by County

RIVER ENGINEERING: BARGES FILLED WITH CORN AND SOY

The military engineers of the Commission have taken upon
their shoulders the job of making the Mississippi over again,
a job transcended in size by the original job of creating it.

—Mark Twain

While the river has been heavily channelized since 1878, the Rivers and Harbors Act of 1930 mandated the Corps to create and manage a navigable channel with a bottom depth of at least nine feet. The Corps operates 37 locks and dams down to St Louis, and up the Illinois River to the south side of Chicago, with most constructed in the 1930s. Nearly all of the rocks that armor levees, most of the concrete constructions, and all of the dredge sand islands were set on the navigable river by the Army Corps of Engineers.

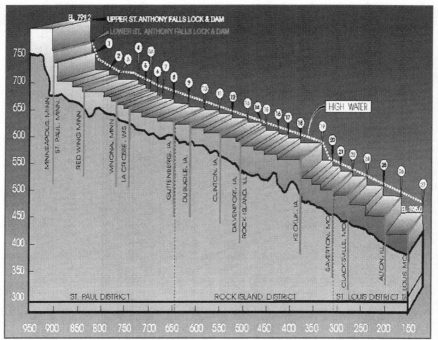

Staircase of water created by locks and dams on the Mississippi River

Longer than the Nile, the Upper Mississippi with its tributary arm, the Missouri River, can no longer freely roam or split into channels and ephemeral ponds or wetlands without the Corps' interference. Engineering keeps 50 percent of the Upper Mississippi separated from its floodplain.

Upper Mississippi flow dynamics depend on the locations and types of concrete restriction in navigation locks and dams, wing dams, closing dams, and levees. On an engineered navigational channel of locks and dams, the river from St Paul rushes and then pools, alternating from moving water to standing water by turns all the way down to the last navigation lock at St Louis. The longest river in the United States, the Mississippi is also the biggest investment in concrete by the Army Corps of Engineers, with 29 locks and dams from Minneapolis-St Paul to St Louis alone. Soil in runoff rapidly disappears into the river but rarely returns to the disconnected floodplain. It joins entrapped river sediments and silt that require periodic dredging, with dredge materials dumped throughout the river system often as sandbars and artificial beaches, blocking or creating side channels and sloughs. Pesticides and fertilizers attach to sediments, although much of it escapes the impoundments to create an enormous deoxygenated dead zone in the Gulf of Mexico at the river's Louisiana delta and mouth. The delta itself cannot rebuild with its sediments held back so far upriver. The Mississippi watershed has been yoked to corn and soy, agricultural chemicals, and petroleum and coal transport for over a century. Cash crops, created from Midwestern soil, water, and sun, fill barges navigating the locks and dams to world markets, never to be seen again in this watershed of their birth.

Engineers refer to the reconfigured river as a staircase of water when it comes to navigation. At the top of the Mississippi River navigation staircase sits Ford Dam, officially known as Lock and Dam No. 1. It occupies a place on the river between Minneapolis and St Paul just north of the confluence of the Mississippi and the Minnesota River. For purposes of navigation, the river is measured in upstream river miles from mile zero near Cairo, Illinois at the bottom of the Upper Mississippi moving to just beyond Ford Dam at Coon Rapids at River Mile 855. In this metric Ford Dam becomes River Mile 847.9 as it now marks the most northern point of the navigable river. The lowest lock, No. 26 at River Mile 200.78 above Cairo sets the pace for barge traffic. These upstream river miles, with locks numbered in the reverse direction, against the natural flow of the river, are rooted in navigational priorities, especially transport of agricultural goods.

Commercial barge traffic now dominates the river. An average tow comprises 15 barges, three abreast, typically carrying 22,500 tons of corn, soy, and wheat. The southernmost and busiest lock on the Mississippi at Granite City, IL processed 60.3 million tons of commercial cargo in 2015, with its 20-year range from 49.8 to 83.8 million tons depending on river conditions and economics. Highest tonnage comes from agriculture, that list topped by corn, most of it destined for export.

When Upper Mississippi zoologist Calvin Fremling began his career in the 1950s, he did not anticipate repeated struggles with the Army Corps of Engineers. A fisherman and a self-described river rat, he noticed and documented the steep declines in mayflies along the river's sewage outflows and pools of water behind concrete barriers. Where sewage entered the river untreated, mayflies did not emerge in the summer disrupting the cycle of life support for native fishes, especially bottom feeders like the endangered pallid sturgeon. Compared to sewage outflows, the mayfly decline behind Army Corps structures was not immediately noticed, since in the beginning mayflies and other important foundations of the aquatic food chain seemed to be thriving in the pools. Over time, however, eutrophication set in, turning the pools into dead zones of deoxygenated water. The crucial mayflies and other macro-invertebrates, so important to the aquatic food web, then plummeted in the Corps pools.

With no fish ladders or ways to connect reaches between the upper river dams, each section has its own tale of ecological loss in decimated fish populations. With the proliferation of invasive species of plants, insects, crustaceans, and animals, ecological chaos ensues. Controlling waters for navigation creates a river in trouble in which whole ecosystems unravel. Longer than land-based food chains, aquatic food webs concentrate toxins in larger fishes such as sturgeon and paddlefish. These points, made in detailed numbers from careful studies, were the subject of talks to the Army Corps of Engineers by Fremling and other scientists. The issues fell on deaf ears of the Corps generals. As a general once told Fremling, "We built them, and we can fill them any way we want."

Things changed with the Corps projects on the Upper Mississippi in the late 1970s. As the environmental movement was becoming stronger, destructive changes on the river due to navigation works and levees were becoming more apparent. Fremling noticed another kind of change with a new administration for the Corps on the Upper Mississippi. The Corps began to set up contracts with respected scientists to assess, mitigate, and, when possible, restore the river's aquatic ecosystems as they were under Congressional mandate to devote significant portions of their budget to environmental work. When asked what he saw as the most important change in the Upper Mississippi over his lifetime, Cal Fremling said, "I never guessed I'd see this change in the Army Corps of Engineers." At an Illinois water conference, I saw this change firsthand as a general literally begged his scientist audience for help with restoration projects. No one knows if the change will last under current and future administrations, but at least for a time, there is progress on the river.

As the river becomes cleaner and environmental programs grow, mayflies are returning to be greeted by mayfly observers proudly wearing mayfly pins on the Upper Mississippi. Swarms of mayflies appear nearly simultaneous at some indeterminate time in spring to autumn in numbers visible on weather radar. Their Doppler radar signature looks like rain falling upwards, rising and spreading out from the river. Emergences crown the lives of adult mayflies in mating dances with males flying vertically up and down, females flying horizontally amongst them. Males clasp a passing female to mate and die soon after. Females deposit their fertilized eggs to the water below, their lives also coming to an end. Long seen as beings who bridge the worlds of sky and water, and a symbol of fleeting life, they rise from the river bottom to fill the sky, cover bridges, vehicles, and buildings sometimes six inches deep. Birds and bats join fish leaping from the water to feast on the sudden plenty. Mayflies take no food in their last moments. Before they burst from the water, mayflies can live for years in the bottom mud of rivers and lake.

Cal Fremling specialized in the study of *Hexagenia limbata*, the giant mayfly common throughout the country. It was their disappearance that called him to action. Scientists of his time did not listen to him, but fishermen heard him. Eventually he published scientific papers on their decline, followed by years of proactive work to see their populations return. These ancient insects constitute an evolutionary wonder. By the time adult mayflies, called imagos, emerge they have undergone several instars (partial metamorphoses in their case) and nymphs with as many as 30 molts. Most of the known 3000 species, with 630 in North America, live for one day to as many as 14 days in the air to mate. These oldest of insects, related to dragonflies and damselflies, came into being during the early carboniferous era, roughly from 360 to 323 million years ago. This period, known as the Mississippian in North America due to dating of rock exposed in the Mississippi River Valley, saw the rise of terrestrial forms that we now mine as fossil fuels. Emergences of mayflies above rivers and lakes, their delicate wings held upright, abdomen curving upward, have returned to signify joy as indicators of clean water and ecosystem health. Mayflies occupy a celebratory place in the circle of life.

FLOOD CONTROL

Ancient impulses of the Upper Mississippi still surge, but the character of floods is different on the channelized river. It can be seen in the trends of major floods since early records starting in 1844 when industry was not present and population was low. In the 1844 Upper Mississippi flood, with no flood control structures in most places, the river spread far from its banks. At St. Louis with its triple confluence of the Missouri and

Illinois, the 1844 flood crested at 41 feet, flow peaking at 1.3 million feet per second, reaching 2 ½ miles wide. River floods are measured in four main ways: discharge, stage, flood stage, and crest. Discharge is the volume of water in a given cross-section of the river. Stage and flood stage are measures above sea level, with flood stage occurring when the river tops its banks. Crest is the highest stage in a flood, but the relationship between discharge and height of the crest are not linear, and crests rise higher on a channelized river. Subsequent flood discharges have not matched that of 1844, but crests have been higher in major floods of the Upper Mississippi in 1851, 1951, 1993, 2008, and 2011. On the armored and constrained river, the flood crests climb ever higher due to the river's separation from its floodplain. Higher crests mean faster rise and heavier battering of the river's restraints. At times, the Corps must deliberately breach levees to relieve the floodwaters. With more frequent climate change storms along with reduced woodlands and wetlands throughout the Upper Mississippi, we can expect water to spill over and breach levees to relieve the furious waters, with or without the help of the Corps.

Upper Mississippi flood news usually comes with numbers of dead people (relatively rare), numbers of people evacuated, numbers of homes lost measured as millions or billions of dollars. Crop damage places high on the list written as acres of lost income. Stories pour in of people awaiting rescue on roofs and debris as they float down urban streets. We draw in our breath when we see wrecked homes, cars, children's toys, and stranded or drowned domestic animals. Little attention is paid to wildlife, trees, insects, and wild grasses. Flood tragedy now, it seems, is all about us and what we believe we own. It would help to extend our concern to all the other wild beings of the watershed. It is easy to lose sight of nature's ecological long view when we restrict our fears of flood damage to ourselves alone.

One of the most important scientific advances in the study of big rivers is the flood-pulse concept. This view sees a river's annual flood as the most biologically productive feature of its ecosystem. It contrasts with previous ecological theories of floods as catastrophic events. Early work on flood-pulse appeared in the 1980s with a seminal paper by Junk, Bayley, and Sparks in 1989. Richard (Rip) Sparks now heads the National Great Rivers Educational and Research Center near East Alton, IL, across from the mouth of the Missouri, near the historic camp of the Lewis and Clark Expedition. These days, Sparks works in an array of projects important to the future of the Upper Mississippi, especially prospects for restoring altered floodplains and reconnecting them to rivers. One of these projects is the Emiquon Project, a collaboration with the Nature Conservancy on the Illinois River. In 1919, Jay Morton, a wealthy entrepreneur, built a levee and drained the land of the Emiquon tributary to the Illinois River. The Illinois River, just as the mainstem Mississippi, was dammed and confined to a narrow channel between artificial banks, causing severe damage to fish populations and ecological diversity. Ongoing restoration of this part of the river and its wetlands shows that floodplain reconnection improves biodiversity, recovery of native plants, fish, and wildlife. It also lessens farm runoff, improves nutrient levels, and reduces flood damage while still maintaining commercial navigation on the Illinois River. The Emiquon Project constitutes the largest wetlands restoration outside of the Florida Everglades.

As for the Mississippi itself, research by Olson and Morton continues to confirm the problems of constraining the river. A recent study states, "Earthen levees and flood-walls can be undermined by sand boils (emergent bubbling springs), fail after weeks of high floodwater pressure and soil saturation, or even be topped... with gullies and land scouring extending into the previously protected lands." Shortsighted navigation engineering and flood abatement constructions routinely backfire. Fortunately, researchers and environmentalists continue to work for watershed restoration, whatever the climate in the federal government. A growing groundswell of voices and hands join in the work as eagles and mayflies return to the river, signs of an improving ecology.

TURNING THE HISTORY AROUND

On an overcast day in late summer my friend CJ and I clear a dusty rise beside dry ochre grasses just over the Cannon Ball River where it joins the Missouri. Below the shoulder of the road, cars and trucks parked in no particular order amidst assorted tents in Crayola colors, tipis, RVs, and hundreds of lightly flapping tribal nation flags tell us this is the *Oceti Sakowin* camp next to the Standing Rock Sioux Tribe reservation. Excitement mixes with apprehension as we enter the main entrance. A camp security volunteer asks us where we are going. "Red Camp," says CJ, who is driving the van. "Oh, Red Warrior Camp," corrects the man dressed in black jeans, orange traffic vest, and a red scarf around his neck. He directs us down the parade entry road toward the end of the main camp and off to the right.

~

Our anxiety stems from viewing footage of pipeline company security guards unleashing vicious dog attacks on the unarmed people who call themselves water protectors. Just before my arrival at the Standing Rock camp in September, CJ and I watched Amy Goodman of Democracy Now! release riveting footage of dogs drawing blood from water protectors near the leading edge of the pipeline excavation. The clutch of people attacked included children and grandmothers. Black and white photos of dog attacks on African-Americans in the Civil Rights movement leapt instantly to mind, along with police actions against the members of the American Indian Movement (AIM) at Alcatraz, Wounded Knee II in South Dakota, and so many other sites where justifiable protection of people and place were met with violence. Peaceful actions to defend the land and protect the water still feel very dangerous.

That same evening, CJ received news of her uncle Johnny's imminent death in her Minnesota homeland. Uncle Johnny died the next day and we carried out our prayer services for him on the banks of the Missouri near Fort Rice, not far from the Standing Rock Sioux Reservation. This place, now a state park, contains the last post of George Armstrong Custer and his two contingents of Seventh Calvary men as they rode out to their deaths in the Battle of the Greasy Grass (Little Big Horn). It was a great victory for the Lakota Sioux Nation and their allies as response to the illegal entry of gold miners and soldiers into the sacred Black Hills that were to be protected in the Ft. Laramie Treaty of 1868. The fight for the Black Hills continues to this day.

We continued on to Standing Rock to be met by a blockade of several police cars and armed National Guard. We were asked for ID and told we would have to take an indirect route to *Oceti Sakowin* camp so we would not be "a danger to the demonstrators on the ND 1806 highway." We knew where the danger really lay, in the militarized police and soldiers. We passed over dirt roads curving through dry hills and over the Cannon Ball River to our first sight of the camp.

Those working to block the North Dakota Access Pipeline (DAPL) from the Bakken oil fields to run under the Missouri at Army Corps of Engineers reservoir, Lake Oahe North Dakota, signal a change in the way this Native-led action works. The issues at Standing Rock are singular: protection of the Standing Rock and Cheyenne reservations' drinking water and all others downstream, honoring tribal treaties and rights, sacred sites, and burial grounds. Throughout the camp there are reminders to stay in prayer, no weapons, no drugs, no alcohol. Prayers in many languages, native and non-native, are offered for all people including the police and hired security firms who attack the water protectors. Energy Transfer Partners and Enbridge own the Dakota Access Pipeline, stretching over 1,172 miles from the Bakken Fields of northwestern North Dakota to oil refineries in central Illinois. They do not own the land.

Everywhere people now know Standing Rock Reservation for the water protectors who faced mace, pepper spray, water cannons, and rubber bullets in freezing weather as they camped for ten months on the Missouri to block the pipeline company from drilling under the river. By the end of the action in March 2017, nearly 800 people including journalists had been arrested at Standing Rock, many held for police processing in dog cages, their rights violated, and significant numbers injured in police and hired security retaliatory actions.

The pipeline, like all oil and gas pipelines, disrupts the lands and waters where it is laid and pollutes land and water when it leaks and breaks—and they all do leak and break. It introduces invasive species and damages existing ecosystems, destroys farms and homes. When corporations control the narrative in the name of jobs and energy backed by a well-funded militarized police force, oil pipelines get permits. For the Dakota Access Pipeline, this process employed a strategy of designating small, contiguous rectangular sections of land along the planned pipeline path to avoid environmental assessment of the entire project. These smaller, mainly rural, sections typically receive ready approval by local cash-poor governments and landowners. Some landowners fight back, but not enough to stop it before reaching Standing Rock. Originally slated to run under the Missouri above the overwhelmingly white city of Bismarck, the pipeline company re-routed to avoid contamination of the city's water. Instead they chose to tear up and pollute the land and water of the Standing Rock and Cheyenne Reservations and everyone else downstream.

The Standing Rock Sioux Tribal government would not have it. What began as a walk to Washington DC by tribal youth grew to over 10,000 people camping out on land near Standing Rock. Direct action ended in early 2017 when water protector camps were cleared (mostly voluntarily on request by the tribal head) and pipeline drilling proceeded. However, the action is not over as legal cases continue and actions to protect water spring up throughout the country. As I learned on a national teleconference with over 5000 attendees in March 2017, actions have grown in 100s of locations, led in partnership with Native environmental leaders like Dallas Goldtooth, a Dakota from Minnesota, of the Indigenous Environmental Network and Tara Houska, Anishinaabe and tribal rights lawyer of Honor the Earth. Many feel this to be a pivot point, a change in how water protection grassroots movements move forward. Standing Rock, a gathering of the greatest number of Native Nations to date, changed the narrative for environmental action to restore and preserve the land and water along with the human rights of all people of the Upper Mississippi and beyond.

In Red Warrior Camp, we found a fence covered in signs and flags, with a decorated Mothers Against Meth car next to the fence. A large sign in black block letters proclaimed, "no pictures." As we pulled into an open camp space, our camp neighbor Diane from Michigan, a Native woman my age, told us she had just witnessed the dog attack at close range. She also informed us we had an awesome camp cook, an older man who called himself Grumble. She pointed to a wiry older man wearing a grey apron and a worn Peruvian cap, veteran of decades of environmental and social justice actions with Seeds of Peace.

During my time in camp I helped in the back lines, cooking and cleaning under the direction of Grumble. And we attended civil disobedience non-violence trainings held daily. We had chosen this camp because we were following Honor the Earth, the organization founded by Winona LaDuke, an Anishinaabe/Ojibwe activist and former US Vice Presidential candidate who ran with Ralph Nader and the Green Party in 1996 and 2000 elections. Her mother, a visual artist from the Bronx, is a friend of mine back in Ashland, Oregon, where Winona was raised until she headed to Harvard and into a life of activism. Honor the Earth and collaborators successfully blocked Line 3, the Sandpiper oil line through Minnesota, and I had long admired their work with water and soil, native seeds, wild rice harvests, health and social justice for the Ojibwe/Anishinaabe, and for all tribes and people.

It is evening, and we finish serving a savory meal of beans, fry bread, potato salad, and mixed cooked greens. We eat in warm camaraderie after prayer led by an Elder. Afterwards, around the campfires, we ready for the next day's front line events. Most slip off into separate planning groups. I speak with Grumble who is next to the kitchen holding his cell phone over which he receives closed-group messages. He tells me of an emergency meeting ordered by the Standing Rock council. I ask, "What is the emergency?" And he drawls in his best friendly but low grousing voice, "Some people need help understanding the 'non' part of non-violence." Where do we draw the line: not defending oneself when struck, or not damaging property? He offered no details. "What do you need me to prep?" I reply.

Amidst whinnying horses, the amplified sound of a man singing the refrain of a Bob Marley tune can be heard from a nearby camp.

> *Emancipate yourselves from mental slavery; None*
> *but ourselves can free our mind. Redemption songs.*
> *Redemption songs.*

"That's a good song," says a man, his face hidden by campfire smoke that rises into the evening sky. Everyone agrees. Indeed it is. Water is life, in all our lives, and in this unarmed action, we have our pure intentions and our strong voices as our touchstone redemption songs. This is the basic foundation of all environmental actions, whether front-line protests, legal suits, canvassing, petitions, or lobbying.

Songs continue through the night and I recognize the American Indian Movement (AIM) anthem. Intertribal, it consists of spirited vowel sounds to avoid association with any particular nation's language. At times, high calls fly over the massed voices, thrilling in its uniting force. Occasionally an energizing war whoop splits the night from those preparing for possible arrest the next day.

In camp, as we clean dishes, a man going by the name of Happy and a woman named Julie test their gear in preparation for locking themselves to pipeline bulldozers. I finish work and sit by a neighbor's campfire where a young boy excitedly tells me where the pipeline company bulldozers are located. After showing me the scars of his eagle offerings at the

Sun Dance from the past summer, he tells me the life story of Tatanka Iyotaka, Sitting Bull. Sitting Bull brought the Nations together, envisioned the defeat of Custer, refused to settle on reservations until forced, and would not give up his rights. The boy did not say Sitting Bull once had a vision he would be murdered by his own people. In 1890, acting on the Standing Rock Indian Agent's orders, tribal police went to arrest Sitting Bull who was killed in a gun fight between his supporters and the agent's police. Two weeks later, one of the most savage acts of the US Army occurred in the massacre of as many as 300 Native people, 50 percent women and children, at Wounded Knee, SD. This was the final step in military actions against the Dakota/Lakota/Sioux.

Two young girls join us and speak of their own Sun Dance offerings. Their voices soft, more centered than the boy's, they also speak of tough gang encounters on Wounded Knee reservation where one girl's father lives. Their voices nearly monotone, matter-of-fact, as they describe assaults I consciously still myself to listen. Long black hair framing sweet round faces, these girls touch my heart, as does the wiry boy who is already becoming a water warrior like his father. Flickering memories of my own daughter at their age, also black-haired and round-faced, along with ancestral ghosts, certainly the ghost of Sitting Bull, inhabit the dense darkness that comes and goes midst the campfire flames.

We rise early to prepare breakfast for those about to risk arrest on the front line. Asked if I will join them on the front, I decline in favor of backline support. I say, "Don't you think it would be bad to have a lot of white faces in the news?" A woman from the Standing Rock tribe with black hair wrapped in a kerchief matching her long red skirt was finishing her breakfast. "It's good to show white solidarity." But I stay in camp as I still don't know enough about my place here or the insider politics.

At the time no one anticipated that Red Warrior Camp residents would be expelled two months later by the tribal council for alleged acts of vandalism against the Energy Transfer Partners pipeline equipment. Spray painting vehicles of the company did occur, but no one really knew who set fires to vehicles. Many in the camp thought the strongest destructive actions were by paid undercover agents of the pipeline company. One man was clearly identified as a pipeline employee wielding a rifle and claiming to be a water protector. This has been borne out in later investigations and news releases.

Red Warrior Camp with its vocal activists provided conditions for embedded subversion and agitation. The high visibility of these acts broke the consistent position in the media of unarmed, peaceful actions of water protectors remaining in prayer. It can be difficult to discern the right level of action, especially in the heat of a moment of police violence. Young high-spirited men in camp were cautioned to stay calm, others asked to help them remain calm. I found many of the Red Warrior Camp self-protective about their personal lives and stories, more so than in other Standing Rock camps. In time, I learned this camp hosted people from many previous American Indian Movement actions as well as Earth First! style protests including tree sits, forest and river dam occupations. No one from Red Warrior Camp used a weapon or injured anyone. But they were accused of damaging bulldozers and setting fire to vehicles in a roadblock. It brought to mind the media storm that came when a member of Earth Liberation Front set fire to SUVs in protest of fossil fuels. For that, Jeff Luers was sentenced to 22 years in prison, later commuted to ten. And he is white. And it was not an "Indian uprising." We have yet to see what harsh sentences will fall on water protectors.

People feared escalation between police and the water protectors and an eventual siege of the camp with no one allowed in or out. One cannot forget the deaths, injuries, murders, and long prison terms of American Indian Movement leaders and their families of the past few decades. Like all environmental actions, I know the world does not pay attention when nonviolent civil disobedience is too quiet. And what is civil disobedience when the invoked rules do not honor the treaties? But there is a time to step back and regroup. Red Warrior Camp has now become Red Warrior Society and stands with others in water protection actions throughout the country.

People around the country were moved by a singular event in December 2016 when over 3000 US military veterans gathered to assist water protectors. In a ceremony at the nearby casino meeting space, Wes Clark, Jr., son of General Wesley Clark, wearing his own Seventh Calvary uniform, knelt before activist and spiritual leaders, Chiefs Leonard Crow Dog and Arvol Looking Horse, to ask forgiveness.

The violations of treaty in the Black Hills led by George Armstrong Custer and his 7th cavalry troops still carry deep wounds. Custer's 1876 defeat and death in a conflict lasting two hours and 15 minutes in an alliance of tribes was a great victory. It brought retribution that forced Native people on to reservations and the takeover of lands never ceded to the US in treaties, especially the sacred Black Hills. Standing Rock Native nation coalitions against the Dakota Access Pipeline continue this struggle for Native sovereign nation rights to unpolluted homelands, self-rule, religion, language, and traditional culture. Prayer and ceremony are the heart and soul of the current coalition of Indigenous nations. Lest we forget, Native religion was not federally acknowledged until the Native American Religious Freedom Act of 1978.

Wesley Clark, Jr., kneeling with other US military veterans, spoke: "Many of us, me particularly, are from the units that have hurt you over the many years. We came. We fought you. We took your land. We signed treaties that we broke. We stole minerals from your sacred hills. We blasted the faces of our presidents onto your sacred mountain. When we took still more land, we then took your children and we tried to eliminate your language that God gave you, the Creator gave you. We didn't respect you, we polluted your Earth, we've hurt you in so many ways but we've come to say that we are sorry. We are at your service and we beg for your forgiveness." It was an important step, not merely token. Outcry against it by other military veterans attests to its power. But there were no dry eyes in the room of over 500 who witnessed the profound act of apology and heard Leonard Crow Dog's reply: "We do not own the land, the land owns us."

Shortly after, in March 2017, the pipeline was laid under Lake Oahe, a reservoir on the Missouri built in the 1960s formed by forcing seizure of over 200,000 acres from the Standing Rock Reservation and the Cheyenne River Reservation. The present pipeline action constitutes a further dispossession of the tribes. At Lake Oahe, a violation of treaty rights occurs each time the Corps works on or issues permits in these un-ceded lands, a fact that is fundamental to ongoing suits by the Standing Rock and Cheyenne Reservations against the Dakota Access Pipeline.

There are important precedents for court action. On June 30, 1980, the United States Supreme Court ruled that the government had illegally taken the land in the Black Hills. It upheld an award of $15.5 million for the market value of the land in 1877, along with 103 years worth of interest at 5%, for an additional $105 million. The Lakota Sioux and other tribes, however, then and now refuse to accept payment and instead continue to demand the return of the territory.

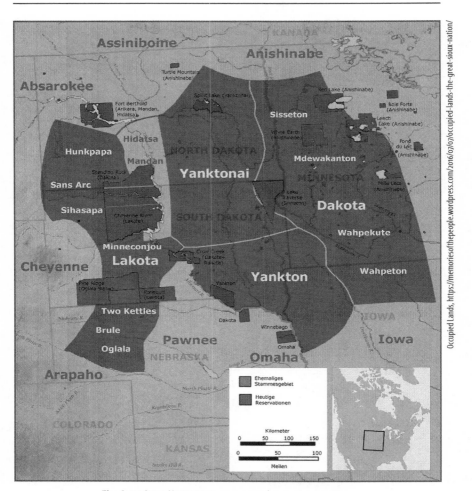

The Great Sioux Nations prior to 1770 and current reservations

RIDING BACK THE HISTORY

The Standing Rock Sioux Reservation on the Missouri River near Bismarck, ND is 500 miles or seven hours in normal driving conditions to where the Minnesota River joins the Mississippi River. That confluence in the Upper Mississippi watershed lives in the hearts of all Dakotas who came to be called the Sioux by their enemies in the early years of colonization. Traveling this stretch of land through what were once wide expanses of short and tall grass prairies, giving way to lakes and woodlands, takes the reverse direction of the diaspora of tribes and broken treaties of the original Dakota nation, including the Lakota, and their Mississippian mound-building ancestors.

The distance from Crow Wing Reservation to Mankato measures 330 miles, an eternity walking or riding horses in the killing winters of the plains. In 2005, Jim Miller, a Vietnam veteran and a descendant of the displaced Dakotas, dreamt of a series of winter horseback rides to raise awareness of the silent impact from the Mankato mass hanging and dispossession, and to bring reconciliation among all people of the region. As a young Army soldier, Jim Miller had killed 38 Vietnamese, and their ghosts disturbed him. His mother told him the story of the Mankato 38, a history at that time unknown to him. The ride was born in Jim's own quest for forgiveness for those he killed and to heal the intergenerational trauma of his people. On the first Mankato 38 ride, participants prayed for forgiveness, then moved on to the site of the hanging to honor the dead. The ride honored the memory of those Dakota expelled from Minnesota and forced to walk or ride to Crow Wing on the Missouri in South Dakota across from the Brule Sioux Reservation. The Mankato ride takes place every year.

I also ask for forgiveness and wish to honor the dead. I carry my ancestors' unborn desires in my genetic heritage though I cannot fully know them. Their hardscrabble lives, shot through with god-fearing family-first values, may never be fully known. Their truth and compassion conveyed through the generations remain treasured gifts, and I am grateful for their hard work and love of family. And I cry with them over their heartaches. It is their ignorance we descendants must dispel and our descendants after us. My maternal line of grandfathers, along with their cohorts of settlers, unwittingly participated in the dispossession of the Dakota by taking possession of the rich soil and pure water of the Upper Mississippi watershed. We can no longer ignore, re-write, or erase this past.

Like the Mankato 38 ride of forgiveness and redemption, my trip to Standing Rock began as an eastward unwinding of the tracks of my maternal grandfather's movements. I journeyed from my mother's home near the California border to Malheur National Wildlife Refuge in Oregon. From the French meaning "bad air," Malheur signifies misfortune. It is here that misguided armed followers of Ammon Bundy held the refuge for 40 days starting early January 2016. Non-government militias and members of citizen movements, mainly ranchers, demanded the

US government turn federal lands over to individual states. Most of the protesters also felt entitled to graze their herds for free on public land, whether state or federal. In a confusing ploy, they took on the defense of two ranchers convicted of arson on public land although the men did not want their help. The siege ended in the death of LaVoy Finicum, a rancher and armed occupier, along with the arrests of its leaders, and surrender by all others in February of the same year. In a completely unwarranted action, Donald Trump pardoned the two arsonists. In contrast, Leonard Peltier, an Anishinaabe and Dakota activist remains in prison in spite of Amnesty Internationals' designation of unfair trial status.

The Malheur protest is diametrically opposite to Standing Rock. The Malheur siege placed individual rights and monetary gain above all others in an armed action. In contrast, Standing Rock water protectors championed the tribe and all people through peaceful prayer. Throughout my journey, the image of Malheur, isolated and closed for criminal investigation, would remain a counterpoint to what we were to witness several days later at Standing Rock. Just as at Standing Rock Red Warrior Camp, a chain link fence enclosed the Malheur campground in which we stayed. The fence was the only resemblance. At the campground near Malheur, we found ourselves surrounded by coyotes outside the fence, while raccoons and bearded, rough men camped beside us inside the chain link fence. There was no talk of protecting water, saving the people, or of redemption songs of freedom.

We traveled through Yellowstone, Bear Tooth Pass, and on through Montana, frequently crossing or following the path taken by Chief Joseph and the Nez Perce on their 1140 mile flight to within 40 miles of freedom in Canada. The Nez Perce had resisted the order to move to reservations, evading soldiers for months in some of the most difficult Rocky Mountain terrain. As the deaths mounted and few remained, Chief Joseph surrendered with the words, "I will fight no more forever." We wept for him and his people in the places of their flight.

We crossed over and sometimes joined the paths of Lewis and Clark who made land claims for the US government, and we also rode back the places of my own family's migration. We passed Williston, ND, center of the Bakken Oil fields, and on to the Standing Rock prayerful water protection of the Missouri. We then traveled on across North Dakota to Minnesota below Lake Itasca, headwaters of the Mississippi, past Leech Lake and innumerable bodies of water, on through the southern stretch of the Boreal Forest crossing the middle of the Upper Mississippi's curling question mark to Duluth. Later we turned down to Minneapolis not far from where St. Anthony Falls bears broken testimony to what ignorance wrought. After that, we followed the Minnesota River to Mankato itself.

In Mankato I ask forgiveness for our ignorance, our unwitting destruction in the name of survival and individual gain. And it is here I vow to help make things right for all people. We do not own the land, but the land graciously holds us. I join hands with all the water saviors before me down through the decades, rippling out from our sincere, determined, and dynamic actions of fluid intelligence to those who will take our places.

Our last day on the road, we travel past the place where my grandfather Bert's first wife and eldest son died in Colorado. His heartache remains with me. We camp high in the Rockies. Secreted in a midnight mountain clearing, invisible even to myself, my eyes widen to scan the stars over the rim of my sleeping bag. I'm snugged all the way down, my cap to the top of my eyes as a makeshift periscope. The tarp above crackles with ice breaking with the smallest movement. From here I spot the North Star, Minnesota's symbol. When I was a child, my father showed me a sextant while he spoke of what he called "shooting the stars" in the early days of aircraft navigation. The North Star, Polaris, stands still in a moving skyscape, as if to hold the sky in place. It reminds us to stand still in our own moral compass on the great earth.

Map of Lewis and Clark Expedition 1804

CHAPTER FOUR

FERTILITY RITES

Upper Mississippi

MOST OF MY ADOLESCENT YEARS were spent living within the St. Louis metropolitan area, not far from the triple confluence of the Mississippi, the Missouri, and the Illinois Rivers. My family resided in a white two-story house in the Smiley Homes subdivision of O'Fallon Illinois in the mid to late 1960s when my father was stationed at Scott Air Force Base. An Equidistant drive between Scott Air Force Base and East St. Louis, O'Fallon then claimed close to 5,000 people amidst cornfields and cows, straight stretches of roads with few trees, and a small herd of rescued buffalo. O'Fallon grew to over 29,000 in the intervening years between then and now.

The assassinations of John F. Kennedy in 1963 and Martin Luther King, Jr. in 1968 bracketed my high school years. It was a time of growing civil rights actions and anti-Vietnam protests. At the same time, a nascent environmental movement found its voice in Rachel Carson after her 1962 publication of *Silent Spring*. She alerted us to the ubiquitous poisoning of land and water from pesticides, especially DDT. "Sprays, dusts and aerosols are now applied almost universally to farms, gardens, forests and homes—non-selective chemicals that have the power to kill every insect, the 'good' and the 'bad', to still the song of the birds and the leaping of fish in the streams, to coat the leaves with a deadly film and to linger on in the soil—all this though the intended target may be only a few weeds or insects," she wrote. Her book, serialized in the New Yorker, brought a storm of criticism, lawsuits against her, and an investigation of her work ordered by then president John F. Kennedy.

For most people in the farmlands of Illinois, the message of *Silent Spring* was scorned, and Carson was reviled as a hysterical, "unmarried woman" who had overstepped her bounds. Monsanto, the manufacturer of DDT in the US, even published a parody of Rachel Caron's first chapter. What did people know of ecosystems and natural farming in rural Illinois, even though methods of natural and pesticide free agriculture were emerging at the time. Little did we understand the that the fertility of the soil and water affected our own health and fertility. It would take decades to unravel the relationship.

Carson did not relate civil rights to environmental contamination. That too would take decades to come to light. Living close to the 96 percent African-American East St. Louis brought the civil rights movement to our doorstep. When H. Rap Brown and Stokely Carmichael, Black Power leaders with the Student Nonviolent Coordinating Committee (SNCC) came to speak in East St Louis in 1967, local white residents bought out all the guns at Kmart. I was far more alarmed by my white racist neighbors than I was by SNCC leaders. The white supremacist James Earl Ray, who assassinated Martin Luther King, Jr. in Tennessee, hailed from nearby Alton IL. It was unimaginable to me that someone from a nearby town could kill King whose words rang so clearly with truth: *Darkness cannot drive out darkness; only light can do that. Hate cannot drive out hate; only love can do that.*

Like Sam Cooke's mellifluous and haunting voice in *Change Gonna Come*, I too believed in change to come. Buffy Sainte Marie's *Universal Soldier* spoke for the change I wanted to see, for all of us to take responsibility for an end to war. It was completely entwined with wanting an end to racism, sexism, and the poisoning of the watershed. Frequent apocalyptic dreams rose in me at that time. In one of them I could see one-third of humanity suddenly cut down like corn stalks before a harvester. Once, when on the verge of sleep while camping at a nearby lake, I seemed to hear the earth's deep resonant songs like the keening of molten rock whales. It remained deeply imprinted in my mind as a message to stop destruction of the land and seek the natural harmonies of nature. In another dream, I entered a cathedral-sized cavern covered with metal emblems. I frantically worked to find the right combination to halt the coming destruction. These images, born of the sensitivity of an adolescent's coming of age on the threshold of taking my place as an adult in the Upper Mississippi watershed, felt like urgent messages and portents of things to come if we did not change.

As it is for most teens, my days were awash in hormonal impulses transmuted into desires for adventure after school and before curfew. We crossed the Mississippi on Route 66 over the Chain of Rocks Bridge with its mid-river 30-degree turn to watch migrating birds follow the river. We did not notice the absence of eagles on the river. The newly completed Gateway Arch symbolized our entry to new experiences across the river in jazz clubs, cafes, and comedy venues in the Victorian buildings of Gaslight Square. We heard Eric Clapton play with his band Cream and classical piano performances by Arthur Rubinstein in the St. Louis Symphony Hall. But Cahokia, a city of the Mississippian indigenous culture that ended in the year 1350, held a sustained magnetic pull for me. My curiosity heightened with the 1967 discovery of the remains of over 250 skeletons in a ridgetop earthwork designated Mound 72. The mound, aligned along the summer sunrise and winter sunset solstices, held mass graves. One contained 53 young women, killed by ligature without struggle at ages 15 to 30, nine centuries before. They had been carefully placed shoulder-to-shoulder, two bodies deep separated by remnants of woven matting. Others, males and females as well as a child, came from various time periods and social classes interred in different chambers of the mound, a few with signs of a violent end.

My friends, spooked by the Mound 72 skeletal revelations, did not want to visit the state park in which the mounds were preserved. Once, a friend drove me to where I could see the mound shapes, but he would not wait for me to explore the grounds. He was far more interested in heading to the Mississippi to look for riverboats, including the remains of the steamboat Gordon C. Greene that sank near the arched Eads Bridge connecting East St. Louis with St. Louis. I wondered if the beauty of this land with its powerful river inspired the Cahokian young women to willingly give their lives for their people. Or had it been like the sacrifice of young men who went on a wave of patriotic ideas to Vietnam, so many to be returned in coffins, or maimed, or mentally damaged. What story were the Cahokian citizens given to believe their deaths for the good of all? Later that late autumn day, I watched the patches of cobalt blue skies between dotted and dashed cloud puffs over the flat Illinois lands and rich soil visible between rows of yellow-brown curling corn stalks. I did not know how I would devote my life to this great earth or what my entry to adulthood would bring; there was still so much to learn.

My opportunity to walk ancient Cahokia and scale the top of its largest earthwork known as Monk's Mound came decades later when I attended a water conference with an O'Fallon high school friend, Doug Meyer. As we approached the state park and visitor center for the Cahokia Mounds, we became acutely aware of the Milam Landfill, the size of two football fields, two miles from the mounds. Three hundred trucks a day dump 5000 pounds of trash at the top of the landfill. Low sections of Milam remain hidden beneath grass plantc ʿ by its owner, Waste Management. But the uncovered upper sections exude a powerful stench while wheeling, strident gulls pick at the exposed trash. By the time of our visit, the garbage pile at Milam topped out at 100 feet, equal to the height of Monk's Mound. In 2017, it is near capacity at 200 feet and 176 acres of garbage. I wondered whether this garbage heap would become our ancient "mound" for future archeologists to ponder along with the Gateway Arch and the buildings of St. Louis that we could see from the top of Monk's Mound.

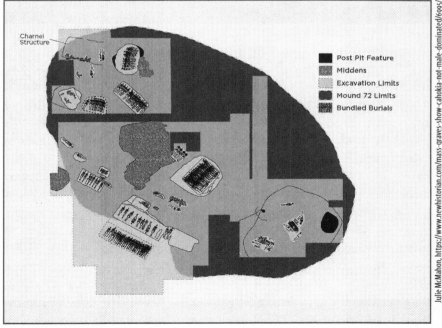

Julie McMahon, https://www.newhistorian.com/mass-graves-show-cahokia-not-male-dominated/6995/

Charnel Structure

Post Pit Feature
Middens
Excavation Limits
Mound 72 Limits
Bundled Burials

Mound 72: excavation and burials

The Cahokia Mounds have been yielding secrets with each passing year. Many view it as a cautionary tale for those who now live in these Mississippi River bottomlands. At first, Cahokia was thought to be a trade center with a dominant male hierarchy. Knowledge grew with each excavation of more mounds, the central city square, borrow pits of clay and soil, trash heaps, and remnants of surrounding villages. Later it became clear that it was an important spiritual center for fertility with both male and female leaders.

Human sacrifices occurred in Cahokia's early years, but ceased in periods of its peak and later decline along with the neglect of Monk's Mound as a center of public ritual. The city that began in 600 CE reached its prime in 1100 CE with abundant aquatic and prairie game along with cultivation of maize, legumes, and squash. Deforestation, over-hunting, possibly floods, and polluted ponds and streams may have contributed to the city's demise. And, like Rome, its fall also may have come from within for its inability to adapt and unite its people. But new evidence points to a prolonged series of droughts that resulted in its final abandonment by 1400 at the beginning of the Little Ice Age, a cooling period that lasted until the mid-1800s. As our climate experiences greater disruption through our heedless burning of fossil fuels and destructive spreading of poisons throughout the watershed, will we become a new Cahokia, a place of far more massive abandoned ruins?

Over the decades, researchers have jointly sketched a Cahokian worldview composed of an Upper World of spirits and ancestors and an Underworld of Earth and animals, with humans in between. Images of falcons or birdmen and women with infants inhabit its artifacts. The worlds were subtly joined, with liminal spaces between as spaces of great power. Rituals of fire and water promoted the fertile union of the Upper World of thunder and spirits, and the Underworld of water and agriculture. Even now at the top of Monk's Mound we can still sense the union of Upper World and Underworld in the dramatic skies above and the Mississippi bottomlands below. Did the young women of Mound 72 stand here feeling inspired and honored to give their lives in their peak fertile years for the continued fecundity of the land and people? With no signs of struggle in their deaths, it's plausible.

Cahokian fire and water rituals have been replaced in East St Louis by toxic smoke emissions, chemical dumps, and severely polluted waters. A Monsanto agri-chemical manufacturing plant, subject of environmental lawsuits, lies in the modern town of Cahokia, a suburb of East St Louis, 18 miles southwest of the ancient Cahokia. The modern Cahokia stands as the shadow side of the union of earth and water for its placement amidst the destruction of natural fertility by agricultural chemicals and toxic waste. Jonathan Kozol in *Savage Inequalities* describes it: "On the southern edge of East St. Louis, tiny shack-like houses stand along a lightless street. Immediately behind these houses are the giant buildings of Monsanto, Big River Zinc, Cerro Copper, the American Bottoms Sewage Plant, and Trade Waste Incineration—one of the largest hazardous waste incineration companies in the United States." East St. Louis remains a landmark of environmental racism. We all live downstream of environmental poisoning, but the black communities of East St. Louis suffer far more.

THE POISONED WATERSHED

While my friend Jeannie and I skipped school to eat pineapple in her backyard, or I rode on the back of a friend's motorcycle up and down steep quarry walls and abandoned strip mines, tried beer and cigarettes, or fumbled clumsily in the back seats of cars with boys, agricultural chemical products were poisoning the Mississippi farmlands and waterways in the name of crop yields. Beginning after World War II, spraying of DDT (dichloro-diphenyl-trichlrorethane), a colorless, odorless, and nearly tasteless organo-chlorine insecticide, peaked in 1963 continuing until 1972 when DDT was banned in the United States. The ban was due in part to Rachel Carson and the growing numbers of studies showing its effects on wildlife. Later we learned DDT and its breakdown product known as DDE to be associated with human preterm birth, spontaneous abortion, impaired thyroid in pregnancy and childhood, and disruption in semen quality among men. Over time DDT came to be classified as a hormone-disrupting chemical, a term that did not appear until the 1980s.

Overlapping the widespread use of DDT, a chemical compound known as Agent Orange arrived in Vietnam as well as the farms of the Midwest. The US Air Force's Operation Ranch Hand sprayed close to 17.6 million gallons of the broadleaf defoliant on Vietnamese jungles and croplands from 1962 until 1971. Vietnamese men, women, and children lost their crops, livelihoods, and their health from its application. US soldiers in Vietnam exposed to Agent Orange went on to win a hard fought lawsuit for compensation against the manufacturers of the herbicide. In the end, 52,000 veterans or their survivors received payments averaging $3,800 per person, poor compensation for the lifelong health effects of Agent Orange. No compensation was given for exposure to the herbicide in the US. At the time few knew that the herbicide 2-4-5-T and a potent contaminant known as TCDD or dioxin, was widely applied as a domestic version of Agent Orange. Used to clear cropland weeds, especially on wheat fields in the once naturally fertile Midwest drainage of the Mississippi, it too is an endocrine disruptor.

TCDD toxicity still tops the present-day list of 419 chemically related compounds under the broad term "dioxins" that are persistent organic pollutants (POPs). All POPs are a subset of endocrine disruptors, their persistence and breakdown stability in the environment making them all the more problematic. Dioxins accumulate in the fatty tissue of animals and bio-magnify in the food web, producing reproductive, immune, and neurological adverse effects along with cancers. Their hormone-mimicking properties interfere with normal human and animal hormonal function. Although various formulations of Agent Orange were banned in 1985, agricultural endocrine disruptors with their subset of persistent organic pollutants manufactured by Monsanto, Dow and other agro-chemical companies remain in many of the EPA's 14 superfund sites in East St Louis. Cleanup actions continue to this day. While the human body burden of DDT and dioxins show declines where it has been banned or phased out, there have been many others to take its place.

With decades of pesticide (insecticide, herbicide, and fungicide) applications throughout the farmlands of the Midwestern Mississippi watershed, we expect to find animal and insect declines. And there are numerous species declining or going extinct although the numbers are not always linked to pesticides, mainly due to a paucity of direct research. Amphibians may be the present leading edge of that evidence. Since the 1970s, and well documented since the 1980s, there are worldwide declines in amphibians. Will there be a time in which we no longer hear the exuberant voices of frogs on a spring night? For millennia, frog choruses have risen in the twilight as males proclaim themselves to females, the males croaking together to a crescendo and tailing off.

Consider the northern leopard frog known for their dark outlined spots and low growls underneath the high notes of spring peepers and boreal chorus frogs. In the Upper Mississippi watershed, an unfolding mystery concerns leopard frogs in particular. A group of children in the company of their teacher set out one day in 1995 to explore Ney Pond in the rural town of Henderson near the Minnesota River. Their open-eyed wonder turned to horror when half the frogs they found had missing legs or multiple legs or with legs branching into multiple sections. Surveys found similar deformities in ponds, wetlands, and fields throughout the Upper Mississippi watershed but with no obvious pattern to distinguish bodies of water with and without deformed frogs.

We have no single definitive answer to what caused the northern leopard frogs to deform in Minnesota or the amphibians of the world to decline. But we have compelling studies and strong multi-layered hypotheses. Ney Pond and other deformity hotspots, sit in the midst of cornfields, and from the very beginning agricultural chemicals were suspected of having a role. The causes appear to be multiple: pesticides, climatological changes in sunlight (UVB), changes in habitat, low immune function, possibly from chemical contaminants, and the rise of parasites and diseases affecting frog reproduction and metamorphosis. The factors do not act singly, but exacerbate one another's effects. A decade-long USGS study published in 2013 reported frequent frog deformity hotspots throughout the country, especially in the Mississippi River Valley, but there was no overall national increase. However, the decline in amphibians, especially endangered frog species and salamanders, was confirmed with an overall 3.7 percent drop in all amphibians each year throughout the country.

One of the first suspects in the Minnesota leopard frog deformities was and continues to be the herbicide atrazine. As one of the world's most commonly applied pesticides, it is the most common contaminant of groundwater and surface water. Up to one half million pounds per year are deposited in precipitation in the United States, and contamination can spread more than 600 miles from the point of application. It is one of the most common contaminants of drinking water. Research repeatedly demonstrates a phenomenon known as intersex from exposure to atrazine. Animals and insects exhibit both male and female characteristics as hermaphrodites and in de-masculinization of male gonads, a form of chemical castration. Of the known pesticides that act as endocrine disruptors in wildlife, atrazine is of special concern because it is a ubiquitous, persistent contaminant of ground and surface water and remains biologically active at low levels. This broadleaf herbicide has been the most commonly used for decades, especially on corn crops.

It is difficult to isolate atrazine as cause since atrazine is rarely applied alone, but rather in combination with a number of other pesticides along with chemical fertilizers that may interact with atrazine. In 2006, Hayes and colleagues conducted a nine-pesticide study (four herbicides, two fungicides, three insecticides) that included atrazine in low concentrations to closely parallel field conditions. The pesticide mixtures retarded frog larval growth, and most importantly, negated or reversed the time to metamorphosis and size at metamorphosis. Damage to the thymus, resulting in immunosuppression and contraction of flavobacterial meningitis infections affected 70 percent of the frogs such that they could not sit upright. Effects of the nine-pesticide mixture inflicted greater harm than single pesticides.

Another piece of the mystery comes in the form of a parasite. In many Mississippi watershed wetlands and ponds replete with agricultural chemicals, lives a flatworm parasite, *Ribeiroia ondatrae*. In 1999, Pieter Johnson demonstrated the role of fertilizer pollution in boosting the number of parasites in lakes and ponds. Parasites attack frogs at the tadpole stage, infecting cells that give rise to missing, extra, and deformed limbs. Snails, the intermediate host of the flatworm, thrive in fertilizer nutrients and increased sunlight. The confluence of agricultural pesticides, fertilizers, and climate disruption with stronger UVB exposures, and parasites leave amphibians vulnerable to disease. The fertilizers likely fostered more parasites, while pesticides depressed host immunity as well as altered critical periods of development that brought on the plague of frog malformations. And it all goes into the mix of multi-causal frog population declines with or without deformities.

Atrazine holds a place in the "Dirty Dozen" endocrine disrupting chemicals listed by the Environmental Working Group, along with organophosphate pesticides, which also cause adverse effects in human fertility, fetal growth and development. There are hundreds of organophosphate pesticides in common use, making the "dirty dozen" moniker a misnomer as each dirty dozen class can include hundreds of chemicals. Endocrine disruption studies increasingly show effects in humans in any system under hormonal control.

The exposures can be massive. An event older residents of St. Louis can recall is the destruction of Times Beach MO on old Route 66 southwest of St. Louis. This popular vacation spot became an overnight ghost town when combined PCB-dioxin oil was applied to suppress dust on roads, which prompted evacuation and superfund designation of the town. The first sign of contamination came in the deaths of 62 horses in a nearby stable. Investigation revealed extraordinary levels of dioxins. Under an immediate evacuation order, people left their homes, never to return to the Christmas decorations and holiday meals left behind. It remains contaminated to this day.

After initial focus on human female and infant reproductive issues, studies of endocrine disrupting chemicals increasingly show effects in males. Notable documented effects are declining sperm motility and quantity, male infertility, increases in testicular cancer, undescended testicles, and congenital malformation of the penis known as hypospadias where the urethra exits as the base of the penis rather than the tip. Often these conditions are found in combination and have come to be called testicular dysgenesis syndrome.

There are limitations on human EDC studies since precise exposure data can be difficult to obtain and must be examined against a background of multiple toxins in food and water. Human studies also require large numbers and long-term follow-up for best results. Difficult or not, the evidence mounts year by year, and now includes multi-generational effects in the descendants of the exposed even when the chemicals are no longer present. The persistence of these chemical exposure effects lengthens the more we examine them.

Agricultural chemical dependence for higher crop yields carries its dark side of human and animal infertility and reproductive anomalies in the disturbed watershed. Some scientists are beginning to ask if we are facing a crisis in human reproduction like the dystopian future in Margaret Atwood's book, *The Handmaid's Tale*. In that novel, humanity faces a world in which most men and women are infertile. This threat to species survival triggers a retrogressive and rigid totalitarian society of elite male rulers, with the rare fertile women hunted and forced to produce offspring for the rulers. We are still far from pervasive human infertility, but we are the creators of a poisoned watershed where all life suffers including us. We are the shadow side Cahokians as we live in the lands of Monsanto and Dow chemical and become unwitting sacrifices to the profits of agribusiness.

Stopping toxic agribusiness requires facing off with what are increasingly powerful multi-national corporations. One of the largest companies occupying a central role in the poisoning of the heartland, Monsanto manufactured not only the insecticide DDT, but PCBs, the herbicide 245-T (Agent Orange), the herbicide glyphosate (Roundup) and many other environmental toxins. It is now best known for creation of genetically modified proprietary and patent protected crop seeds. Through a process of divestment and mergers, Monsanto now focuses only on biotechnology, especially genetically modified seeds, leaving its "legacy" of poisons behind.

Still headquartered in the St. Louis metropolitan area, the current business arc for Monsanto follows from being one of four groups to introduce genes into plants in the early 1980s and the first to conduct field trials of genetically modified (GM) crops in 1987. Recently, the German-based multinational company Bayer bought out Monsanto. Bayer's areas of business include human and veterinary pharmaceuticals and consumer healthcare products. The combined Bayer-Monsanto sells farmers glyphosate in its trade name Roundup to kill unwanted broadleaf plants and grass, and sells its branded Roundup Ready seeds to survive the patented product. And its pharmaceutical arm sells treatments for the health consequences of long-term exposures to its pesticides and herbicides. We now have a company to fit Samuel Beckett's delegates for an uncommunicative god in *The Unnamable*: "Low types they must have been, their pockets full of poisons and antidotes."

Since its creation in Monsanto labs in 1970, glyphosate, a broad-spectrum systemic herbicide and main ingredient of Roundup, has become the most heavily used herbicide worldwide. In Europe, glyphosate is limited to a five-year license starting in 2018 after which it will likely be banned in Europe. The US is far from eliminating the manufacture of Roundup. With so much of the Upper Mississippi planted in genetically modified seeds including Roundup Ready and *Bacillus* modified corn (Bt-corn), federal farm regulations require farmers to plant 20 percent of their acreage as a refuge with non-GM crops. The measure aims to protect against the development of further pesticide resistance as well as for the protection of potentially beneficial insects including bees, butterflies and other pollinators. Initial compliance by farmers reached 90 percent when the ruling was first introduced, but dropped off after 2008. Current federal administrators are not interested in enforcement of the ruling.

Like Monsanto products, atrazine has been subject to corporate mergers making its regulation and environmental mitigation difficult if not impossible. It was first formulated in 1958 in Geigy labs, later to become Ciba-Geigy, renowned for the 1960s chemical dye pollution of Tom's River, NJ, an EPA superfund site to this day. It later merged with Sandoz to become Novartis. In 2000, Novartis divested its agro-chemical and GM operations, merged with Zeneca to form the Swiss-based Syngenta, the company that still holds the atrazine formula. However, ChemChina, now poised to take over Syngenta, could make regulation even more difficult in this labyrinth of international mergers and dissolutions. Most often, unmitigated "legacy" environmental poisonings get left behind in our rivers, lands, cities, and homes with no one held responsible for damages and cleanup. How can one hold ChemChina responsible with its provenance of so many folding houses of chemical company cards? The land and water of the Upper Mississippi watershed, including drinking water, remain contaminated with decades of atrazine application to fields. The elevated levels of atrazine in drinking water throughout the watershed attest to its ubiquitous and continuing presence alongside a host of other agrichemicals such as glyphosate.

Resistance by crop pests and weeds to all forms of pesticides, including herbicides, results in development of new poisons and antidotes arriving in the nation's storage barns and fields and throughout the watershed. As resistance sets in to a pesticide or herbicide, farmers resort to using additional chemicals. This process termed a "pesticide treadmill" keeps a dizzying supply of chemicals pouring over and throughout the watershed. No one can keep up with the changes. Fertilizers, mainly chemical, flow along with herbicides and pesticides into the waterways of the Mississippi watershed down to the Gulf where they create an enormous dead zone year after year. EPA regulations require farmers to abate run-off but have left it up to voluntary compliance. Research shows consistent reductions over time in agricultural pesticide and fertilizer runoff, but levels of nitrates, atrazine, and Roundup remain well above regulatory thresholds throughout the Midwest.

There are those who fight back, who work for the good of the land, who give their life energies to the health of land and people. My return to the Mississippi watershed to walk ancient Cahokia and to speak with watershed protectors, from scientists to environmentalists, tells me we can and often do succeed.

CHANGES SINCE RACHEL CARSON

One hundred years after the US Army's evicted the Dakota Nation from their traditional lands in Minnesota to partition the Upper Mississippi watershed into homesteads, we heard and saw the words *Silent Spring* in magazines and on television screens. That year, I was 11 years old and rode my bike with the rest of the neighbor kids, laughing in a cloud of DDT spewing out the back of a truck. No one chased us away from the pesticide sprays. DDT spray trucks and planes appeared in countless towns in the name of mosquito and pest control. As kids, we choked on the fumes but kept trailing after the truck. And so did the rest of the country. We were in a collective fog over this wonder substance that killed mosquitoes, was said to control malaria in the south, and kept crops free of pests in the Midwest. Or so we thought.

What the public had not seen before the Carson book was the growing body of evidence of wide-scale contamination that was poisoning not only wildlife, but our own bodies. This was Carson's message. No one was as quietly eloquent or spoke so directly to us, the uninitiated public, about the environmental crisis as Rachel Carson. Hers was a call in the wind, lifting the curtain at night to find our sleeping ears. Even as an 11-year-old, I understood her message of the pending loss of eagles and osprey, peregrine falcons, and the silencing of the spring dawn chorus of robins and songbirds.

Through the din of outrage, criticism, government inquiries, and industry propaganda, the quiet and firm voice of Rachel Carson called all generations to come and see what we have done. She called it a river of poisons. Her poetic writing held more power than diatribes or recitations of facts and yet the careful science was clearly in her writing as well. Just a year and a half after publication of *Silent Spring*, Rachel Carson died of breast cancer. She had written her book in agonizing pain, fully aware of her own impending death. Rachel Carson was 56 and would not witness the widespread growth of the environmental movement she helped foster.

Before Carson, the environmental movement was poised for change although its numbers were still relatively small. Nature mystic and founder of the Sierra Club John Muir was long dead by 1962; Aldo Leopold, wilderness philosopher and the father of ecology, had been dead for 14 years. And the forest service conservationist Gifford Pinchot had died two years before Leopold. David Brower emerged as the most influential heir to wilderness preservation. Fifty years old in 1962, Brower was navigating a tumultuous fight for Sierra Club leadership. Under charges of recklessness by Ansel Adams and others, Brower was forced to resign, but went on to found Friends of the Earth in 1969 and many other organizations thereafter. John McPhee wrote about him in *Encounters with the Archdruid*, recounting Brower's many heated confrontations. Brower bridged the movement divide between wilderness protection and a form of environmentalism we recognize today, starting with actions against the Alaska pipeline, nuclear power, and Agent Orange. He was one of the first to effectively use militant tactics such as locking one's arms or legs to pipelines and logging equipment, striking mass media campaigns, lawsuits, and lobbying in defense of the environment.

Brower's methods remain in the armamentarium of the environmental movement, especially in groups like Earth First! founded by Dave Forman who was 15 in 1962. In addition to Leopold, Carson, and Brower, Forman found inspiration in the writer and naturalist, Ed Abbey, particularly his book the *Monkey Wrench Gang* that launched nonviolent sabotage as a form of protest. Abbey's stance and tone is expressed in his oft-quoted saying: *If wilderness is outlawed, only outlaws can save wilderness.* Earth First! protests often involved dozens of people who physically locked their bodies to trees, bulldozers, and officials' desks. These methods spread to numerous other groups and actions since. I have witnessed them at many environmental protests, including against the Dakota Access Pipeline. This recently completed pipeline was built to transport shale oil from the Bakken oil fields of northwest North Dakota, under the Missouri River at Cannonball ND on the Standing Rock Sioux Reservation land, under the Mississippi River near Keokuk IA, and down to an oil tank farm near Patoka, IL not far from where I went to high school. Native water protectors locked their arms through chained padded tubes on to pipeline company bulldozers in an effort to block the pipeline.

Over time millions raised their voices to preserve the land and stop the poisoning of the water and soil. The first Earth Day in 1970, just eight years after *Silent Spring*, brought an estimated 20 million people throughout the country to what was billed as an environmental and world peace teach-in. Earth Day, celebrated every year at the beginning of the northern hemisphere spring on April 22, continues to this day worldwide.

On the Mississippi River, scientists and watershed protectors abound. The research of Dr. Calvin (Cal) Fremling, who fought to restore aquatic ecosystems, was knowledge Carson knew as evidence in her work. When Rachel Carson's book landed on bookstore shelves in 1962, Cal Fremling was 33 years old and had published evidence of the disappearance of mayflies around sewage outflows on the Mississippi. Later, Dr. Richard (Rip) Sparks who developed the flood-pulse concept, the science that underlies the role of floods in biodiversity, found inspiration in Carson. Rip Sparks was 20 years old in 1962. Others working for the Upper Mississippi included Mark Van Patten, nine at the time *Silent Spring*. Van Patten created the Missouri Stream Team program with its now more than 70,000 citizen scientists and waterway advocates who monitor contaminants, plant trees, and stabilize riverbanks. Mark attributes his inspiration to God, Rachel Carson, Ansel Adams, Aldo Leopold, and his grandparents. At the age of 12, Mark escaped from his violent street gang in LA to live with his grandparents in Missouri on a five-acre farm. They taught him to live simply on the land with care and gratitude, and he carried these lessons into the lives of thousands as Stream Teams grow and younger generations join each year.

Chad Pregracke represents a younger generation of Mississippi River defenders born in 1974 long after Carson died. Chad noticed the abuse of the river at age 19 when he and his brother were freshwater mussel fishermen. After fruitless calls to government and other groups to help, Pregracke began to clean up the Illinois River himself, retrieving tires, automobiles whole or in parts, refrigerators and all manner of trash near East Moline, not far from St Louis. He then went on to found Living Lands and Waters in 1998. With a laugh, Chad tells me his inspiration comes from Chuck Norris, skateboarding, and his parents. He is serious about his parents who are actively involved in his rivers work He was not around when Rachel Carson spoke so directly to us, but her message ripples through the generations whether or not younger water protectors know it. Chad surely knows many other older Carson-influenced Mississippi River activists such as Mark Van Patten. Pregracke's organization now hosts 98,000 volunteers with cleanup projects on 23 rivers and on-going river education projects on its headquarters river barge. In 2017, the group planted the millionth tree in their river bottomlands *Million Trees* project. There are many others, men and women, all ages, most unsung, quietly doing the work of river and watershed restoration throughout the

Upper Mississippi watershed. It is as if the Gateway Arch to Jeffersonian westward expansion and colonization changed its role to a gateway for a growing environmental movement.

So much has changed since Rachel Carson's time. She would have been amazed to learn where science has taken us since her death: plate tectonics, evolutionary genetics, and biodiversity pathways billions of years old. She did not know of the rise in greenhouse gases, acidification of the world's oceans, disruption and collapse of so many co-evolutionary ecosystems. In *The Sea Around Us,* a book published prior to *Silent Spring,* Carson tells us we live in a special period of a slight natural rise in sea levels. In fact, the seas continue to rise to the present, the result of global climate disruption. The science of greenhouse gases was then in its infancy, with the most well known early measurement of CO_2 rise by Charles David Keeling taken at the Mauna Loa observatory just beginning to show an increase in the middle atmosphere. The longest continuous measurement of CO_2, in what is called the Keeling curve, now shows a dramatic rise of CO_2 from 315 ppm in 1960 to over 400 ppm at present. The rise constitutes one of the basic facts of human-generated climate disruption from the burning of fossil fuels. We can change this if we work together in multi-pronged actions just as we did to halt DDT and dioxin.

DDT and dioxin were banned and restrictions or bans placed on other pesticides. We can directly witness the effects of bans on DDT and dioxin in the watershed. Over 2000 eagles now make the triple confluence of the Missouri, Illinois and Mississippi Rivers at St. Louis their largest North American over-wintering grounds. Osprey and peregrine falcons have returned, and the avian dawn chorus of birds and evening frog songs still rise each year, although they remain in danger. The beauty we found as adolescents in the snowy fields and streams of the Mississippi watershed near St. Louis can still be seen, though we must work quickly to maintain the environmental gains as well as end the continuing river of poisons in the watershed.

We can make these changes. We have already made so many changes. May we continue to give our lives in activism to restore the fertility of the watershed and all its dependent lives.

CHAPTER FIVE

SALT FRONT OF THE RIVER THAT FLOWS BOTH WAYS

Lower Hudson

WHEN I FIRST ARRIVED IN New York City in 1969, like most of the city's inhabitants, I was unaware of the Hudson River's tides. At age 18, I had come to stay with a friend's family in Manhattan's Washington Heights for the summer. It was the summer Viet Nam troop withdrawals began, followed by the Stonewall Riots in the city for gay rights. At the end of summer, the first Woodstock Festival in Bethel, NY became a symbol of my generation. While these signal events were unfolding, the Hudson River received ocean tides twice daily just as it always had.

From the tip of Manhattan, designated Hudson River Mile Zero, the Hudson's estuary runs up to the federal dam at Troy, Hudson River Mile 153 just above Albany. New York Harbor is the doorway to moon-driven ocean tides surging upriver to be met by the down flow of freshwater. Their meeting is layered, the denser seawater on the bottom, with freshwater from runoff sliding over the top of the salt layers. The salt in the water mingles through turbulence and chemistry, the direction of change between dense to a less dense solution of salts. The point at which salinity drops enough to declare the river drinking water safe is called the salt front. The salt front changes with the height of tides, strength of waves, downstream flow dynamics, and the power of storms. Plots of the salt front show wide seasonal swings over the years, from periods of heavy rains to droughts, like the etchings made by a seismograph recording ground movement in an active earthquake, but with a time-scale of years and seasons rather than hours and days. Most days the salt front is near the Tappan Zee Bridge at Hudson River Mile 25, but in times of drought, it can be close to Poughkeepsie, River Mile 75.

Mid-way in the range of the salt front at Hudson River Mile 55, a weathered granitic mountain juts into the channel the Dutch called the "Wey Gat," the wind gate to the Hudson highlands. The mountain called Storm King rises 1,340 feet above the river, overlooking prime fish spawning nurseries. Storm King is a crucial river milestone in both the story of the near-death and resurrection of the Hudson for aquatic life, and in the engineering of New York City's drinking water. The two tales span over two centuries, with my own story coming into the period of the greatest threat to the Hudson and the growth of the movement to save it. I'll start with my own migrations, just like the fish, over oceans and upriver struggles into growing awareness of the plight of the Hudson.

I got a job at Saks Fifth Avenue in 1969, my first summer in NYC. To her mother's delight, my friend Susan took a job at Gimbals, the sister store to Saks. She was a feminist anti-war activist who admired Workers' World Party, a Marxist-Feminist organization. We could speak openly of her activism at Susan's place with our backs turned to her parents, as both were deaf. As marriage counselors in the deaf community, they knew marital discord, their own and others. Susan, her brother Benjy, and I would huddle in the grey-green back bedroom listening to their uninflected staccato voices, imagining their wild gestures. We heard the metallic tings of hurled wedding rings at the conclusion of their fight.

My retail "career" ended later that summer, and I made it to Seattle on the back of a friend's motorcycle. Cashing in my college insurance money, I boarded a plane for a one-way flight to Japan. In a dank Kyoto jazz coffee shop, I met and later moved in with a long-haired Japanese jazz musician. We lived with his family in a tiny hamlet beside rice paddies northwest of Tokyo until we could travel to the US. At the American embassy in Tokyo, we were married without the approval of our families, followed by his application for immigration the same day. But my husband's US residency was denied due to an underage marijuana arrest. With Les Paul guitar in hand, we headed to Canada to find a way to enter the US.

The final leg of my return journey to the city at the mouth of the Hudson occurred four years of Canadian residency later. An ACLU lawyer told us our best chance would be to petition from within the US no matter how we managed to get in. At a Canada-US border crossing in early January of 1978, a shivering US border agent asked for my ID. Then he asked my husband if he too was an American citizen. He said yes, and the border agent let us through. The light reflected from mounded roadside snow accompanied us to Seattle for the flight to NYC.

We were young parents of a one-year-old without jobs in an overpowering city. We moved into a sixth-floor walk-up apartment in Hell's Kitchen at Hudson River Mile 5 where the river is heavy with salt. For us the Hudson was a view from our building and NYC drinking water a short trip through the apartment's plumbing. My unemployment checks barely sustained us until I obtained a job at Columbia University. It had been a ten-year full circle migration since I first entered the city at eighteen.

We continued to live five miles north of New York Harbor until our marriage fell apart in 1980. The end came when we were living in Manhattan Plaza, a midtown performing arts building. For a time, my life was borne in tidal shifts, a salt front of tears, and upstream travel like the shad, herring, sturgeon, and striped bass to freshwater spawning grounds. I moved by incremental river miles until I completed a masters' degree in environmental epidemiology. Had I not already been working at Columbia, I would not have gone to school. Perhaps it was the Hudson River's tides rocking me in my grief that made me quiet enough to hear the sound of lapping waves urging me upriver.

Partway through a doctorate pieced together from on-the-job work and publications, I moved over the bridge from Manhattan to the Bronx. I had moved from Hudson River Mile 5 to Hudson River Mile 15, a fifty-minute ride on the Broadway No. 1 train, but it was 15 years between adolescent to researcher of epidemics. I continued to shift in and out of school while working and raising my daughter in a time so many NY epidemiologists came to be needed for the AIDS epidemic. It was dizzying, pressured, and by the end, I was heading into burnout. Giving up my faculty appointment, I moved to the Catskills where the NYCs drinking water starts out as rain. By then, I had spent close to five decades off and on traveling the watershed of the Lower Hudson, the source of our bounty, recipient of our abusive ignorance, and birthplace of a precedent-setting legal victory in favor of the beauty of the land.

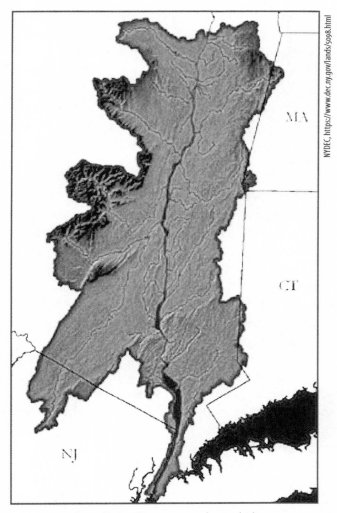

NYDEC, https://www.dec.ny.gov/lands/5098.html

Lower Hudson River estuary and watershed

ASCENDING THE RIVER

Below the surface of the Hudson River live uncounted finned beings of shadowy dappled hues and silvery flashes revealed by sunlight. They move in watery layers, some bottom or benthic feeders, others near the surface. They have been in the Hudson estuary since the river first filled the glacier-carved Hudson Fjord 26,000 years ago. Except for spotting the occasional fisherman on the riverbank in Harlem or to buy Hudson River fish in west side markets at Citarella's or Barney

Greengrass, I was unaware of the life beneath the surface when I lived in Manhattan. As my personal vortex of life dramas lessened, I began to hear the tragedy of fisheries as they came to light in the late 1970s and 1980s. Anadromous fish, those migrating upriver from saltwater to freshwater, were in trouble. Their ability to live in the ocean and the brackish estuary, and to spawn in fresh waters above the salt front was no longer an evolutionary advantage. On the Hudson, just 300 years into post-European Contact, most fisheries were already in steep decline. In my lifetime, it became far worse.

Unlike the salmon that spawn and die upstream, the Hudson River's upstream running anadromous shad, striped bass, and sturgeon travel up and then back downstream after spawning in the river's fresh water. In good conditions, many make this difficult passage from their birthplace upriver, maturing as juveniles above the salt front, and then move down, waiting out high tides to swim with the retreating ebb tides. They join the fish and sea mammal migrations, a complex food web feasting its way up and down the ocean's continental shelf and back again in seasonal cycles.

It begins with the spring thaw. Schools of American shad, herring, and alewives enter the Hudson estuary followed in time by Atlantic striped bass and sturgeon to travel upstream to the edge of the salt front and beyond to their spawning grounds. They must make adjustments to their speed of water intake, chemical osmotic processes in their gills, and change their rate of fat metabolism to survive the round trip. They are finely attuned to changing river salinity, currents, tides, temperature, and channel geomorphology. No one knows how the fish find their way back to natal rivers, but if they survive their time in the ocean, nearly all return for the seasonal run. Some say they smell the unique mineral mix of the river water. In the past 100 years, a time for which records have been kept, close to 80 percent of historic Hudson River anadromous fish populations went missing. In some cases it was 90 percent loss or 97 percent and even 98.5 percent. It is hard to hold these shifting numbers.

Not acts of nature, not freshwater fish disease epidemics like "ich"— *Ichthyophthirius multifiliis,* and not food chain competition— the failures are human-caused. We built ecologically unsound dams, dumped agricultural and industrial pollution along with storm and sewer discharges, and overfished for most of the past two centuries. These days the Hudson is in a recovery phase. A massive environmental movement to foster its recovery lives here, and its birthplace is the Wey Gat at Storm King.

ENVIRONMENTAL TRIUMPH AT STORM KING

The year my marriage ended also saw the end to a proposal to destroy a major section of Storm King Mountain for a fish-killing Consolidated Edison (Con Ed) hydroelectric plant. It was four days before Christmas in 1980 when the news came. With daytime temps in the low 20s and winds 30mph on Broadway and 112th St, I fought my way through the door into Tom's restaurant. Over a bagel and egg breakfast, I saw a headline at the bottom left side of the front page of the New York Times: *Con Ed to Drop Storm King Plant as Part of Pact to Protect Hudson.* If I had turned to the person on the seat next to me to share this good news, I most likely would have been met with a don't-bother-me shrug. It was a singularly important watershed decision. Consolidated Edison, the company that made the lights and everything electrical work in Manhattan, had proposed a new power plant at Storm King 17 years prior. It would have blown up a third of the mountain's base to lift water to the mountaintop for down-flow hydropower in a cost-ineffective plan.

Most people were unaware of the fight by Hudson River citizen-activists against the Storm King hydroelectric plant. For me, the news that the Storm King power plant was at last blocked cheered me on this wintry day as I ventured out to shop for Christmas groceries. Its details and importance did not fully sink in until I was living outside of NYC not

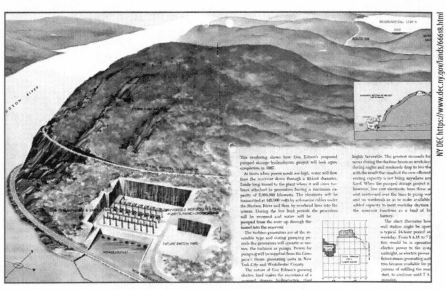

NY DEC https://www.dec.ny.gov/lands/66618.html

Consolidated Edison 1962 power plant proposal for Storm King far from Storm King and learned the full account of the 17-year battle from local residents and river activists. That history is so important it is taught as a module in law school course curricula even for those not going into environmental law.

The first drawings of Con Ed's proposal to blast apart the mountain evoked feelings of appalling desecration and violation in 1963. Completely unaware of potential outcry, the company published the drawing which intensified opposition to the plan. A bald and worn yet glittering mountain, Storm King had become a temple in the American landscape under the brush of Thomas Cole and other nineteenth century Hudson River School painters. It was equivalent to announcing the destruction of a third of the base of El Capitan in Yosemite. Just as John Muir, the naturalist founder of the Sierra Club, had been heartsick literally unto death over the 1914 damming of Yosemite's Hetch Hetchy valley, so too were a handful of determined citizens of the Hudson River lower watershed heartsick over Con Ed's proposal. They created the organization, Scenic Hudson, to fight the power company, dogging the company in all of its meetings. Scenic Hudson's volunteers, referred to by Con Ed representatives and lawyers as "those birder women in sneakers," hired brilliant lawyers to sue Con Ed, winning after 17 years in court.

Founding members of Scenic Hudson joined with Bob Boyle, sports writer and fisherman who founded the Hudson River Fishermen's Association (HRFA), progenitor of Hudson Riverkeeper. To this day, Hudson Riverkeeper, a watchdog group funded and run by citizen activists, defends the Hudson and protects New York City drinking water. The initial small numbers of activists in the front-line against the Con Ed belied their strength. Perhaps the fish, birds, and the mountain itself came into their dreams at night, infusing them with strength. Certainly the crows had a role. Called by circling cawing crows, fishermen found piles of dead striped bass a dozen feet high near the Indian Point nuclear plant 15 miles downriver from Storm King. It too a Con Ed company, managers had secretly piled the fish beside the river after they had been killed by the utility plant's cold water intake machinery and warm water discharges. Indian Point nuclear power plant destroyed over a million Atlantic striped bass when operations began in 1962. The proposed Con Edison plant at Storm King would have similar cooling water intake and outflow structures as the Indian Point nuclear plant, enough to double the fish kill.

The two plants operating in close proximity would destroy the prime fish nurseries and juvenile fish habitats of the Hudson.

The case against Con Edison grew to 11 environmental groups and government agencies before the last court decision was finalized. Its period, from 1963 to the 1981 final signing, marks unprecedented victories in the history of the American environmental movement. In the first year, the Clean Air Act was passed by Congress and became a template for other major environmental laws to follow. Then came passage of the National Environmental Policy Act of 1969. The following year saw the creation of the Environmental Protection Agency. Shortly after, three more legislative jewels appeared, the Clean Water Act of 1972, the Endangered Species Act of 1973, and then the Toxic Substances Control Act of 1976. The environmental groups fighting for Storm King and the Hudson River fish were deeply involved in crafting legislation, and were especially instrumental to the National Environmental Policy Act (NEPA).

The voices of the First Earth Day in 1970 brought greater numbers to the movement. That year also saw the founding of the Natural Resources Defense Council, and the environmental law clinic at Pace to train lawyers expert in the growing body of new rulings and legislation. By 1980 there were more than 100,000 visibly strong citizen voices in NYC alone on Earth Day against those who would destroy the life of the Hudson's estuary. There are now millions of voices united with Hudson watershed grassroots collaboration of fishermen and citizen's groups, a powerful alliance to this day. For ordinary citizens, the true innovation in these actions grew into our inalienable right to invoke the laws and, when needed, initiate lawsuits in the name of the land, for its beauty and its wildlife. The natural world continues to win in so many places of the Hudson watershed and throughout the country, thanks to our profoundly intelligent and passionate citizen activists who took on Con Edison at Storm King.

There will never be a utility plant at Storm King or any other new location on the Hudson as a condition of the settlement. From the battle against Con Ed emerged the first truly strong environmental rulings that still serve as a cornerstone of environmental law. When the final Storm King agreement came in 1981, few could anticipate the spectacular growth of the environmental movement to come. And few could anticipate the enormity of the challenges that also came to light during and since that time. Yet every day, multiple environmental groups wielding powerful laws in grassroots activism counter the destruction. The Storm King Settlement shines a beacon light throughout the land just as lights atop Beacon Mountain across from Storm King in the Wind Gate of the Hudson Highlands once alerted the countryside to the movements of the British troops in the American revolutionary war.

We owe the Storm King Settlement an incalculable debt of gratitude. Each time I traverse the Hudson by Storm King, I pay homage to the Hudson River saviors who changed the world. When I am on the east side across from Storm King, I stand in silence at Cold Spring to give thanks to Franny Reese at the place she died on the roadside across from Storm King. She began her adult life as an artist and poet who taught herself law in order to stand up for the land and act as inspired leader of Scenic Hudson. She remains ever etched in my memory from a photo of her slender form and wavy hair pulled back at her neck, an "F" on her lapel jacket, as she sits next to the balding Bob Boyle to sign the Storm King Agreement. She died in 2003 at age 85 when her driver lost control of her car and hit a utility pole in full view of Storm King.

The names of the environmental laws may not resonate with most, and their acronyms are certainly not poetic, but I believe their names should be invoked, chanted in a sunrise service at Storm King: CAA, NEPA, EPA, CWA, ESA, and TSCA. And a memorial should be created for those who fought this good war, a memorial as great as Maya Lin's Viet Nam memorial, atop Storm King beside its fine art park.

WHO HEARS THE CRIES OF THE FISH?

Restoration of the Hudson fisheries comes in long-term sequences of steps against the history of sustained ecological tragedy. The New York Times declared the Storm King Agreement successful except for "a few fish deaths." The requirement of closed systems on utility plant water intake and discharge came years later. Even a few fish deaths matter in the perspective of decades of multiple fisheries decline. "Who hears the fish when they cry," asked Henry David Thoreau during his time at Walden Pond in the latter half of the 1840s. Even then massive takes of fish, especially American shad, the largest of the herring, took place. Shad, the first to appear in the Hudson in the spring thaw, fed the Lenape nation, early settlers, and the fledgling United States. George Washington himself was a farmer and a commercial shad fisherman. Some say the spring shad run rescued the revolutionary army at Valley Forge.

The fishermen on the Hudson directly witnessed fish stocks plummet since their grandfathers' time and with that the end of livelihoods. Only a handful of commercial fishermen remain on the Hudson. Factory-scale fishing operations, especially on the ocean side of the river before the fish have a chance to swim upstream, destroyed fisheries and ruined the lives of subsistence fishermen and small companies. Atlantic sturgeon fisheries were closed in 1996, after which all Atlantic seaboard states imposed a 40-year moratorium. The American shad fisheries closed in 2010, though Atlantic striped bass fisheries re-opened close to that time on a limited basis.

Fish and river scientists work tirelessly to restore fish populations beyond simple survival. We fail even if they do not go extinct but become ghost species, those fish not extinct but no longer with sufficient numbers to occupy their pre-industrial age ecological niche. Recovery is a moving target. Current population level comparisons do not address peak populations or the carrying capacity of a healthy river. We do not know what healthy populations comprise since most Hudson River fisheries experienced their catastrophic collapses well over a hundred years ago. There is no absolute measuring chart, just a process of long-term protection, observation, and research. Attuned to their movements, we find welcome signs of recovery. Striped bass, alewives, and herring have been increasing their populations since 1990. The American shad fishery can be expected to follow given its current fishing moratorium.

A fish I especially love is the sturgeon. With 27 species throughout the world, the two native species of the Hudson remain in steep decline. I pray that the sturgeon logo of the Hudson estuary posted up and down the river does not become the grave marker of its local extinction. This living fossil fish sports tail fins resembling those of sharks, and possesses barbels, rake like projections at its mouth, for dredging the river bottom sediments. Except for its jaw and its armor plates of scutes, it is cartilaginous, a marker of its evolutionary path before the rise of bony fishes. The ancestors of sturgeon, once more plentiful than Passenger Pigeons, survived the dinosaur extinctions over 60 million years ago. And they came from a far earlier time.

Sturgeon predecessors from the Devonian age of fishes 500 million years ago survived the Great Dying of the Permian-Triassic mass extinction event. They outlived the over 50 percent of marine genera with all their sub-classed species suddenly extinct 252 million years ago. Sturgeon survived the Great Dying's 14-degree rise in global temperature, heavy ocean acidification, oxygen at 80 percent of present levels, and CO_2 at 2000 ppm, five times current concentrations. These ancient ones could not foresee a time in which female sturgeons would become fertilizer after being taken solely for their eggs as caviar. By the early twentieth century, sturgeon had been nearly clear-cut from the Hudson and the Delaware Rivers by commercial fishing in the caviar craze of the late 1800s. Long-lived at up to 60 years, typically six to eight feet in length and weighing 200 pounds, aged 20 at their first spawn, sturgeon recovery takes time. No one knows when and to what extent sturgeon populations will rebound in the Hudson. At present sturgeon juvenile numbers show increases thanks to the Atlantic sturgeon fishing moratorium and the endangered species act designation for the short-nosed sturgeon. We thrill to the sight of scarce young sturgeon in the river. Their photos taken by fishery scientists are like pictures of grandchildren, lovingly passed on.

OUR OWN LIVES AT STAKE

Like the tragedies of the river, my early life in New York City was challenged by living at the edge of the abused Hudson near Sputyen Duyvil in the Bronx. And just like the river, I received many hands reaching in to help me, but not until I felt the destructive forces deeply. The plight of the fish and our own health are inextricably interwoven as are the movements for social justice and environmental change. The year I first arrived in Manhattan in 1969 was a time of widespread activism: anti-war, civil rights, gay and lesbian rights (other sexual rights issues came later), women's equality. The following year, the first Earth Day arrived to mark this change in awareness. In my mind, it is one movement of compassion, inclusiveness, and the end to the poisoning of ourselves and all those around us. In Zen Buddhism there is a saying: how we do one thing is how we do all things. There remains a lot to undo.

In the 1980s, the city became an assault on my peace of mind through its noise, pollution, and crime as well as the unbearable grief of knowing what we had done to the land and water. Daily survival anxiety stuck sharp knifepoints into my awareness. Everyone I worked with had been mugged, robbed, assaulted, or scammed at least once and some multiple times. I was mugged and robbed, sexually assaulted, groped on the subway, experienced an apartment break-in, and my car stolen while I lived in the city. Others had it far worse. In the mid-1970s, the streets were littered with crack-cocaine vials and people sleeping it off on building stoops.

And beginning in the late 1970s, but not recognized until the early 1980s, New York City became the North American center for the AIDS epidemic. Like so many epidemiologists, I was called away from environmental work to the front lines of the epidemic. As an HIV/AIDS epidemiologist with friends, neighbors, and study patients dying every week, my research work tracking the epidemic often felt ineffectual. It was like looking for patterns in post-mortem entrails, too late to make a difference. The reality was far more hopeful, but it was a feeling I had when in the throes of unrelenting hard work. In decades of time, the threads strung by activists, scientists, clinicians, and epidemiologists began to control and slow the AIDS epidemic, like a malevolent Gulliver strapped by Lilliputians. But in the day-to-day experience of work, I felt like a foot soldier in a losing war. So many died, especially the poor. In my old Manhattan Plaza performing arts building at Hudson River Mile 5, black crepe-draped photos of dead friends and neighbors appeared every week.

BEYOND STORM KING: GENERAL ELECTRIC AND PCBS

During the 1980s, environmental activism for the Hudson grew as a continuous stream of problems surfaced. In 1983, The EPA declared the 200-mile stretch of the river from Hudson Falls to the Hudson Harbor a Superfund Site under the 1980 law with a name nobody says in full—the Comprehensive Environmental Response, Compensation, and Liability Act (CERCLA). It is simply called "the Superfund" a name that underplays the dire nature of its function to manage and pay for mitigation of extreme environmental destruction.

Most people have heard of the polychlorinated biphenyl (PCB) contamination that made the Hudson a Superfund Site although the story bears retelling in the context of Storm King. Thirteen years after the Storm King fight began and five years before the public news of PCB contamination by General Electric in 1975, Bob Boyle, leader of the fishermen's association in the Storm King fight, tested Atlantic striped bass from the Hudson. Results showed PCBs at abnormally high levels. The data were shared with government regulators but nothing was done. Fish were still caught, sold, and eaten. After a ban on PCBs throughout the US in 1977, contamination levels decreased, but not enough for safe consumption of fish.

The damage from the General Electric capacitor plants dumping of PCBs in the beloved Hudson River imprinted deeply in public awareness. It was a personal assault, especially when the state banned harvest of all commercially viable fish species, with the exception for a short time of large adult sturgeon below the federal dam at Troy. No one was allowed to swim in the river. Mid-water column and bottom feeding fish, striped bass and sturgeon, in particular, were hard hit by PCB pollution of the Hudson, as the oily molecule tends to attach to river bottom sediments. At General Electric's Hudson Falls capacitor manufacturing plants at River Miles 193 and 178, more than 1.3 million pounds of PCBs were actively dumped and passively streamed into the Hudson River from 1947 to 1977.

By 1975, there were 171 scientific papers on PCB contamination in fish, birds, domestic animals, and humans. Monsanto, the only US manufacturer of PCBs, knew of its toxicity as shown by internal documents from at least the 1960s and probably as early as the 1930s. In thousands of studies over the decades, PCBs have been shown to harm humans, domestic animals, and wildlife in a long list of conditions that can be roughly categorized as immune and thyroid dysfunction, hormone disruption including effects on fetal development, neurological and skin conditions, and tumors in animals domestic and wild. PCBs are classed as a probable human carcinogen.

PCB dredging and removal, declared successful by those monitoring the Hudson, ended in 2015, although some river advocates say it is not complete. The next phase of work may prove intractable: dismantling the GE plants from which discharge into the river continues from a mile long underground lake of PCBs that no one yet knows how to staunch. Like Con Ed, General Electric fought judgments against them. It took two decades before GE agreed to the cleanup. And even then, the EPA made concessions to GE to clean up a third less than originally agreed.

PCBs are the dark side of the electric age. Widely used in everything electrical, including transformers and the ballast of fluorescent lights, the stable, hydrophobic yellow oil settles into river sediments, attaches to particles, and can become airborne in turbulent water. They persist in the environment for centuries. If PCBs were a visible unique and indestructible pigment, one could see the man-made molecules mapping the entire world in plants, animals, and in bodies of water, ice, and rainwater. The most concentrated pigments would be in the animals at the top of the food chain, darker than the most contaminated river water, especially in big fish and mammals eating fish from the Hudson. We would see them stored in my body fat, that of my daughter, and everyone we know.

PCBs brought increasing numbers of people into environmental activism. It was PCB contamination that called forth the Sloop Clearwater and folksinger Pete Seeger to travel up and down the Hudson. The Clearwater organization asked people to unite, to educate one another, and to end river contamination. This elegant nineteenth century model sloop still sails its mission from port to port, festival to festival, its environmental vision emanating in song. From clean-up efforts and 25 years of EPA and citizen science monitoring, we can now safely swim in some places in the Hudson, eat limited quantities of river fish, and hope for a time when the songs calling us to action might turn to celebration. But even as we celebrate victories, we must remain vigilant and ever ready to defend the Hudson.

LET'S NOT FORGET THE ZEBRA MUSSEL

I could list all the harms done to the river, but it would take a lot of mind-numbing words and depressing numbers. However, I am intrigued by the story of the zebra mussel. In an unexpected stroke of luck from the zebra mussel's perspective, the shellfish arrived one day in the ballast of ocean-going vessels from Eurasia sometime in 1991. By the end of 1992, the coin-sized striped mollusks dominated the Hudson above the river's salt front, filtering a volume of water equal to the entire estuary every two to four days. Dissolved oxygen levels plummeted as the zebra mussel joined forces with the water chestnut, an earlier arrival in the watershed. *Trapa Natans*, or water chestnut, a native of Eurasia not to be confused with water chestnuts used in recipes and restaurants, was inadvertently introduced into the Hudson-Mohawk watershed, where it spread unchecked. *T. Natans* form dense mats blocking sunlight to aquatic plants below the surface, and its yearly die-off decreases dissolved oxygen. As the zebra mussel and water chestnut both flourished, phytoplankton fell by 80 percent and zooplankton by 70 percent. Native freshwater pearly mussels and clams nearly disappeared.

For reasons no one completely understands, long-term monitoring of zebra mussels now shows a decade-long decrease with a countering rise in native mussels along with a return to earlier levels of zooplankton, albeit little recovery as yet in phytoplankton. The water chestnut, ever more common in the Hudson and extending its range south to Virginia and north into Canada, may be responsible for the continued loss of phytoplankton. As for the zebra mussel, it may be the blue crabs expanded their menu to include the invading mussels along with native species. And zebra mussels may have filtered too many toxins with adverse effects on their offspring. No one knows for sure. Sometimes unseen nature guardians of the Hudson take a hand.

MID-HUDSON TURNING POINTS AND TRANSITIONS

In the early 1990s, I moved away from the city to the country on a line nearly straight across from the Beacon-Newburgh Bridge above Storm King in Dutchess County. Still I commuted most days to the city to work in epidemiology. It felt like I was in post-city rehab in the farmlands and woods while I still carried my toxic life burdens like hidden poisons in river sediment. On the parkways running parallel to the Hudson, the long wave sounds of wheels on pavement accompanied me to and from the city to collapse in exhaustion each night.

After a summer of near-deafening frog and insect choruses outside my window, I found hidden stores of inspiration and unexpected resilience. In 1993, my resurgence upriver brought me to create a nonprofit called Bronx Community Works. Friends laughingly called it "The Works" for the plethora of programs, environmental and social. Although the nonprofit work cut into my research job duties, my good friends and colleagues in epidemiology work cut me a great deal of slack. They told me to consider it their donation to my nonprofit. And they assisted me in getting grants as well. This unstinting support especially buoyed my spirits.

Every day I had new program ideas. It was hard to stop the flow seeded so many years before in environmental and social justice movements. We worked with the parks department on restoration of meadows, forests, and the Bronx River, a 24-mile stream in the Hudson watershed that empties into the East River. We brought this work to those at the very bottom of the social order. One Community Works' program, called Planet Hot Plate, hosted festive healthy cooking groups for those living with HIV, many of whom also participated in the parks and waterways programs. Some of the people attending had triple diagnoses: HIV/AIDS, diagnosed mental illness, and drug addiction. Add to that the heavy burdens of poverty, racial bias, and high crime neighborhoods in the city. For the people in my research programs and in the nonprofit, many of them Viet Nam veterans, the city didn't just feel like combat, it *was* combat. To counter the surrounding din of impending disease and death from HIV and so many complicated adverse conditions, we held gatherings to work in the watershed, cook, tell stories, and create gardens for Bronx schools.

The Community Works garden group and peer educators, Carlos, Mark, and Ronald, became especially dear to me. I recall a woman who joined us but refused to speak. After digging a new trail in Van Courtland Park in the Bronx River watershed, we learned she had been raped, then stabbed and left for dead in an alley two weeks before. At lunch, she was soon playfully laughing with the others. Another time, new participants showed up to help remove invasive bittersweet vines the team called "strangulation vines." At the end, with loppers and shovels in hand, the newcomers threatened me when I told them it was volunteer, no pay, though we gave everyone lunch and subway fare. My regulars, many of them Vietnam war veterans, surrounded me, forcing them to drop their tools and leave. Later we set up a certificate program for the core participants through the New York Botanical Gardens and parks department. The award ceremony was small yet unforgettable in its outpouring of joyful accomplishment.

One summer, a man named Ritchie came to us. A bone-thin Gulf War veteran in his 40s, Ritchie soon developed weakness with intermittent fevers. Still, he would show up to work, although he could barely manage sitting in the sun while the others planted and weeded a South Bronx school community garden. When the group learned Ritchie was hospitalized, we all went to visit. He was hooked up to intravenous blood and fluids that the nurse bungled, spraying blood all over his sheets. His only comment was to apologize for not coming to work with us. When Ritchie died of HIV/AIDS and tuberculosis, no relatives came forward. We located his daughter and collected money for his burial.

I hear that some of these Community Works men and women survived long enough for the improvements in HIV treatment, and are thriving in their renewed lives. They and I would remember Ritchie and others who did not survive.

These days, the river is far cleaner and crime much lower than it was in the 80s when I fled the city. The city moved to restore neighborhood beauty and pride, one trashed-out neighborhood at a time. It is my hope this spirit continues. In my life, the threads of social and environmental movements have never been separated. While the city worked on the built environment, a long, low hum of greening appeared in the Hudson watershed that is now flowering in manifold ways. My own community program exemplified this integration of care for one another and the earth. We grew organic vegetables in schoolyards, and brought nutritious food to low-income neighborhood food deserts. Community Works people would go from cooking meals to meadow restoration to river cleanups in an unbroken sequence. At the beginning of a session, we meditated for five minutes together. At times we read poetry or did yoga while sitting on chairs. Those leading yoga had to be aware that so many came from traumatic childhood abuse and war, such that lowering one's head below the heart felt dangerous. We told one another our stories when we gathered for the meals that ended each session. Each awakening affects everything else. These people, scorned and abused throughout their lives, gave more to the city than most NYC residents at the time.

PURE WATER FOR THE CITY

The people who brought about the defeat of Storm King power plant and the cleanup of the Hudson were also active in resolving the problems of the city's water in reservoirs above the city to the East of the Hudson. Conflicts began with external water grabs by the city under DeWitt Clinton, sixth Governor of NY (1817-1822) and builder of the Eire Canal. He selected the Croton River, which empties into the Hudson River Mile 35 at Croton-on-Hudson, as a water source. The first reservoirs of the Croton system were finished in 1842, long after Clinton's death in 1828. Engineering of the Catskills streams away from their natural destinations in the Hudson watershed began 65 years later. By the time the Catskills system came about, the city had plenty of experience in securing rights by any means. Using eminent domain powers to take private property for public use, the people of the Catskills were forced to submit to NYC watershed ownership in 1905.

The Catskills forests and streams came to be protected as an add-on to an 1885 bill curtailing logging in the Adirondacks around the headwaters of the Hudson. At the time, Catskill streams were considered unimportant but local politicians saw a tax benefit and managed to append its protection at the last minute. Once tangible plans to appropriate Catskills water were laid out just 20 years later, the city could not be stopped. With its powerful financial centers and political ties, in spite of the Catskill Forest Preserve protections, it acquired rights to the land and water. The building of the system moved quickly, not waiting for settlement of lawsuits by those living in the newly designated watershed. By 1916, NYC residents in all five boroughs began to drink and bathe in piped-in Catskills rain.

It took less than a generation after completion of all the systems' reservoirs in 1964 for city residents to forget where the water came from. Everyone believed the hype that it was the best water in the world. The first major jolt to that belief came in the 1980s when Hudson Riverkeeper and the Natural Resources Defense Council (NRDC) ran a shocking ad campaign to alert New Yorkers to the sewage contamination of the Croton System to the East of the Hudson. The ad bore the image of a cup on which a man sat with his pants down. Raw sewage was pouring into the Croton Reservoir and mingled with other reservoir waters to the city. Hudson Riverkeeper and others forced the cleanup of the Croton system. A smirking David Letterman on his late night David Letterman Show spread the news nationally by proffering a mug of NYC water with the words, "Bottom's Up. Literally."

The legal actions moved up to the Catskills. In 1997, the Hudson Riverkeeper organization, represented at that time by Robert Kennedy, Jr., was a signer to an agreement made between NYC Department of Environmental Protection (NYC DEP), the Catskills Coalition of Towns, and 15 other groups and organizations. It is called "The M-O-A," the same way one calls NYC "The City," as if no other memorandum of agreement or city exists. The agreement came about to avoid an EPA-ordered nation-wide ruling: filter the water or prove water quality standards can be met without filtration. By then, the older east of Hudson Croton system was too polluted and required filtration. But the Catskills reservoirs, Ashokan and Schoharie in particular, had a chance, provided the city's watershed protection could be stepped up.

With the active presence of NYC DEPs water police in the Catskills, upstate residents do not forget that the city claims the water. The brilliant farmers and ranchers of the Hudson Valley, anticipating the potentially damaging action to come, drafted their own plan ahead of the city. That plan was modified by the Watershed Coalition of Towns to become a central foundation for the agreement with NYC. With a NYC water commissioner they could respect in Marilyn Gelber, upstaters did most of the heavy lifting. The role of upstate plan writers and negotiators that included economic assistance to compensate for curtailment of polluting industry and development in the Catskills watershed was another crucial turning point in watershed environmental history.

REBIRTH IN PURE WATER

By the end of the 1990s, I was compelled to move yet further upriver. My home in Dutchess County, a converted farmhouse next to the Appalachian Trail, burned down. Later we learned that mice had eaten through wire insulation, sparking a conflagration when a space heater was turned on. In the building's second floor, a young mother with an infant at home, stepped out of the shower to see flames licking her apartment window frame. The floor on which she had laid her son was hot to the touch. She grabbed him up to outrun the fire into the yard. Then she alerted the elderly couple in the end apartment unit. One-third of the building blazed into charred ruins within an hour. That day I left work sick with a sudden onset of flu, only to find myself facing the blackened wreckage of my home. I arrived just as the pumper trucks put the fire out. The fire marshal did not allow me entry, but later I arranged to collect what belongings had escaped the fire, smoke, and water. In the ruined kitchen I found the remains of the vegetarian empanadas my neighbors helped me fold the day before. Through the kitchen window I could see the yard still green, the pond still shimmering. It was incomprehensible, like getting pushed over an unseen cliff.

After the fire, exhaustion deepened in a way that could not be explained by hard work or the difficulties of the sudden home loss and move. Some of my clinician friends thought it might be chronic fatigue or low thyroid or Lyme disease, though no diagnosis could be confirmed. But help can come from unexpected places. For me, it came from the community program participants who wore strings of tiny red, white, clear, black, or blue brightly colored beads. I noticed those who wore the beads were sober, reliable, and would step up to help anyone in need. They engaged in their community with ethical nature-based values through Santeria, an Afro-Caribbean religion brought to America by Africans kidnapped as slaves.

Rita Morales and a few other community program leaders, noticing my failing health, urged me to go to a *Santero*, a spiritual reader and healer of Santeria. They thought a healer from their own culture would help when western medical doctors could not. On a late November night, I made my way to a building in Chelsea near 23rd Street, its entry a plain metal door in an empty alley. When I pushed the apartment door button, a crackly voice asked *"Quien es*, who is it?" and I was buzzed in before I could say my name. A door opened to a brightly lit loft space across from the elevator. An African Grey parrot once again asked, *"Quien es?"* Scanning the room I saw a few people near a floor to ceiling altar. It was covered with a red cloth, flowers and candles, bowls of cornmeal porridge with okra, bananas, and mangoes. I was told the altar was for Chango, the lord of fire and lightning, music, drumming and dance, a deity or *orisha* in Yoruba West African culture.

People kidnapped in Africa and sold in the Caribbean brought their ancestral Yoruba culture, language, and seeds of sacred foods with them across the Atlantic. In the Caribbean, Santeria and other Yoruba culture-derived practices are syncretic, joined to Catholic saints, but not merged with them. Adherents live throughout the city, not all of them of Caribbean descent. The santero, a man in his late 60s with slightly labored breath, told me that he was a child of Chango and that he had recently suffered a heart attack. "The Christian saint, Santa Barbara, served as a front for Chango," he said. "People could pray for their captors to be struck dead while looking pious."

Refusing payment, the santero, cleared the room for my reading. After a long invocation of gods, goddesses, and blessings, he opened the reading through Elegua, the orisha of the roads who holds the keys to past, present, and future. Tossing cowry shells in set sequences, he said that my health would continue to decline if I did not take steps to help myself. I learned that I was a child of Oshun, the river, and I was given the beads of Oshun along with those of Chango, Elegua, and Yemaya, the orisha of the ocean. The beads, worn round the neck as I had noticed on my Community Works people, were for protection. The next requirement was to make a doll to take the sickness from my body. I made her from my own clothes, embroidered a face beneath her long brown yarn hair, and gave her tiny turquoise earrings along with a matching turquoise necklace. After consecrating rituals and a cleansing bath of herbs and rum, I went down to Pier 25 in what is now the Hudson River Park, just above the Battery. I offered this doll of myself to the Hudson where the salt is most dense. She lost an earring on her way down, and then she floated on ebb tide toward the sea before disappearing beneath the surface.

Next came the most surprising advice of all. The santero suggested I go live in a Buddhist monastery. When I made the doll and gave her to the river, I thought of her as the mad Ophelia on the waters, a path I did not have to take. Instead, it seemed I was urged to take Ophelia's father's order to "get thee to a nunnery." The santero may have known some of my history from the community people who referred me. In any case, he had no stake in this advice. In the months before the house fire, I had visited an upstate Zen Monastery near Woodstock in the Catskills. The Santeria reading and rituals, whether or not I believed in them, made me stop long enough to see my own short mortal thread and seriously reflect on it. I had gone to the santero to honor Community Works people in an open-minded inquiry into non-western forms of healing. Following my own intuitions to reduce stressful ways, to seek solace in nature, and to establish a meditation practice, I eventually moved near the monastery in Mount Tremper in the Catskills where NYCs drinking water begins. And I moved into the monastery itself in late 1999 to stay for over three years.

"Oh how relaxing!" people would exclaim when I told them I moved to the Catskills, and had taken up a meditation practice. Meditative self-inquiry in the beginning can be about as relaxing as intensive psychotherapy. Sincere and honest engagement brings dissolution of unnecessary self-concepts and long-held defenses. Stepping outside the world I had known, including all of the good works of research and community programs, afforded a chance to see my life more clearly, though at first it was as through muddy pond water. That changed over time, aided by the still wild nature of the Catskills. Breezes over verdant mountains and rocky streams became instruments in the great choruses of green. I realized how much exists beyond our blunted senses, and below the range of ordinary hearing. It was the opposite of St. Paul's vision of

God that blinded him on the road during his conversion from persecutor to holy man. Saul of Tarsus, later St Paul, was struck down from his horse. My conversion was more like T. S. Elliot's "patient etherized upon the table" slowly coming to through the mental fogginess of years of sensory overload and taxed adrenals.

The songs of the Catskills grew in my awareness, penetrated my sleep and filled my days. Eventually I could hold still long enough to feel them through my whole undivided being. Like so many naturalists, there was a turning moment of direct contact with the natural world. For John Muir, it had been two wild orchids that changed his life; for Aldo Leopold, "the fierce green fire" in the eyes of a dying wolf. For me, it was a sycamore tree—the light of the forest with its upper white branches reaching into the sky and its mottled trunk into deep roots below. Its radiance filled me with love such that I could barely see its ordinary form, just its radiance. This enormous tree connects heaven and earth, stands at the threshold of both life and death, its sap and seeds life-giving to insects and birds, its branches nesting sites for high flyers, its shade a resting place for travelers and seekers. I had come to the green temple of pure waters, renewed myself in them, and awoke to new life by the light of the sycamore. And I soaked in the healing waters for three years to emerge realizing to my marrow this aliveness, even in the rocks over which the Catskills waters run down and underground to the city. The inspiration of the sycamore, its hollow trunk and sturdy wood so often used for dugout canoes, would transport me from then on.

DESCENDING THE WATERS

Early morning on the Esopus Creek in the Catskills, a lone angler wades into the rising mist to cast his line. It is not a creek by most standards, being wider and stronger than most western rivers. The Esopus fills Ashokan Reservoir to supply 40 percent of NYC water. The spring surface of the reservoir glistens through roadside birches not yet in leaf. Rounding a curve, there is an expanse of watery stillness, surprising even when you know it is there. But for the low hills and the line of Panther and Slide Mountains in the distance, the colors of sky and water merge. It looks as if it has always been here. Yet 12 towns lie hidden beneath the waters, unseen until periods of prolonged drought reveal a house foundation, a lost toy, or a plow in the margins.

The captured cycles of rainfall keep the city rich in clean drinking water, an increasingly scarce resource worldwide. Gathered through forests on porous heavily vegetated land into channels to enter holding and settling reservoirs and into the long tube of the Catskill Aqueduct, the water here requires no further filtration. With the problems in the Croton system resolved, this natural filtered water coming from the Catskills is the envy of cities everywhere.

I love the waters of my Catskills home and know many of their paths in surface streams through forests, meadows, and stony cloves. Gradually I have come to know them as Catskill Aqueduct Miles, like Hudson River Miles, but instead measured in water flowing through the aqueduct that runs underground down to the city. At times I follow the path of the water from the Ashokan Reservoir for over 100 miles downriver to the places of the earliest water sources in Manhattan of the pre-European contact Lenape people. In a story that sharply differs from the centuries of abuse of the Hudson, the Catskills drinking water is revered, protected and consecrated by massive outlays of money to secure its pathway down to the city.

Here and there clumps of roadside grave markers jut from overgrown grasses, small squares like mile markers corroded by acid rain. They mark the nearly forgotten dead removed from cemeteries before the water was impounded in the Ashokan reservoir. When the reservoir was built, the disinterred dead outnumbered the displaced living.

When the Ashokan reservoir dam was first planned, Teddy Roosevelt was president and the city thrilled to its first electric lights and skyscrapers. By then, NYC's population had leapt to over three million and stressed the city's water supply from the Croton system 41 Hudson River miles above the city. In 1907, if one did not have a farm, business, or home in the path of the Catskills reservoirs and aqueduct, the reservoirs and dams appeared to be a steam-powered machine triumph. While immigrant workers toiled on the dam, their European nations of origin went to war and the United States joined in. But World War I did not stop the city. After the war came the Great Depression with ground zero in Wall Street just above the Battery in Manhattan. Under Teddy Roosevelt's cousin, Franklin, monumental public works became part of the cure for the Great Depression. The city did not stop building its water infrastructure, and the process of displacing towns for reservoirs continued into the 1960s.

Just as in 1916, the trapped rainwater of the Catskills still leaves the Ashokan Reservoir to enter the Catskills Aqueduct in the town of Olive; we can call it Catskills Aqueduct Mile 0 just as the Battery in Manhattan is Hudson River Mile 0. The water in the aqueduct heads down the west side of the Hudson watershed to New Paltz through the Shawangunk Mountains. The top of the aqueduct's trenches can still be seen beneath tangled vegetation on hiking trails near Mohonk Preserve around Aqueduct Mile 26 across from Hudson River Mile 80. Catskills pure water moves unseen past hikers and technical mountain climbers of the Gunks to Storm King at the intersection of Catskill Aqueduct Mile 55, counting down from the Ashokan Reservoir and Hudson River Mile 55, counting up from the Battery.

Long before the environment won a major victory at Storm King, this same mountain was the site of a massive public work for the sake of the city's holy water. It is here that the captured Catskills streams still enter a tunnel dug by descendants of slaves 1000 feet under the river bottom into the bedrock below. Here fish swim above, and Catskills rainwater flows below. While the river-running fish traverse this transition zone in both directions, the Catskills fresh water travels one way only, underground and downward by gravity to the nine million people in the city.

From the tunnel's exit gate, the aqueduct angles east to Peekskill, then parallels the Taconic Range on the east side of the Hudson down through Dutchess and Putnam Counties into the older reservoir systems in Westchester.

Above ground along the hidden watercourse there are cemeteries ever greater in number and magnificence as one approaches the city, scale-model Greek and Roman estates of the dead. The names carved in stone are a who's who of politicians, musicians, actors, gangsters, builders, scientists, and the city's elite. And they contain the far greater numbers of ordinary people in simple plots. For over two miles, cemeteries cover the low hills with tombstones and monuments near Valhalla at Catskills Aqueduct Mile 86. The graves hold Fred Friendly, Lou Gehrig, Herbert H. Lehman, Sergei Rachmaninoff, Flo Ziegfeld, and so many other great talents now buried near Kensico Reservoir, the gathering place of Catskills waters.

It is at Kensico the Catskills Aqueduct waters meet the Delaware Aqueduct waters, an event never meant to occur naturally in the adjacent

Delaware and Hudson watersheds. And Kensico itself stands as the grave-marker of the headwaters of the Bronx River, now forced to arise in and around the parking lot of Westchester Hospital. Here too houses were demolished, residents displaced, and the dead disinterred. As one crosses into the hamlet of Valhalla, the sight of the narrow valley incongruously stopped up with granite blocks can be but a fleeting image from the parkway, unless one gets closer.

I turn off the parkway to come face to face with Kensico Dam. The granite blocks look as if they had been stolen from a cathedral to be jammed for no good reason into the V-notch of the hills. As I walk closer taking pictures, an armed guard stops me.

"You can't be here," the guard shouts.

"Why?" I ask.

No answer.

"Are you from the city's water police?" I ask.

No answer. Then he tells me, "Stop taking pictures and move on."

After the destruction of the World Trade Center towers by Al-Qaeda in airplane attacks on September 11, 2001, the reservoirs serving NYC were actively protected by armed guards. Attacks on the city's water could potentially inflict far greater damage to New Yorkers than the over 3000 people who were incinerated or jumped to their deaths in the World Trade Center. As I leave to the parking lot, I see two brightly clad young girls pushing their baby doll strollers, the stones carved by Italian immigrants visible at their backs. I wonder if they will ever learn the story of the water. It all feels a lot less secure now than when I lived in the city and took tap water for granted.

Downriver from Kensico I pass more graveyards: Thelonius Monk, Paul Robeson, and Malcolm X in Ferncliff Cemetery; Woodlawn Cemetery, last stop for Fiorello LaGuardia, George Bird Grinnell, Joseph Pulitzer, and the parkway builder Robert Moses. Catskills water moves underground into Jerome Park Reservoir in the Bronx, near Montefiore Medical Center where I once worked and many of my community programs took place. It moves on beneath the East River to Manhattan. In Manhattan, Catskills rain courses beneath Central Park and down the West Side past Ulysses S. Grant and his wife in their federalist style mausoleum in one of my former neighborhoods. Then it moves on to Brooklyn past Hudson River Mile Zero.

In the tunnels of NYC's underground realm, subway riders head to

Brooklyn in tandem with the water. A music student sits on her way to the Brooklyn Academy of Music. She silently mouths an exercise from Bona's *Rhythmical Articulation*, Schirmer edition, held tightly in her hands. Coming up from the subway, from tinny headphone overflow can be heard: "I'm a loser, baby. So why don't you kill me?" Above ground near Schermerhorn and 3rd Street I find a manhole cover with the words "Catskill Water." The terminus of Catskills Tunnel No. 1 lies below.

BURIAL OF THE CITY'S ORIGINAL WATERSHED

With early 1800s technology, before the creation of the Croton dam of 1842, the people of New York had varied though inadequate water sources. The city would not have grown past its 80,000 residents of 1800 without drastic changes. In Manhattan, there are no visible remains of the 40 streams, numerous springs and ponds of pre-European Manhattan of the Lenape. The Dutch and English settlers' Collect Pond, an early water source, now lies beneath the Criminal Courts Building and remnants of a reservoir can be found in the basement of the main public library. The original springs, streams, and ponds all lie encased in concrete, and the city must pump water from the subways and all underground utilities which would overflow in three days if pumping ceased. The original springs can also be released by storm damage as occurred with Hurricane Sandy in 2012, an event more likely to be repeated with the increasingly erratic climate disruption of our time.

In all the city's five boroughs, the Bronx River, with its headwaters in Westchester, is the city's only freshwater river. In 1799 it was the proposed water source for the Manhattan Company, the predecessor of JP Morgan Chase Bank. At the outset, the Manhattan Company, founded by Aaron Burr, delivered as little water as possible, only enough to keep the license for its bank. The water company was the pretext for creation of New York's second bank to rival its first, which had been created by Alexander Hamilton. An 1808 *New York Post* article describes the Manhattan Company: "Some wells have been dug in the filthiest corners of the town; a small quantity of water has been conveyed in wretched wooden pipes." The Manhattan Company's failure to deliver clean water was said to have fostered the cholera epidemic of 1832. In our times, its mega-bank market manipulations nearly toppled the world economy.

LOCAL AND GLOBAL ENVIRONMENTAL ACTION MERGE EVERYWHERE

In the late Devonian period, 375 millions years ago, a meteorite half a mile in length struck the Catskills in the place we now call Panther Mountain, from which the Esopus begins its descent to fill the Ashokan Reservoir. The impact created a crater six miles wide, which geologists found buried under vegetation, rocks and debris below the mountaintop. It surpassed the potential energy released by the greatest thermonuclear bomb ever created. Yet this impact was but a small change in the upheavals, collisions, mass extinctions, ocean and climate changes to come. A relative period of stability, called the Holocene, goes back only 11,700 years, the most recent inter-glacial geologic period. More importantly, it brought conditions for agricultural stability, and the logarithmic rise in human populations. We now arrive in the Anthropocene, a period characterized by general global warming and erratic local weather patterns largely due to human activity, especially fossil fuel combustion. I leave the logic, chemistry, and evidence to others in the very near unanimous consensus of scientists, but I am fully convinced by the growing body of research from the earliest work until now. Whether or not we believe the science—not an act of faith but an acknowledgement of facts traced in numbers and projections—we must address the problems visible all around us.

On a visit to an Esopus watershed stream restoration on Stony Clove Creek near where I now live in Phoenicia, one can see the remains of glacial till in moraines left by receding ice before the Holocene Era. Even though the Catskills enjoy protection in ways so many places do not, the changes due to the growing battery of storms and erratic rainfall are apparent. When roiling waters tear at degraded stream banks, especially where the land was deforested in the 1800s and the surface geography altered for resource extraction and industry, glacial till turns the water a turbid reddish-chocolate. Stream restoration is a necessity here if the water is to remain clean enough for NYC. But can we keep up with the storms?

In Phoenicia, I ascend the steep trail in the middle of town, where old growth hemlocks unwillingly yielded their bark for the tanning industry. The great hemlock forests never recovered from the tanning industry. The tanbark trails on which the hemlocks were sacrificed later saw massive blocks of stone descend to awaiting trains and river barges. The forest filled with oak and pine in place of the missing hemlocks.

On the Tanbark Trail, trees grow around the quarried rock outcroppings and broken-off blocks embedded in trees ascend with new growth in eye-catching inversions in the wake of hasty resource extractions.

Apart from rare areas of inaccessible terrain, there are no first growth woods, intact meadows or marshes in the watershed. Its water-filtering services are not secure in the Anthropocene Era of too little water, and too much water, with water in the wrong places at the wrong times. And the system of reservoirs, aqueducts, and tunnels faces widespread breakdown of the aging infrastructure. In the Delaware system, a crew lives and works from a submarine to staunch the heavily leaking cracks in its aqueduct. Long-overdue repairs to Catskills water Tunnel No. 1, the receiving tunnel from the upstate Catskills aqueducts, are scheduled to start in 2020. Meanwhile the Ashokan Reservoir, initially built for a 90-year life span, needs a 150-year extension from the Army Corps of Engineers.

Hurricane Irene in August 2011, followed by Hurricane Sandy in October 2012, forcefully ravaged the watershed such that some areas will not recover. My home on Stony Clove Creek near its confluence with the Esopus had no egress on flooded roads, no power for 11 days. Others lost everything, and some lost their lives. Previous streambank restoration projects on the Esopus suffered setbacks, leaving the watershed worse than before. There will be more unpredictable patterns of rain and drought, snow and wind. Global warming is not a gradual change into a sweet tropical paradise but an erratic and stormy confusion of extremes in which adaptation is thwarted and resilience hard to define.

Storm surges, high tides, and flooding during Irene and Sandy are a foretaste of our future in the Hudson watershed. Sandy went all the way up the estuary throughout the natural Hudson watershed. Its imprint shows in sharply erratic salt front graphs. While Irene brought heavy rains moving the front down, Sandy brought more ocean water upriver. For the Hudson, erratic weather with unpredictable rain, wind, and snow patterns changes the salt front graph from a slow earthquake pattern to the shape of a full heart attack. The swings of extremes widen in longer droughts alternating with erratic heavier rains—sometimes with a month's worth of rain in two days.

These forces will remain in motion even if we end all fossil fuel and atmosphere polluting industries today. However, the speed of change will accelerate if we don't stop. Even for me, steeped in this knowledge, the reality eludes my grasp on a sweet autumn day, sitting by the stream across from my home. In the lazy flow, I can see the riverbed rocks. Yet it could violently change tomorrow, with churning muddy forces tearing at the stream bank and flooding the town. We do not know how the multiple interacting ecosystem forces change when the climate affecting everything rapidly unravels.

We can learn something of our future from the story of Hudson in deep layers of marsh sediments. Researchers from Lamont Doherty, NASA/Goddard, and Lawrence Livermore extract core samples from Hudson estuary marshes to show changes in vegetation, periods of drought, and heavy metals over a roughly 7000 year period. A senior researcher, Dr. Dorothy Peteet, invited me to speak with her at her home in Suffern, New York. It is a warm summer afternoon, and Dorothy invites me to sit on the swing overlooking the large natural pond in back of her post-revolutionary war period home. I note her trace of Georgia accent ask, "So is New York going to turn into Georgia, wetter and warmer?" Without hesitation, she says in the same friendly lilting voice, "No, it's probably just going to become more erratic. We are in a long wet period at the moment, but historically there have been many long periods of drought." A palynologist, a botanist who studies spores and pollen both ancient and modern, Dorothy has compelling data on the changes before and after Europeans came to the Hudson. Strong evidence exists for a prolonged period of drought lasting 550 years during the European Warming Period (800-1350), followed by damp and cool periods with shorter duration droughts during the Little Ice Age from 1400 to 1850. Vegetation shifts mark these periods. After Europeans first appeared in the Hudson Valley their calling cards show up in the sediments from the effects of deforestation, rise of permanent agriculture and industry, channelization of the river and destruction of wetlands.

Just as with the rest of the country, the Hudson watershed has lost at least 50 percent of its natural wetlands, important sponges for the aquifer, fish nurseries, and bird nesting sites. A signal marker of European settler effects comes in the rise of *Ambrosia* or ragweed after 1697. Ragweed, though native, thrives in full sun rather than shade, and heavy increases come just after widespread deforestation. George Washington noted that by the end of the revolutionary war in which the forests were cut down for battlefields, a waist high species of ragweed dominated. In more recent reforestation periods, ragweed shows decline, but the forest profile has changed to include more invasive tree species such as Norway maple and European silver birch. Industrial processes also show up in the sediments: as a rise in copper and lead in particular from mining and smelting.

Dorothy Peteet says the Piermont marsh and other treasures of the Hudson will likely be lost due to human effects if we do nothing. She believes removal of dams and side channels could help as they hold back sediments and alter natural flows needed to build up the marsh. Traditionally, marshes serve as the poor man's river access, and turn into landfill dumps that hamper natural deposition to the marsh. In fact, one of the striking findings of the ancient core sediment library is the constancy of carbon and the heavy post-European losses of non-carbon sand, silt and clay. Displacement of plant diversity also marks the present, with Piermont and other Hudson marshes now dominated by *phragmites*, a monoculture grass species that is not native. In fact, invasive species in the east tend to be a one-way journey to North America from Europe. The final blow to the marshes may be from the climate altering burning of fossil fuels that melt glaciers and ice sheets producing sea level rise. From my first meeting with Dr. Peteet to the last talk I heard given to the Sierra Club, Mid-Hudson Chapter, in 2017, I noticed her deepening concerns for the Hudson Valley where she lives and works.

When I first started work in environmental epidemiology in the late 1970s, global warming was known in the scientific community. But complete polar ice cap meltdown with an attendant 20-foot rise in sea levels was rarely mentioned. Rachel Carson's 1951 *The Sea Around Us*, noted that we lived in a marvelous time of "natural sea rise" and warming temperatures. In all likelihood, she was actually witnessing the beginning of human-caused increase in the planet's global temperature. Global climate disruption from burning fossil fuels had been posited by Arrhenius in 1900 but largely ignored until the late 1960s. In the five decades since, we see the details unfolding in real time around us. We see it in videos of arctic ice calving, ski resorts closing from lack of snow, record-breaking heat days and months, prolonged droughts, more frequent major storms, stressed forests and trees succumbing to pests and blight. The reality is hard to grasp, leaving us all in some level of denial.

We are like landscape painters who use a black mirror. With back turned to the actual scene, we look into the mirror. It brings down the

light and dark contrasts and emphasizes basic shapes with few details
in a softened romanticized image. We see the changes in our world
this way—softer, less extreme, without disturbing details. When our
backwards vision turns direct, we are shocked by what we find.

I recall a night in 1985 when a colleague came into my office and
noticed a set of jars in the metal cabinet behind my desk. They contained
varied small objects in liquid. I watched shock and revulsion streak
across her face the moment she realized the jars contained malformed
human fetuses. The collection of spontaneously aborted fetuses formed
part of a multi-disciplinary Columbia University study of environmental
and genetic causes of fetal malformation. These deaths of youngest
among us, the canaries in the global mine, speak volumes as evidence
of environmental toxic effects, among them PCBs. As we keep looking,
the full realization can be shocking, staggering, and even revolting.
In our salvage job, we fall on our knees in hope that natural systems
will join our committed efforts to bring about a renewed habitable
earth.

The rise in ecological thinking and environmental action gives me
great hope. A lot depends on how we see global as local, that what we do
affects everything and how each thing we do is how we do everything.
Just as there can be a synergism of destruction and collapse in living
systems, there can be a synergism of restoration and health.

There have been victories, reversals and restorations large and small.
Some, like the Atlantic sturgeon, are ICU patients just waking up to be
moved to another hospital wing. In others, like the Atlantic striped bass,
the patient is better but requires lifelong monitoring and aid as needed.
No action is too small and no action too big. All count. My bead-wearing
stigmatized community program participants worked hard to restore a
meadow to native grasses in the Bronx River watershed, part of the larger
Hudson River watershed. As they healed themselves, their work brought
back native butterflies and bees and birds as part of the watershed's web
of life. Can we measure the size of their work? One small group working
a few months becomes life for generations of wildlife.

Restoration of the Bronx River itself, for decades one of the most squalid
and poisoned places in the city, began with one determined woman in
the 1970s. Ruth Anderberg, who died in 2016, had been an Army Air
Corps aviatrix as a young woman. Around the time of Vatican II, the
Catholic Church's 1962–1965 ecumenical council that brought it into

open dialogue with other religions, Ruth's brother served as a priest at the Pine Ridge Reservation in South Dakota, and Ruth worked as a Catholic lay minister. She moved to the Bronx near Edgar Allen Poe Park, where Poe rented a farmhouse and wrote *Annabel Lee* in 1849 in the last year of his life.

When Ruth's Bronx police precinct chief called on local Bronx residents to step up to clean up the river, she volunteered. She was given a desk and a phone in her precinct police station. She called on towing companies to help remove cars, furniture, appliances, and even a piano from the river. She herded boy scouts to clean up the stream bank and rebuild it with discarded tires. Successive leaders from the changing demography of the Bronx stepped up behind her to save the Bronx River. In their wake, the river became healthy below its thwarted headwaters, with beavers and alewives returning home.

Ruth Anderberg invited me to her home in the last years of her life. She knew the changes in the river since her time working on it, and rejoiced in them. A sturdy-boned woman with more determination than muscular strength, curly grey hair tumbling forward, she could no longer navigate the stairs to her Victorian home in the Bronx and required help with the basics of living. As her many white cats circled our feet and jumped up onto the plastic covered table, she cheerfully instructed me in her life view. She reminded me that in her Catholic religion there are sins of commission and sins of omission. A sin of commission is an active violation of moral and ethical codes. Sins of omission occur when we fail to do the right thing. It happens when the river cries out for our help, and we ignore its cries. It is as Martin Luther King, Jr. said, "In the end, we will remember not the words of our enemies, but the silence of our friends." Rooted in her moral and ethical life, Ruth loved all creation. When I asked what should we tell younger people who inherit this world after us, she said, "All is a gift—rain, snow, our bodies. Treat your neighbors as friends. Appreciate what you have. The only thing that matters is how we live." Ruth heard the cries of the Bronx River watershed in which she lived, an example to us all, until her death in 2016 at age 89.

A photo posted in the Bronx River Alliance newsletter to honor Ruth Anderberg shows her in hip waders near the river shore. In her forties at the time, she stands with noble bearing beside a canoe filled with officials in white shirts and ties. Stephen DeVillo in *The Bronx River in*

History and Folklore writes of the impossible task she took on and yet, "today her vision is fulfilled by new riverside parklands, a Bronx River Greenway, and an increasingly revitalized Bronx River."

As of 2015, thanks to so many acting to save the entire Hudson watershed, there will be no shale gas drilling anywhere in New York State. New York State banned high-volume hydraulic fracturing (fracking) for shale gas for its environmental destruction to land and water as well as its dangers to public health. The victory came at the end of a seven-year fight. The documents and reports developed in this struggle are now serving as templates for activists in other states. Catskill Mountainkeeper, along with 400 other New York organizations, joined together in the struggle. When the state first undertook a study of fracking, 260,000 public comments and multiple hearings flooded the Department of Environmental Conservation. Like all environmental laws and bans, this ruling can be revoked, but vigilant citizen groups stand ready for any attempted reversions.

We. Are. Strong. Together. In 2007, Paul Hawken wrote *Blessed Unrest*. Hawken created a video simply listing all the known environmental groups at the time. Running day and night, the full video takes four days of 24-hour viewing. And these were only the most well-known groups at the time. My own nonprofit, and many others like it, did not make the list. As this movement grows, and we honor each person who awakens to action, we could offset the list of every being we have harmed, every tree unsustainably taken, all creatures great and small to whom we owe our lives. We work to reverse the inversions of our times; we hope to turn the over 90 percent missing Hudson River fish to its opposite of less than 10 percent. The changes we bring, when broad enough and long enough, can be carried forward by the healing ecosystem itself. I pray each drop of Catskills water be heard in the heart of each person who drinks it to spread the light outward far beyond our small vessels.

LIVING LIGHTLY ON THE LAND

Returning downriver to my old neighborhood, I close my eyes and see a Dutchman on the cliff-edge meadow at Spuyten Duyvil. It is the first break in the weather in March 1647 when two 70-foot fat Finback whales swim up the river on their sides, mouths open, scooping up the spring run of shad and herring. A strong spring freshet brings the edge of the salt front all the way down to the harbor. Later the man learns that one whale stranded itself forty miles upstream, the other turning back stranded 20 miles below the first. The townsmen where they were found boiled the dead whales for oil and left an oil slick on the river for three weeks.

The spring brings an abundance of shad, alewives and blue herring, striped bass, and sturgeon upriver past the Spuyten Duyvil. They head north to spawning grounds and birthplace nurseries upriver near the Wey Gat before the highlands. Smelling the changes in the minerals of the water, the fishes know they are home. They eat little in anticipation of spreading uncounted eggs to meet equally unmeasured quantities of sperm-filled milt, churning the water frothy before they turn back downstream.

There are as yet no pipes pouring sewage into the river, none of the 80,000 chemicals created 300 years into the future, no zebra mussels from Eurasia, no invasive water chestnut. The channel is not dredged or filled, not dammed. It has no banks of riprap. There are not millions of people living beside it.

But by this time in 1647, most of the 15,000 Munsee Lenape in 60 nearby settlements are gone. The Director of New Amsterdam, Willem Kieft, had driven them away. In just 20 years time, the agreement the Lenape made and sealed with beaded wampum in Spuyten Duyvil in the 1620s to share the land between the Dutch and Lenape is broken, while the streets of the Dutch settlement in lower Mannahatta fill with trash, pigs, horses, manure, and drunks. In two months time, the one-legged former slaver Peter Stuyvesant will rule the colony until the British take over in 1665. At the time of the British arrival, Adriean van der Donck, the man on edge of the cliff at Spuyten Duyvil, will be dead. His peaceful ways of learning from his Lenape neighbors end, along with most of the oral indigenous local knowledge of the land and water.

Lenape ancestors go back 10,000 years. By the time of Adrian van der Donck's whale sighting, they had been cultivating beans, corn, and squash for thousands of years. They made clothing, pottery, and everything needed to hunt, fish, and live well. They had no overpopulation, no financial crises, no water company bank scams, no massive air pollution and greenhouse gases. There was no coal or nuclear power grid, no trains and cars, no skyscrapers, no terrorists flying airplanes into buildings.

It is just 20 generations in time since the Lenape were forced out of Manhattan, ending their 500 generations of village life on the island. We cannot go backwards. But still, somewhere between what was then and what will be, the Hudson watershed natural and not so natural needs us to change our ways for all the generations to come.

CHAPTER SIX

THE RIVER OF PAINTED ROCKS

Chattahoochee

TURKEY VULTURES ABANDON THEIR PERCHES on the twisting branches of an ancient oak in a rural Georgia pull-off. A limping brindle hound bays at my car. It is deer hunting season in rural Whitesburg on the Chattahoochee River, 40 miles downriver from the 5.5 million people of Metropolitan Atlanta. As I pull up in a cloud of fine clay dust, my friends Sybil Rosen and Glyn Thomas rush out from their late 1910 rough-hewn cabin to meet me. "Come on in, dearie," Sybil croons in my ear. Glyn joins in, "Good to see you, darlin'."

My arrival in Whitesburg, Georgia begins a quest to learn about contaminants and infectious microorganisms of the Chattahoochee River. It is part of an on-going journey started in 2006, beginning with the Klamath River in Oregon and going on to four other watersheds in different regions of the country. Atlanta claims its place as the home of Centers for Disease Control and Prevention (CDC), and part of my career landscape as an epidemiologist. The CDC campus lies just 12 miles east of the river in the city. Nearby, highways converge in a tangle of crisscrossing ramps and roadways, in some places 16 lanes across, amid the soaring glass and steel that make up so much of Atlanta's downtown.

My first glimpse of the Chattahoochee River comes over concrete bridge barriers early in the day. I find her green and lazy, tree-lined and inviting even in winter. The effects of the past few drought years followed by a record-breaking autumn flood are barely visible. In Whitesburg, an hour from downtown, I get a better look at the river from the deck of Sybil and Glyn's porch on what was once a fishing camp. He calls it,

"The Waller—just like pigs in shit." I feel like I had dropped into a time before automobiles when people gathered to fish, gamble, drink, and shout across the river for the ferry.

Glyn, a white-haired retired professor of history, economics, sociology, and political science is like a rumpled blue shirt you just never want to take off. He is comfortable, ready to crinkle into laughter, to hold you lightly in his warmth. There is the daily political Glyn rant, brought to an end by a throaty "Glyynnnn" from Sybil if it goes on too long. Sybil, a writer and actor, has stories woven into the fabric of her being—stories you hear like a kid who doesn't want the tale to end. The stories unfurl slowly, generously until they are no longer hers but ours. I spent two separate month-long periods at the Waller learning about the Chattahoochee watershed.

Glyn tells us he once took a college class all over the county to trailers, teepees, tents, tree houses, barns, discarded boxcars, and sheds where people lived. He wanted to expand his students' views of life, to help them understand that one can be rich with little money. Sybil became his finest example. In her early adult years, she lived in a tree house with the musician Blaze Foley, who was later shot to death 12 years after they split up. Among the many great Blaze songs, "If Only I Could Fly," was written out of longing for Sybil, later recorded by Merle Haggard and Willie Nelson. The tree house hosted Sybil and Blaze for many months including through a winter when water froze in drinking glasses overnight.

Decades later, Sybil, full-lipped with the curly dark hair of her Jewish forbears, returned to Waller to research and write a book about her life with Blaze Foley. In the living room, Sybil's photo portrait from the Blaze days had been quietly residing there all along. As Glyn tells it, before anyone knew Sybil would return, he had started a shed building frenzy, boxcar wood joined into sheds, sheds connected into a guesthouse, somehow knowing "some writer or artist was going to show up." After a time living at Waller, Sybil told Glyn she felt "kinda shy" around him. He too felt the growing love mixed with sexual tension between them, and soon they became a couple. In a ring of friends and neighbors, Sybil and Glyn "jumped the broom." When country preachers could not get through the snows in Appalachia, couples would jump the broom. Black folks, for whom marriage was illegal back then, also jumped the broom for all to know their bond and joined lives.

"The homes of the First People here," Glyn says, "were not teepees; the tribe of Southern hippies brought teepees in the nineteen-sixties." He laughs, then, with sober countenance, tells us the history. The Cherokee spoke an Iroquoian dialect, and had their own Cherokee syllabary by 1821 that was created by tribal member Sequoyah based on English, Greek, and Hebrew letters. Colonists called them one of "the Five Civilized Tribes." Their homes resembled the long houses of Iroquois-related bands throughout the eastern US, although in the late eighteenth century many adopted settler style homes, attire, and farmsteads.

When settlers found gold and squatted on Cherokee land in 1829, Cherokee leaders took it to the US Supreme Court. The case resulted in a foundational ruling on tribal sovereignty for all tribes. In Worcester v. Georgia (1832), the US Supreme Court Chief Justice John Marshall ruled that American Indian nations were "distinct, independent political communities retaining their original natural rights," and entitled to federal protection from the actions of state. Nonetheless, forcible removal was enacted by President Andrew Jackson under the previous Congressional *Indian Removal Act* of 1830 in which all eastern tribes were to be evicted to unsettled lands west of the Mississippi.

In northwest Georgia, the Chattahoochee River once separated the Cherokee lands from those of the Creek, Cherokee to the west and Creek to the east. Creeks and Seminoles originally of Alabama, Georgia, and Florida spoke Muskogee, as different from Iroquoian as Vietnamese from French. The river's name, Chattahoochee, comes from the Creek for "River of Painted Rocks." Occupying this part of the country far longer than the Cherokee, the Creek likely descend from the builders of the Ocmulgee Mounds, a place of continuous habitation for 17,000 years, near Macon just south of Atlanta. The end of Creek territory in Georgia came when Chief William McIntosh and others signed the 1825 Treaty of Indian Springs ceding all Creek territory in Georgia and Alabama. Deeming the treaty fraudulent, tribal police executed McIntosh and other Creek signatories. The treaty was overturned and replaced in 1826, but Creek land in Georgia was never returned. About four miles downriver from the Waller, McIntosh Reserve Park holds the remains of Creek Chief William McIntosh on the site of his home.

I ask Glyn what has happened to the river since the time Georgia wrested the watershed from the indigenous people. My hosts and their water activist friends say the deepest cuts came with deforestation and power generation in the early 1900s. Georgia Power, the utility company, was still ruining the land and water with its coal-fired plants spewing smoky air contaminants that return in dirty rain. And they tell me of the incinerated coal ash kept in acres of storage ponds, contaminated water seeping into the groundwater. And then there are Atlanta's sewers. Some say Georgia Power's polluting power plants created Atlanta's sprawl that turned the Chattahoochee into a sewer, contaminating everything downstream.

Right up to the river's edge, there is a Georgia Power utility near Glyn and Sybil's home. Below the old-growth wood of the house, the river's smooth surface flowing toward a short stretch of riffles and rapids belies its strength and depth. Just downriver, past a rope swing, locals say a bus lies completely submerged. We hike through the winter woods of dormant dogwood, redbud, white oak, box elder, and birch. It is warm enough for light sweaters and jackets this January day. The invasive kudzu, wisteria, and privet, winter shorn and cut back by foresters, form the backdrop to Dayglo chartreuse Georgia Power property signs spiking nearby fences. In the most damaged areas, first-growth loblolly pines and sweet gums rise amidst the broom sedge. Behind those skinny trees, two smoke stacks loom above us from Georgia Power's coal-fired power plant.

The waning light paints the smoke stacks a luminous salmon against deepening amethyst cloud shadows. Leaf litter crunches underfoot as we stoop beneath thorny bittersweet vines to reach the edge of a power-line right-of-way. No longer obscured, the stacks grow gargantuan above the building's turrets and walls. Lights blink out of sync. Beyond them an earthen dam holds back the slurry of the plant's ash pond. "Someday that dam's gonna break," Glyn sighs, as Sybil gently clasps his arm.

Awareness of coal ash ponds was sharpened by a 2008 break in the Tennessee Valley Authority's Kingston power plant near Harriman, Tennessee. Over five million cubic yards of wet coal-ash broke through its earthen dam covering the land, destroying homes, and filling waterways with arsenic, mercury, lead, and other toxins. It brought alerts to boil water for bacterial pathogens coming from flooded sewage systems. Another major incident occurred in North Carolina in 2014 from a Duke Energy pipe break that dumped 140,000 tons of wet coal ash waste into the Dan River. During the flood of 2009 in the Chattahoochee watershed, the floodwaters rose to within inches of the top of the Plant Yates earthen dam. "It isn't 'if' but 'when' that dam will break," says Glyn, "hopefully not in my lifetime. It would take out my home, the Waller."

In Whitesburg, I stay in my host's guest house, created from adjoined sheds that Glyn built without knowing Sybil would be the anticipated unknown writer and his future wife. The river, here known as "the Hooch," flows just a short walk down from the path by the guest house. Everyone I meet delights in showing me this watershed. Just as "darlin'" does not jump naturally to my tongue so too "the Hooch," though I feel I could live the rest of my days beside this river.

We kayak a stretch of the Chattahoochee just below Plant Yates along Class II and III rapids. I nearly lose my kayak amidst shouts that if I don't get to the bank now the next pullout is six miles downriver. Eyes wide with panic, I paddle furiously across the strong current that wants to take me away to the next town. The float guide's eyes, as wide as mine, form a tractor beam drawing me to outstretched arms as I am pulled to safety. My rescue comes with a circle of hugs. We retreat to eat in the local "Meat 'n Three" where the okra along with most of the veggies and meats are deep-fried comfort.

In "the Quarters," as Glyn calls the guesthouse, the forest presses up to the windows, and occasional shafts of sunlight break through cracks in the walls. Evenings I can hear hunters with their dogs. Deer are still present, bears long gone, turkey and pheasant only sometimes seen. Coyotes, long gone, are just beginning to reappear. A pack of stray dogs led by a big mixed breed dog, a poodle among his followers, can be heard after dark. And I hear the trains pull into Plant Yates, the sound of machines pulverizing coal permeating the night air.

Within an 80-mile circle of downtown Atlanta, Georgia Power still operates seven coal-fired plants. All have earthen dams with coal-ash ponds. All are among the top 100 coal waste producers in the US with Plant Scherer the nation's largest single source of CO_2 emissions. If coal deliveries from as far away as Wyoming and North Dakota stopped today, the city would halt. But there are changes afoot. As of 2017, Georgia Power has taken down one of the stacks at Plant Yates. It tends a 500 acre green-way nearby, and is four years into a ten-year conversion of Plant Yates to gas and solar. Glyn, who died in 2014, would approve.

THE CHATTAHOOCHEE AS ATLANTA'S SEWER

Each day the City of Atlanta draws millions of gallons of water from the Chattahoochee below Lake Lanier, the unnatural impoundment of the river's headwaters. After quenching everyone's thirst, watering lawns, washing clothes and cars and sidewalks, racing through business and industrial processes, the system flushes all the urine and feces, medical and industrial waste, runoff from pavement and sidewalks and every surface of the city. When it reaches sewage treatment plants, it is filtered, chlorinated, de-chlorinated and returned to the Chattahoochee and everyone downstream. As in most sewage systems, hundreds of microorganisms and thousands of toxins can evade this process. Everyone along the 400-mile run of the river from Atlanta to the Gulf pays attention to what Atlanta does with the Chattahoochee's water.

With no natural boundaries, Atlanta and its suburbs keep swallowing nearby towns. As with most eastern American cities, Atlanta's growth came in the wake of the second industrial revolution in the late nineteenth century. In the cities of the 1800s, human and animal waste overflowed cesspits and open sewage ditches. Cholera, a fecal-oral disease, came in epidemic waves. The first worldwide cholera epidemic appeared in the 1830s. Two decades later, in the second cholera pandemic, 10,000 died in London with similar numbers in New York, although Atlanta was spared. Cholera mainly traveled through navigable waterways at that time. But by the 1860s, the third cholera pandemic arrived via travelers riding newly built rail lines inland. This time cholera came home to the people of Atlanta shortly after Georgia joined the Confederacy. Atlanta, the railroad hub of the south, had ditches but no sewers, and cholera thrived.

The science linking raw fecal contaminated sewage and cholera spurred the sanitation movement of the late 19th and early twentieth centuries. But Atlanta had been burned to the ground and its citizens forcibly removed in the mid-1860s Civil War. William Tecumseh Sherman proudly wrote, "Behind us lay Atlanta smoldering and in ruins, the black smoke rising high in the air and hanging like a pall over the ruined city." It took decades to rebuild. The first city sewers in Atlanta were simple storm-water ditches into which household waste was thrown. Later covered ditches served both storm-water and sewage with raw human and animal waste and trash emptying into the Chattahoochee. Over time, pipes like randomly strewn pick-up sticks were laid but sewage was not separated from storm water run-off. Atlanta's system of cracked and leaky sewer pipes, along with its overburdened combined sewer and storm overflows, poured raw sewage into Atlanta neighborhoods every time it rained for nearly a century.

Whenever I ask about Atlanta's sewers, everyone says, "You've got to talk with Sally Bethea, the Chattahoochee Riverkeeper." Sally Bethea and I agree to meet on the banks of the river in Marietta, a primarily white middle-class neighborhood of Atlanta. I find her sitting on sun-warmed rocks beside the river, a fit woman with shoulder-length light brown hair. She looks like my image of Wendy caring for the Lost Boys in Peter Pan. Behind us fly fishermen wade into the water. Breathing multi-layered scents of forest, rock, and water we watch a blue heron in the shallows.

Sally Bethea describes herself firstly as a mother of two boys. She adds she is an ordinary person with a big job, fantastic staff, thousands of supporters, and generous financial support. If you met Sally on the street, her description of herself as ordinary or normal would hold true. For those who know her, she is anything but ordinary. It is Sally Bethea's 50th birthday. She laughs about having to think like a lawyer in her work. In the middle of our conversation, Shirley Franklin, the first female black mayor of Atlanta and any Southern city for that matter, calls Sally's cell phone. After their brief conversation, Sally turns to me to say how Shirley calls herself "the sewer mayor." She appreciates her close relationship with Shirley Franklin to speed the work forward.

Before Sally met Shirley, she met Laura Turner Seydel who co-founded Chattahoochee Riverkeeper with funds from the Turner Foundation. Laura is a daughter of Ted Turner, founder of Cable News Network. In the wake of his divorce from Jane Fonda, Ted Turner obsessively turned to environmental activism. He kept himself busy by acquiring parcels of what would become two million acres, mostly in the high plains, for 51,000 head of bison in eco-conscious ranching. Inspired by John Cronin and Robert F. Kennedy Jr.'s book, *The Riverkeeper*, Sally and Laura joined what is now called the Waterkeeper Alliance, a national and international organization of citizen activists who patrol waterways focused on clean water. As with most of the 270 river, bay, and sound keepers, Sally Bethea's learning came on the job.

Under a lawsuit Sally Bethea initiated, the City of Atlanta paid $2.5 million in the largest one-time penalty ever assessed under the Clean Water Act at that time. The federal consent order in this lawsuit required

Atlanta to mitigate pollution, redesign its sewer system, and create a greenway corridor. A heroine to those who love the Chattahoochee, Sally received numerous awards including an honorary doctorate. She retired from her Chattahoochee Riverkeeper position in 2014, though she remains an advisor to the organization she co-founded. The next generation of Chattahoochee River saviors continues the work. And what of the new system? A full 4.5 billion dollars later, Atlanta's sewer project was successfully completed in 2014. It features a new, larger combined storm water and sewer tunnel beneath the city. Sewer separation, the engineers said, would be too expensive.

Like all large city sewer systems, the sewers in Atlanta, even in its updated form, are hidden things and forbidding places. Two older combined sewer and storm water overflow system (CSO) tunnels pre-date the new tunnel, all of them with diameters sufficient to carry a phalanx of men carrying other men on their shoulders if the tunnels were empty and such a crazy notion occurred to anyone. Instead, an equivalent volume of urine, feces, and everything else that goes down Atlanta's drains flows through the tunnels to one of seven treatment facilities. In concrete buildings with no windows, the foul slurry gets stirred and raked of trash, degreased, pushed through grates to be decontaminated before turning into biosludge and sold as compost. At least we think this happens. There is no description of what actually goes on in Atlanta for the public to read. We do know that the 2009 flood of the Chattahoochee nearly destroyed one of two new sewage treatment plants, sending tons of raw sewage into the river just like the old days. But the city promises there will only be an average of four overflows per year rather than the 12 to 15 per year of previous decades. The projection includes the erratic weather patterns of climate disruption with its more frequent extreme weather. But no one really knows how long-term forecasting will match reality.

While cholera outbreaks have not occurred in Georgia's cities for decades, *giardia lamblia, e.coli, cryptosporidium, legionella* and other water-related pathogens are certainly present along with many of the 80,000 chemicals created since the 1930s. Studies of waterborne illness outbreaks over time show that since the 1950s most outbreaks are due to system deficiencies and breakdowns in the distribution system, especially water pipes to and from the sewer mains. In addition to bacterial and protozoan infections, chemical poisonings have increased. Chemicals can readily evade the treatment process founded for the most part on bacterial decontamination. Their appearance in city tap water depends on how the entire system works anywhere upriver or upstream from one's faucet. These problems plague all cities, new systems or not.

ENVIRONMENTAL RIGHTS ARE CIVIL RIGHTS

The story of Atlanta's sewers is not complete without looking at its black neighborhoods. Black neighborhoods, congregations, colleges, and civil rights activism make Atlanta a citadel of black culture. The Martin Luther King Jr National Historic Site in Atlanta contains his boyhood home, the Ebenezer Baptist Church where King's father and he first preached, and now his martyred body lies next to his wife, Coretta Scott King. Just as in the rest of the country, efforts to end racism continue. The old south still shows up in the way the city celebrates Stone Mountain with its monumental bas-relief of Robert E. Lee, Jeff Davis, and Stonewall Jackson. Depicted astride horses with hats over their hearts, the images bear witness to the founding of the Ku Klux Klan at Stone Mountain in 1915. There are restless civil war and civil rights ghosts all around Atlanta.

It's a "whiter Atlanta," the Atlanta Journal-Constitution headline announced in 2006. A whiter Atlanta does not mean there are more white faces throughout the city; it is still largely segregated by neighborhood. There is Marietta and Buckhead, mainly white, to the northwest, and African-American neighborhoods to the southwest. In the black neighborhoods of Atlanta, I met African-American leaders of neighborhood environmental action. The sewer protests in black neighborhoods of West Atlanta shook up the city beginning in the late 1980s with wins for sewer upgrade and sewer separation in Utoy Creek and partial victories for other black neighborhood sites. And all of this occurred a full decade before Sally Bethea became Riverkeeper.

As I travel these areas of the city, I recall that one hundred years nearly to the day after Georgia seceded from the Union, the Freedom Riders, including Congressman John Lewis, passed through Atlanta. Later they were beaten and their bus torched in Anniston, Alabama by an anti-segregationist white mob. A local environmental activist, Sherrill Marcus was not a Freedom Rider, but he was a student in Birmingham at the time. He chose to become a civil rights activist and put a career in biology on hold. With a smile slowly spreading over his deeply lined face, eyes twinkling, he chuckles as he tells me he once brought his white shirts to a laundry for "whites only." He took part in the major actions in Birmingham and later headed the National Association for the Advancement of Colored People voter registration for the Southeast. But NAACP activities, illegal in Alabama until 1964, meant relocation of headquarters to Atlanta. When the main voter drive ended in the 1980s, Mr. Marcus took a job in a Bosch auto parts warehouse then moved on to environmental activism. Sherrill Marcus and other civil rights veterans became the experienced leaders and mentors for what came to be the Environmental Justice (EJ) sewer and other protests in West Atlanta.

Sherrill Marcus and I meet in West Atlanta near a place once branded "the Little Berlin Wall," separating the white and black parts of the neighborhood before most of the whites moved to the suburbs. The homes here are modest, single-story ranch styles, many painted in quiet colors. The tree-lined streets, with little traffic or urban noise, hold sweet flower scents from residents' gardens. We speak of the importance of *Toxic Wastes and Race*, a 1987 study sponsored by United Church of Christ for Racial Justice that details higher levels of toxic waste in African-American and Hispanic neighborhoods compared with white neighborhoods regardless of social class or income throughout the country. This document has been followed by other confirming studies, evidence used in the Environmental Justice movement to bring attention to the high rates of toxic dumping in black communities. There are literally thousands of black "Love Canals" including that of Hooker Chemical contamination of the original Love Canal in Niagara Falls. Lois Gibbs, then a young white housewife resident of Love Canal, became and remains a great environmental leader, but black Love Canal residents in Griffin Manor public housing, largely ignored by the media, also stood up against the chemical company.

In West Atlanta, I meet the next generation of EJ leaders. Bruce Morton, avid bicyclist and father of five, grew up near Cascade Springs in southwest Atlanta. He tells me that when he was a boy his family had to close the windows at mealtimes to reduce the sewage stench until the sewer protests changed all that. As he imparts this history, we walk through a restored park to a waterfall. There are boardwalks to make it easier for elders and disabled to enjoy the park. I too am grateful for the easy walk over the stony ground. "Here," he says, "my brother and I used to play soldiers—Union soldiers," he says with eyes sparkling, "but we didn't really know that history as very young kids, just soldiers." They often found civil war artifacts in the park when they were young. Bruce led others in preserving this 220-acre preserve in the city. Bruce says that in the seventies, "We had our 'kumbaya' moment—whites and blacks together, but it is really black activism that saved these urban preserves." Hampton Beecher Nature Preserve, another conservation effort led by Bruce Morton, holds treasured old growth trees. Later, I saw a photo of a 200-year-old Tulip Tree curving forward from its wide furrowed trunk as if putting its arms around Bruce's family gathered in front of it. Miraculously, so many trees made it through the early days of settlers, the Civil War, Reconstruction, and even contemporary urban development.

Another emerging young leader is Na'taki Osborne Jelks. At the time of our meeting, she co-led efforts with the West Atlanta Watershed Alliance and later became its board chair. She sits at a table with a laptop, her greeting bringing the corners of her mouth upward and her eyelids gently downward. Her steady soft gaze under her unwrinkled brow and thick smooth hair serves her broad knowledge well when she speaks. One quickly comes to trust her. She starts our conversation by saying, "Sally Bethea is all right, but there is an older history here." It was the black neighbor to black neighbor grass-roots effort in west Atlanta that brought an end to raw sewage running through playgrounds and backyards. "No one else was going to step in, so families did it themselves." Na'taki, a public health graduate of Emory University, has received numerous awards, especially for youth outreach to foster the next generation of EJ leaders after her.

She discloses her own family history in our conversation. They could have been, and probably were, one of the points of data in the *Toxic Wastes and Race* study. The family of Na'taki Osborne Jelks suffered from environmental poisoning in African-American neighborhoods of her childhood in "Cancer Alley." This is the name give the petrochemical corridor between Baton Rouge and New Orleans, where her mother was diagnosed with breast cancer at a young age. With her strong environmental science background, Na'taki knows there is no proof of cause for her mother's cancer that a court would accept, but the multiple carcinogen exposures there have been well-documented. Her measured recounting of this history carries an undertow of the family's health crisis history, evidenced in a slight quaver in her voice. This family and so many others experienced tragedy wrought by unrestrained industrial polluters in places considered worthless dumping grounds, in spite of the residential areas and schools nearby.

Feeling inspired by these dedicated Environmental Justice advocates, I drive out of the neighborhood to return to Carroll County and an event at McIntosh Park on the river. At the corner, a fresh-faced young man probably in his late teens, wearing a smart grey uniform, leans in to hand me a leaflet. He hesitates when he sees I am white. But he hands me the leaflet anyways for an upcoming rally. He is a member of the New Black Panthers. *The Southern Poverty Law Center* and the original Black Panther Party call the New Black Panthers a racial hate group with some members advocating death to whites. Maybe one day this young man will find a better way to fight injustice. I hope he will meet and work with people in this neighborhood, especially Bruce Morton, Na'taki Osborne Jelks, and Sherrill Marcus.

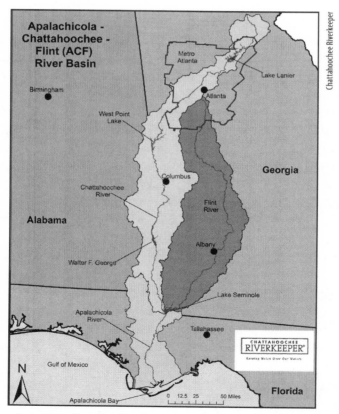

Apalachicola-Chattahoochee-Flint River basin in relation to Atlanta, GA

INFECTIOUS DISEASES AND OUR FOREST CLEARING

My own journey in public health did not begin with noble intentions to help a disenfranchised community. Until I was 21, I spent my days painting, playing music, writing poetry, and sometimes I wrote apocalyptic fiction. If it were not for my marriage to a jazz musician and a much-needed job as a secretary for a professor who studied epidemics and brought new computer tech into medicine, I would have stayed in the arts. As my work in epidemiology ripened with intensive training, the CDC campus in the Chattahoochee River watershed became a strong pull on my life. I worked in New York City with CDC partners and I worked in Washington DC as well as Bethesda, MD at the National Institutes of Health with CDC partners. Serum samples, phone calls, data, jointly authored papers, colleagues, and I frequently found our way to Atlanta throughout my career. It took decades to stop long enough to see the river running through it all.

When I first took a job in epidemiology, I was without a science background. My infectious disease knowledge, other than my mother's instruction on colds and flu, came from the Disney film *Old Yeller*. The adopted stray dog, Old Yeller, defends his prairie settler family from a rabid wolf only to contract rabies, or "hydrophobia," as they called it in the film. Pierced to the heart with love for Old Yeller, the oldest son, Travis, holds back tears as he fires his rifle ending the life of his heroic dog. And I learned the power of rabies. Later, Edward Jenner's work on smallpox vaccination showed up in a children's book. The memory of a pastel-colored drawing of a young English milkmaid and her cow remains etched in my mind. And I read the story of Ignaz Semmelweis in a young adult book. He taught hand sanitation after discovering that medical students were infecting women in a maternity ward as they came from their cadaver studies. There was little else in my memory stores when I landed in epidemiology.

In the beginning, my primary motivation was escape from a job as a secretary. My gadfly university employer, Ted Sterling, thought I could replace his graduate research assistant. He did it to prove "native intelligence can beat out rote book education." As a mischievous eccentric, this gambit suited his image and his budget. He spoke of exploiting me with a twinkle in his eye, although I did not find it amusing. Nonetheless, he remained a steadfast supporter for me in the years ahead through research projects, first publications, and my formal education at

Columbia University. Sterling also brought me into my first investigation, a waterborne infectious disease and a meeting with the CDC.

Happy to be off the hook from answering phones, typing, and filing, I spent hours in the library learning statistical analysis and basic principles of epidemic investigation. I read Bradford Hill's classic 1965 paper on "The Environment and Disease: Association or Causation?" This paper signals the beginning of what has since become increasingly sophisticated causal reasoning in biomedical research. Hill drew on many sources including John Snow's detailed investigation of 1854 Soho district of London cholera deaths. Germ theory had not been put forward, and no waterborne pathogen was posited by medical experts at the time. On the contrary, the *miasma* theory of bad air as cause of cholera and many other diseases we now know to be infections held sway. An agent in the water was a long shot, yet Snow expended great personal effort in gathering data to thoroughly examine the idea. With the help of Reverend Henry Whitehead who knew the people of the affected Soho wards, Snow visited homes and carefully mapped water use for the 13 wells in this area. On the same map, he placed a black bar at the address of each cholera death in what Steven Johnson calls *The Ghost Map*. When Snow meticulously plotted the least distance service area for each well, the deaths clustered strongly around the Broad Street (now Broadwick) pump.

With the hypothetical exposures mapped for each potential water source, the living and dead could be compared. It turned out to be key to discovering the then unknown pathogen carried in fecal contaminated drinking water. Yet there were anomalies for the suspected Broad Street Pump. No cholera deaths were reported in a workhouse housing 500 near the pump, and cases were not found in a brewery one block east of the well pump. The workhouse had its own well, but the brewery remained a mystery as it used the suspect water. Not until knowledge of the pathogen, *vibrio cholerae*, and the development of germ theory publicized by Robert Koch 30 years later, did an explanation appear: the bacterium was killed by alcohol. Apparently few drank water at the brewery.

The John Snow investigation of the 1854 outbreak illustrates what have become basic outbreak investigation principles. Simple counts of case numbers alone are poor clues to potential causal patterns. Snow's case mapping, while not accounting for the population size in each place, made incorrect default assumptions of population uniformity. While some areas of Soho were less densely inhabited than others, mapping the areas by water source became the unit of comparison. Comparison of disease rates generated in this way underlies the first major principle for Bradford Hill and the foundation for what we call "strength of association." It tells us how much greater the rates in the hypothetical exposed group are compared to rates in the unexposed.

Despite the unrefined enumeration and the data anomalies, the preponderance of John Snow's evidence pointed to an agent in the water of the Broad Street pump. With epidemic detective work, unknowns such as the anomalous uninfected brewery workers always cloud findings. In the case of Snow's cholera data, the evidence was strong and favored his hypothesis. Snow left us with an example of an ingenious outbreak investigation, although he died in 1858, not living long enough to know the biology of his mysterious waterborne agent. Re-analyses of data from the 1854 cholera epidemic using modern mapping methods confirms Snow's results.

There are six more Bradford Hill criteria, among them consistency of findings across studies, and biological plausibility. These principles essentially still hold. Investigation still requires the combination of educated guesses, data collection, and skeptical testing of the results. We still use shoe-leather methods along with statistical and mathematical models, some based on ecology of living systems.

My first water-borne outbreak investigation came in 1976 when I was 25. Legionnaires who had attended a meeting in a Philadelphia hotel were getting sick and dying in noticeable numbers. At first the outbreak was attributed to H1N1, a swine-to-human viral disease at the root of the 1918 Spanish flu that killed up to 100 million people or three to five percent of the world population. Periodically H1N1 resurfaces. It showed up at Fort Dix, New Jersey in a limited outbreak in early 1976, lending credence to its hypothetical role in Philadelphia. But the Philadelphia epidemic turned out to be a far more complicated water-borne infection. By the time it was over, 211 Legionnaires had been hospitalized and 29 had died. We now know that Legionnaire's disease comes from a pathogen of water tanks, cooling equipment, warm water pipes, showerheads, and other places in which we bring the water into our built environment.

Back in 1976, the process of elimination ruled out person-to-person infection transmission as no cases were found in household contacts or the community outside the convention events. Those hospitalized presented with an atypical pneumonia that was somewhat greater in older ages but could just as easily kill 30 year olds—a pattern not seen in most respiratory infections. Rates of cases among the hotel occupants by place and time in the hotel were generated just as Snow had done to study cholera. Food-borne diseases were also ruled out as no pattern emerged. Attention turned to contaminants in the hotel building itself. As the investigation proceeded under public scrutiny and pressure, there were many theories but no conclusions. It would be a year before an infectious agent was identified. It turned out to be a bacterium that lived in the buildings water systems. Extensive testing confirmed it as cause of the epidemic among the Legionnaires.

When attention first turned to the building environment, before the pathogen was identified, my research group was called in to consult with the CDC. I had given birth to my daughter in January of that year, and it would be my first trip away from home since her birth. A jazz musician friend, Teruo Nakamura, and his girlfriend, Jackie, were visiting as I prepared to travel to the CDC-sponsored meetings. While I made garlicky Japanese dumplings for our guests, Jackie leaned her head with her natural afro over my sewing machine, and hastily made a red jacket and pants for me to wear to the meeting. The hotel sported red curtains, carpets, and chairs in its ballroom, and I nearly disappeared in all that red in my new outfit. I could be the invisible "fly on the wall" listening to everyone in the room, a role I savored as I was new to outbreak investigations.

Our group first explored airborne toxins of the ventilation system as potential causes of what we were by then calling Legionnaires Disease, but quickly ruled that out. The next major system examined was the building's water. The hotel had an enormous evaporative cooling water tower with a maze of water pipes, faucets, and showers throughout the building. In principle, the evaporative cooling system worked like a household swamp cooler—ideal conditions for what we would come to know as *Legionella*.

In the years following the outbreak, we learned the bacterium was not new but was newly opportunistic in the increasing numbers of large buildings with massive water systems, hot tubs and spas. It grew in its ideal temperature range of 95 to 115 degrees F. We now know *Legionella* even grows in engine-heated windshield wiper reservoirs that do not contain disinfectant.

Thirty-eight known major outbreaks surfaced since the Philadelphia convention, including one in Atlanta shortly after the Legionnaire's meeting outbreak. The Chattahoochee River water piped into buildings hosted *Legionella* in Atlanta, as a disease of the built environment's artificial waterways. In Atlanta and other cities, the river water enters into a labyrinth of pipes, to be heated and stored at the right temperature range, and later returns to the river, causing infections in buildings between intake and outflow. Many of the outbreaks since the first one in Philadelphia carried higher case fatality rates, the ratio of fatal cases to all cases. The highest death rates to date occurred in 2015 at Lincoln Hospital Concourse Plaza in the Bronx, NY.

William Foege, head of CDC at the time of our first meeting on Legionnaires' Disease, uttered words indelibly etched in my memory: "With infectious diseases, we live in a clearing in a forest." He continued: "the wild pathogens are all around us, and can reenter our clearing in spite of our feelings of security." We listened closely to Bill Foege, a 6'7" tower of intelligent kindness with an unswerving gaze, as he was heading the global plan to eradicate smallpox. The last known case of smallpox in the world was documented in October 1977, the year after our Legionnaires' disease outbreak, during which the global smallpox eradication effort had long been underway.

Foege strategized new epidemic control principles borrowed from fire fighting. Long before his work at the CDC, Bill Foege worked as a fire fighter. His team of firefighters would set a containment ditch or ring, removing fuel for the fire, then move from one hot spot to another. He said, "When your house is on fire, you do not prevent fire in the neighbor's house first." Given this principle, his plan first quelled hotspots of active smallpox cases through quarantine, contact tracing, and supportive therapy, followed up with vaccination. His team used these principles to eradicate smallpox, centering the global effort in the hands of the local affected communities. Practical over-arching plans implemented with local knowledge by first responders stand out as important principles in so many things from epidemics to environmental disasters. These methods have become central to waterborne and water-related diseases of watersheds in Georgia and around the world.

For the people of the Chattahoochee watershed, waterborne diseases such as cholera were among the most historically important causes of death. The first major drop in infectious disease mortality in this watershed, as it was for the whole nation, proceeded from sewage treatment and chlorination of public drinking water in the 1920s. Later, antibiotics dropped infections to yet lower levels but not as steep as the initial drop brought about by chlorination. Thanks to decades of public health researchers, Americans have come a long way from the conditions of my grandparents' times. Born before the turn of the last century, they knew that infectious diseases stalked the land and spared no one. In 1900, the top three causes of death in the United States were pneumonia, tuberculosis, and diarrheal diseases mainly from bacterial and other microorganisms in water. Heart disease stood in fourth place. A century later in 2000, the order reversed: heart disease, cancer, and stroke landed in the top three causes and in sixth place pneumonia. Deaths due to contaminated water no longer made the top ten.

The pattern of low rates of infectious disease deaths continues into the twenty-first century for richer nations while for low-income nations one-third of all deaths can be attributed to infectious diseases. For Sub-Saharan Africa, infections claim half of all deaths. The topmost causes of death in low-income countries are HIV/AIDS, tuberculosis, malaria, along with lower respiratory infections, primarily pneumonia. For young children, diarrheal diseases from contaminated water claim lives among the 2.5 billion who lack adequate sanitation and safe drinking water. It is an unprecedented public health triumph in wealthy nations and still a global health crisis in low-income nations. Yet, ancient diseases still circling the globe, coupled with economic instability and widespread resource depletion, can and do come back to our clearing in the forest.

FROM PRE-COLONIAL TO POST-WAR GEORGIA

The history of water-related infectious diseases has a role in wetlands mismanagement of the watershed. Early sanitary engineer methods included drainage of wetlands and spraying of pesticides. These are the same methods that came into heavy use in agriculture, and the mid to lower Chattahoochee watershed was ground zero for these methods in controlling mosquito-borne infections and in conversion of wetlands to dry land agriculture.

The story begins in pre-colonial Georgia before malaria arrived. Changes began in colonial times to bring so many mosquito-borne infections to the southern waterways and wetlands although now there are no longer epidemics of malaria or yellow fever even with the same mosquito carriers still present. We need to understand what happened between then and now. Near the Chattahoochee confluence with the Flint River lies a much older Georgia still host to remnant longleaf pine woodlands and nearby wetlands. It is the birthplace of the original CDC infectious disease field station.

Margery Boris and Angie Stober, people I met through Sybil and Glyn up in Carroll County outside of Atlanta, accompany me to a place 200 miles south of Atlanta on the Flint River, the Chattahoochee's major tributary. We wake long before dawn in the home of a member of Angie's family. As we open the kitchen window, stale indoor air meets moist outdoor air droplets as we pack our bag lunches. Backway roads roll on in darkness along with our quietly held excitement. We are headed to a long-leaf forest grove. These woods and wetlands represent so much of the southeast as it once was.

Our arrival in the ancient long-leaf forest intrudes upon a conversation whispered above us. The trees seem to say, "Shush, your elders are speaking." The sienna and yellow-brown carpet of winter wiregrass clutches our trousers below the knees. Interspersed in this understory, spindly rods hold long pompoms of young green long-leaf pine needles. Mists like smoky cats curl around tree trunks neatly spaced as if by design. Swooping crones' bones of branches crowned in long sap green needles appear above us, but only if you crane your neck to see them. It is winter and mosquitoes are not present. They are overwintering in tree hollows and knots.

Within the fungus-softened heartwood of these trees are lodged critically endangered Red Cockaded Woodpeckers nesting in community clusters. Excavation of the tree heart in the still-alive trees takes up to three years of woodpecker hard labor. Even the multiple sap holes drilled to keep rat snakes and corn snakes away from the nest take valuable head-bashing work. We hear but do not see woodpeckers this morning though the nesting holes are visible through a spotting scope. The trees provide everything for the woodpeckers that feed on insects, including mosquitoes caught in the tree pitch.

As the mists slink away, I see reddish-gold lights high against the pearly morning sky. They streak along branches and momentarily outline ten-inch long pine needles. The forest owes its greatness to the lightning-ignited fires that clear the understory along with the young deciduous trees. No old deciduous trees live here. The long-leaf pines shed their green fingers and the young pines their spritely tops to feed the fires. Fire-resistant bark of the trees and long taproots of the young keep them alive to regrow needles after cleansing blazes. On seeing the dancing streaks of red lights, I realize we had stumbled into a morning ceremony in praise of fire, with the sun officiating for the trees, air, clouds, and lightning.

Before European settlers showed up in the southeast, there were vast stretches of this unique ecosystem of longleaf pine and wiregrass plant communities from East Texas to Virginia. They thrived in periodic lightning struck burns or, when lightning was scarce, in controlled burns by their indigenous caretakers. These woodlands and nearby wetlands hosted mosquitoes but there was no malaria or yellow fever until the Spanish and then English settlers arrived in ships. Ship builders arriving in Georgia from Europe across the Atlantic discovered the long-leaf pine's fine oils for tar, pitch, spirits of turpentine, and rosin for caulking ships and waterproofing sails. We can say the long-leaf forests were forced to build the ships that brought Atlantic trade to Georgia, including kidnapped Africans and old world diseases like malaria and yellow fever. The long-leaf forests of the southeast gave their oil and pitch to make 70 percent of the worlds' supply of *naval stores* as they were once termed until the forests thinned and their domain shrank. Later, in the age of railroads, the tall straight and dense long-leaf wood made ideal railroad ties and trestles. One could also say the long-leaf pines were conscripted into building the railroads that built Atlanta mostly in the Civil War and brought old world diseases on rails throughout Georgia.

Broken remnants of these woodlands exist in isolated nature preserves, old quail plantations, and military reserves. By chance, practice military war maneuvers would ignite the longleaf pine forests. The military became the surrogate for the Cherokee, Creek, and Seminoles who once cared for the forests with periodic burns before they were driven away by soldiers. These tribes were among those hardest hit by old world infections riding in the appalling conditions of cross-Atlantic ships long before soldiers and settlers drove out most of the remaining indigenous people.

Near the confluence of the Chattahoochee and Flint Rivers, one of the greatest old growth stands of longleaf lives on. They are rooted in the largely undisturbed quail and hunting plantation of Robert W. Woodruff, an early executive of Coca-Cola. Woodruff, a reclusive but powerful businessman, had turned the nearly bankrupt Coca-Cola into an economic colossus. His name adorns buildings and institutions all over Georgia. Quail hunts, popular among southern gentlemen of the late 1800s and into the twentieth century, resembled the sports of English kings. Hunters on horseback, following a cart from which quail were dropped, shot in polite rounds. The quail were picked up by prize hunting dogs, descendants of which still live at Woodruff's plantation. These quail plantations constitute the prime reserves of an older Georgia ecosystem of the lower Chattahoochee watershed.

If not for Woodruff and his plantation, there would have been no early CDC work on mosquito vectors of disease. Noticing his plantation tenant farmers suffering from malaria as were workers clearing power line rights-of-way for Georgia Power, Woodruff set aside land and buildings for a malaria treatment and research field station on his property. It became the Emory University field station and treatment center for malaria, mainly funded by Woodruff from 1939 until 1954. During World War II, the station was operated as the Office of Malaria Control in War Time, the predecessor of the CDC. After Woodruff's death in 1985, the Joseph W. Jones Ecological Research Center at Ichauway was established in the same site.

MOSQUITOES, WETLANDS, AND THE CDC

Anopheles quadrimaculata. Her wings make a high-pitched whine as she lands to get her flexible needle into the deliciously scented neck of a warm-blooded animal. She detects carbon monoxide, ammonia, and octenel, assurances to her that blood will nourish her eggs. After the lightning quick jab, she grows quiet. The magnificent mosquito with a fancy name, *anopheles quadrimaculata*, has always been here in the Chattahoochee watershed. She has relatives everywhere—in Northern Mexico, all over the American south, New England, Canada, and in western mountains all the way up to the continental divide. She and all her kin sport a four-pronged headdress, two sets of front legs, and a pair of delicate wings. There is one set of back legs behind the wings, just enough to pitch her body to the correct needle insertion angle. Her mate lives on plant nectar, as does she with the one exception of blood feedings for her eggs. Her partner doesn't stick around and dies a week before she does. A week is one-third of her lifetime. She lays 250 eggs carefully, one at a time. They have floaters attached to make a bassinet in the water to hold the eggs on the surface until they hatch into larva. They molt four times. The final metamorphosis brings adult males and females on the water drying out their wings, but the mother will not live to see her adult descendants.

She does not intend to carry malaria. Rather, she is hijacked by a protozoa that evolved to survive life within her body. The protozoa uses ingenious biochemical means to last long enough to be injected with saliva of *anopheles quadrimaculata*, containing anesthetic to ease the host's painful reaction and anticoagulant to keep the blood flowing.

The Centers for Disease Control and Prevention started with *Anopheles quadrimaculata*, the primary carrier of malaria's protozoan parasites *plasmodium falciparum* and *plasmodium vivax* in North America. Mosquitoes and the pathogens they carry became a crucial factor in the American Civil War. The stories of mosquito-borne infection epidemics converge with poor water drainage and open sewage outflow ponds fostering infection-carrying mosquitoes near human populations.

How did we get to this, our clearing in the forest of water-related mosquito-borne infectious diseases? The story involves innumerable sick and dying. It involves movement over continents and oceans, mistaken ideas, and false containment efforts, breakthroughs in science, and environmental control until the circle could be declared closed. When one speaks of "eradication" or "local extinction," the disease and vectors are not literally extinct everywhere. The disease may reappear due to remote reservoirs of infection, outside our infection clearing. Only smallpox has been officially termed "eradicated" globally, but it too still exists in laboratory freezers, and even in bodies defrosting in the arctic global climate meltdown.

The protozoa that causes malaria, an African import in the blood of infected sailors and kidnapped human slaves, has been around for 100,000 years, originating in African tropical forests. There is still a parallel form in African chimpanzees. Malaria carried by mosquitoes increased with the spread of agriculture and human settlements starting 10,000 years ago, speeding up with wet rice cultivation in West Africa and later in the Americas. The protozoa, first identified in 1880, had its complete cycle worked out by the end of the nineteenth century in time to institute control measures for Panama Canal work sites. Work on the canal, in fact, brought increases in mosquitoes due to environmental disruption. Without mosquito control, the work on the canal would have stalled if not halted altogether as occurred earlier for the French due to yellow fever and malaria. We think of malaria as a swamp dweller through its name, "malaria" from "mala aria" or the bad air of wetlands. In truth, it exists beyond the swamp, just needing enough water to propagate, and sufficient numbers of infected people to carry to others. It does not need to fly far, just short flights, person-to-person, household-to-household, along transportation lines.

At its North American epidemic peak, malaria occurred throughout the eastern US, even traveling west with soldiers to California. The greatest epidemics of malaria, along with murine typhus and yellow fever, occurred during the Civil War affecting both north and south. Like good bankers, the Union army kept counts of soldier diseases. They counted 1,315,955 cases of malaria excluding typho-malarial fever and including multiple occurrences for individuals among Union soldiers, second only to diarrheal diseases such as dysentery with multiple pathogens including cholera. The numbers, collected midst chaotic circumstances, can never be fully certified or tracked as episodes of malaria recur and soldiers entered and left military service throughout the conflict. We do not know the differences in occurrence of infection between North and South, but we do know that the North still provided quinine and medical treatment to its soldiers long after the South could not. Overall, disease deaths exceeded combat deaths by five to three. In the post-war period, the south suffered from malaria in the ravaged land to an even greater degree than during the war.

Malaria brought pesticides to the forefront of public health. Pyrethrum, an insecticide derived from the chrysanthemum flower, was first used in 1901 by William Gorgas in Cuba where it was burned inside sealed dwellings. Mosquitoes entirely disappeared from many parts of Havana. Later control methods followed this lead. Mosquito control stepped up around southern military training camps of World War II. These were the early years of the CDC, and its officers applied tons of DDT to kill mosquitoes. DDTs broad health effects, not fully known at the time, were later revealed as a ubiquitous killer that included bees, bird embryos, and fish beyond the targeted mosquitoes. Human health studies, still accruing to this day, show adverse effects on male and female reproductive health, breast and other cancers, nervous system toxicity, and liver damage. Moreover, insects have developed resistance to its effects.

The CDC also drained swamps and millponds as mosquito breeding grounds. With the disappearing wetlands, agricultural land expanded and housing developments moved in. The sick were isolated from uninfected people and from mosquitoes with netting and indoor insecticides. Livestock herds appeared in great numbers to become mosquito blood hosts and a dead end for human malaria, as livestock do not carry the disease.

Official narratives state that, taken together, these measures effectively ended the spread of malaria's plasmodium protozoa in North America. But there are other explanations, and the mosquito populations, now resistant to DDT and other pesticides thanks to heavy applications in agriculture, have all rebounded to their historic distribution. At the time of the malaria control work based on sanitary engineering of wetlands and widespread pesticide applications, there were dissenting scientific voices. Work at the Ichauway experimental research station went in a different direction that deemed widespread pesticide spraying and wetlands drainage were unnecessary and destructive. In fact, drainage ditches were observed to be better mosquito breeding areas than natural wetlands with intact wildlife ecologies that kept mosquitoes relatively low.

Centers for Disease Control and Prevention

Current Anopheles quadrimaculata distribution in the United States

The field biologists of the inter-war and post-war years, approaching the problem from the perspective of ecology, held a different view on malaria. First, malaria had been declining since the 1930s for reasons that included use of anti-malarials, such as chloroquine given preferentially to pregnant women, and dismantling of the sharecropper and tenant system of agriculture. This change in populations altered the dynamics of transmission, reducing contact with carriers of malaria. Ecological changes to the land, however, remained problematic. Agricultural still water pools, coastal rice and upland cotton fields provide ideal mosquito breeding grounds. The karst geology of the southwestern Chattahoochee and Flint rivers hosts limesinks and water-filled ridges, devoid of insect-eating fish. These places can and do host the mosquitoes that carry the malaria protozoa. In fact, while malaria prevalence was high, the mapping of malaria to karst geology provided a basis for the Ichauway field station's turn toward ecology. With careful study, lead researcher Goodwin wrote that draining mosquito-habitat, carried out "promiscuously" and without regard to its effect on water and conservation, had negative impacts on the watershed without being effective for mosquito and malaria control. Moreover, the team found pesticide application works best mainly indoors where people suffering from malaria lived, rather than broad indiscriminate spraying of the land. Separating infected people, treating them medically, and controlling local indoor exposure to the mosquito proved a key strategy.

MOSQUITO AND WETLANDS STUDIES AT ICHAUWAY

Where are the mosquitoes of the Chattahoochee watershed now? And how much infection do they actually carry? The Chickasawatchee Swamp, at the confluence of the Chattahoochee and its tributary, the Flint River holds answers. It is February and free of biting female mosquitoes, yet it is warm enough to explore the lowland bald cypress swamps and upland pine forests. Islands in the Chickasawatchee still have potshards and other remnants of the Creeks who hid from the settlers and soldiers bent on their extirpation from these lands. Periodic slave rebellions were launched from its dark, hidden islands. Bald cypresses, hundreds of years old, rise from conical trunks in watery darkness, their branches sheltering countless wildlife and insects. At the edge of the swamp, the damp ground bristles with winter grasses. In February the trees are bare, deciduous unlike other cypress. Their rough grey waterproof bark bears streaks and speckles of brown, with the darkest marks showing previous high water levels. Mosses adorn the trunks.

Low winter sun sends spindles of light into openings through the dense trees. Light streaks above and in water reflections below where patches of blue appear. It gives the illusion of lifting the whole forest into the air. Emerging above the water line, the ancient trees display what botanists call their "knees," like abstract sculptural forms rising from water-bound roots. The trees point the stumpy projections, more like arthritic hands than knees, upward to the tree crowns 100 feet above. Where leaves once sprouted, tiny branches feather the tree crowns, pink-tinged in morning light. It is a community of all ages, the deceased elders lying in the water to feed the living ecosystem. Mosquitoes make this place home, both in wetlands and nearby forests.

Studies in the JW Jones Ecological Research Center at Ichauway bring us up to date on mosquitoes of the south central Georgia swamps. Research shows no single pattern of mosquito habitat by degree or size of wetland, forest, or savannah or by vertical distribution from ground to treetop for all mosquitoes and no one-host-fits-all for mosquito feedings. Common hosts in this region include deer, cows, passerine birds such as crows and thrushes, cottonmouths, and bullfrogs. The vast majority of mosquitoes play no role in the cycle of human disease.

The Ichauway research center is in a humid sub-tropical region with relict longleaf pine and cypress forests. A large-scale mosquito study in 2008 collected 58,000 mosquitoes of 30 species in nine genera, among them *aedes*, *anopheline*, and culex genera, the latter being the primary vector of West Nile. The *aedes* genus can carry yellow fever, chikungunya, dengue, and zika viruses. The most abundant species, *aedes vexans*, dominates throughout the May to November mosquito seasons. It is a vector of dog heartworm and a deadly rabbit disease but carries no human pathogens in America. We simply find it annoying, hence its name.

Only 190 blood-fed mosquitoes, three-tenths of one percent of all 58,000 collected mosquitoes, were found in this mosquito season study. The most common among the blood-fed, *anopheles quadrimaculatus*— the malaria mosquito, drew blood from cows, horses, deer, and a chicken.

Plasmodium protozoa, the pathogen of malaria, were not detected in any mosquitoes. *Aedes albopictus* showed up as a single mosquito blood feeding on a white-tailed deer. The *A. albopictus* mosquito competes with *A. eqypti*, the carrier of zika and other flaviviruses, resulting in increasingly sterile populations of both when they crossbreed. West Nile Virus was detected at very low levels in *Culex quinquefasciatus*, the main carrier of West Nile that circulates mostly in birds. In Georgia, human infections with West Nile tend to show up in urban or populated areas with large numbers of birds that feed on mosquitoes breeding in sewage outflows, such as the combined sewage and storm outflow of Atlanta. No *aedes egypti* mosquitoes were caught in traps, confirmation of their scarcity in the wetlands of south Georgia.

The potential mosquito-borne epidemics of this watershed remain quiescent. Future surveillance efforts would benefit from mosquito surveys, and from an ecological approach that takes into account the health of the whole ecosystem before fears of epidemics bring out risky and environmentally damaging control measures.

PUBLIC HEALTH SANITARY ENGINEERING

"We don't have cholera anymore, why do we still need chlorination?" asked a sanitation engineer whose name I can't remember. But I do recall his hulking frame, hunched over a heaping plate of hamburger and fries at the water conference we were both attending. "Apart from the long list of pathogens treated by chlorination and de-chlorination, cholera is not so far away," I responded, "It can come back if conditions shift." He was not convinced yet we watched cholera enter earthquake-devastated Haiti, coming in with Nepalese UN workers who unknowingly contaminated water near their camps. The epidemic continues with an official total of 9,200 deaths in 2016. A *Doctors Without Borders* study demonstrated deaths to be four times higher than official counts in some areas, as so many died before reaching a doctor. Cholera was recently in Cuba and Mexico, though quickly contained there.

With economic and infrastructure breakdown, situations like Haiti can occur anywhere the organism enters drinking water. It is not necessarily a disease of the poor but it is a disease of unsafe water infrastructure in which the microorganism is introduced and survives. In cholera, water is both disease carrier and cure with hydration key to survival. This makes conditions all the more challenging in emergencies such as earthquakes and fires that destroy potable water systems.

And what of malaria with its still abundant mosquito carrier? People still travel to and from malaria endemic areas. Though rare, there are still locally acquired cases of malaria in the US, the most recent case in Colquitt, GA, between the Chattahoochee and the Flint Rivers. Malaria can re-enter the population in large numbers when conditions are right from nations with on-going endemic infection as we see in Central and South America, and especially in Sub-Saharan Africa. The World Health Organization in 2016 put global malaria eradication back on the table after previous failures. Its success will be dependent on funding and international cooperation, especially in low-income countries. And how is cooperation possible in war and famine de-stabilized countries, and with millions of refugees? It seems insurmountable, but without the effort, malaria will continue to kill and cause suffering globally for millions. The World Health Organization put the number for malaria in 2015 at 212 million cases and an estimated 429,000 malaria deaths.

In the United States, surveillance and early containment remain plausible defenses against waterborne and water-related diseases. We do need sanitation engineers for sewage treatment and the return of clean water to the rivers. We do not need sanitary engineering for wetlands drainage. In fact, the health of the ecosystem needs to shift toward wetlands restoration, and to de-fragmentation of the natural ecology. The real mistake is clearing the forest and converting the swamps for dry land farming to punch holes in the ecosystem's equilibrium.

And it is a mistake to think that we are so intelligent, so defended that cholera or malaria or any other ancient pathogen cannot come back. They sit at the edge of our unnatural clearing in the fragmented land. No, cholera did not vanish. It just lives somewhere else right now—most recently Haiti, Iraq, Zimbabwe, and Yemen. The World Health Organization estimates 1.3 to 4.0 million cases of cholera, with up to 143,000 deaths worldwide due to cholera each year. Yellow fever lurks nearby, with recent major outbreaks in Brazil. In North America, just like all the wild creatures of the forest that took their dwindling populations and moved away, all the wild diseases can return as habitat becomes increasingly fragmented and scarce, and as our public health infrastructure becomes strained

DRAINING SWAMPS, PUMPING GROUNDWATER, DEWATERING RIVERS

Draining wetlands and spraying pesticides in the name of public health fit the agricultural agenda of the south. Agriculture in the Chattahoochee watershed shows a history of destructive practices, with both the Chattahoochee and the Flint landing on the list of America's most endangered rivers. The combined problems of Atlanta's water use and agriculture downriver resulted in the Apalachicola-Chattahoochee-Flint designation as the number one endangered watershed in the country in 2016.

For people in the southeast, the Apalachicola-Chattahoochee-Flint watershed signifies a never-ending tri-state water war. The three joined names constitute the official watershed name covering a long slice of eastern Georgia, a narrow strip of western Alabama, and a little over 100 miles of the Florida panhandle. Where the Chattahoochee flows over the Georgia state line into the Florida panhandle, the name changes to the Apalachicola before it empties into the Apalachicola Bay and the Gulf of Mexico. As for Alabama, Georgia claims the Chattahoochee from eastern riverbank to its western bank of Alabama, creating water problems for Alabama, which owns a nuclear plant on the river. The three states have been locked into water wars for over 25 years, most centered on the water withdrawals of Atlanta at the head of the system where the river's watershed is most narrow.

All the plumbing into and out of Atlanta affects the once thriving oysters and fisheries of Apalachicola estuary and bay nearly 400 miles away. Revered as one of the most ecologically diverse river basins in the Southeast, the Flint River is also at risk from pollution; absorbing storm water, agricultural and industrial runoff as it flows south starting just below Atlanta. Heavy agricultural withdrawals of surface streams and ground water in the Flint River basin dewater the Flint and reduce flows to the Apalachicola. The state recently halted new groundwater requests from farmers in the midst of this water crisis. Florida, in its effort to save the aquatic life in the Apalachicola estuary and bay, presses for sufficient water releases from reservoirs in Georgia. It needs to alleviate the severe ecological stress resulting from low water flows and heavy salt intrusion. As of 2017, with no resolution, decisions for Florida and Georgia regarding water allocations remain in the hands of a court-appointed Special (Water) Master. He believes no one will be happy with his decisions. The whole system reflects poor management, overuse, and degradation at all levels.

Like so many rivers, the Chattahoochee hosts Army Corps of Engineers dams and navigational locks such that, for management purposes, the river is divided into manmade dam "watersheds." The Flint, running mostly parallel to the Chattahoochee, fares somewhat better. After its partly paved over headwaters under the Hartsfield-Jackson Atlanta airport, the Flint flows free for 200 miles until it reaches small impoundments before joining the Chattahoochee at Lake Seminole reservoir at the Florida border. System-wide water management requires the Army Corps of Engineers to re-assess their inland navigation and reservoir management as well, but the Corps does not see it that way, and sits outside of the litigation.

The Chattahoochee and the Flint rivers have common geography, with their upper reaches in the red hills of the Piedmont, then flowing down through channels below their fall lines etched into crystalline rocks. They spread out to broad, forested swampy floodplains, then move through limestone rock above the Upper Floridan Aquifer. Historically the Flint joined the Chattahoochee directly as its tributary, but now the Flint terminates in Lake Seminole. The Floridan Aquifer, an enormous open aquifer in which recharge from surface water and rain but also pollution can take place, is the major source of groundwater in the agricultural areas of the Flint River. Groundwater has been dropping precipitously over the past two decades. Increasingly, wetlands have been drained, paved over, and developed for housing, tree plantations for paper pulp, and agriculture, mainly corn and peanuts in recent time. In this historically wet country, even the streams sometimes dry up.

The land here long sustained agricultural damage, especially when intensively planted in cotton, a notoriously thirsty crop. Cotton became profitable to produce on small farms as well as large slaveholding plantations. Both types of farmers grabbed up this "Land Between the Rivers," and by 1860 Georgia was the world's largest producer of cotton, with much of that production coming from the Flint River Valley. Plantations were divided into tenant farms. Farming diversified into corn, tobacco, and peanuts, but cotton still ruled until the 1920s. Farmers ignored agrarian leaders across the South who warned of cotton's effect on the soil and the farmer's dependency on cash crops. By the 1920s, severe erosion, soil depletion, the boll weevil menace, and the

Depression wreaked havoc on the state's agricultural economy. Between 1920 and 1925, 3.5 million acres devoted to cotton were abandoned then reclaimed for other crops in Georgia alone. In the land between the rivers, agricultural withdrawals from ground water in the Floridan aquifer were not a problem until the 1990s. Irrigation from both ground and surface water has been increasing ever since. A somewhat hopeful note comes from recent data showing a relative drop in groundwater use per acre of harvest.

Between the middle and lower Chattahoochee and the Flint, and above Seminole Lake reservoir that feeds into the Apalachicola, a town called Plains hosts a population of less than 700. In it, Jimmy Carter, the 39th president of the United States and his wife Rosalynn, still reside. The people there call him "Mr. Jimmy." They are proud of their Nobel Prize winner neighbor. The prize came in 2002 for the work of the Carter Center, with its international peace-keeping and work on infectious diseases including malaria. Carter was the first sitting US President to oppose a large number of water projects as unnecessary failures of engineering. Water projects, such as large dams and hydroelectric works, have long been unopposed pork barrel bills in Congress. When faced with heavy opposition, Jimmy Carter lost his battles to end these projects. Marc Reisner, in his seminal work on the history of western water projects, *Cadillac Desert,* details Carter's efforts and the importance of the southeastern politicians in the country's wasteful and environmentally destructive water projects. But Carter has been successful on the Flint River of his home state, protecting the river for decades. In 2009, in opposition to a newly proposed dam and reservoir on the Flint, Carter joined with the Flint Riverkeeper, and other defenders of the river. The dam, proposed as a measure to alleviate Chattahoochee River withdrawals affecting Florida, would not remedy the situation and has not been approved.

The former president and the Flint Riverkeeper know that saving the Flint requires a hard look at agriculture in its basin. Carter's farm no longer grows peanuts and soy, but now harvests solar energy. In February 2017 he unveiled solar panels on his land, sufficient to power half the town of Plains. Carter, always an environmental progressive, favors water and energy efficient sustainable agriculture in his home watershed. In many areas of the country, including the southeast, ecologically sound farming practices are taking root with pesticide-free crop diversity replacing row crops and mono-cropping, soil replenishment without artificial fertilizers, and silviculture with diverse and wildlife-friendly forest crop management. This change is long overdue and how it will impact the water resources of the whole watershed remains an unfolding story.

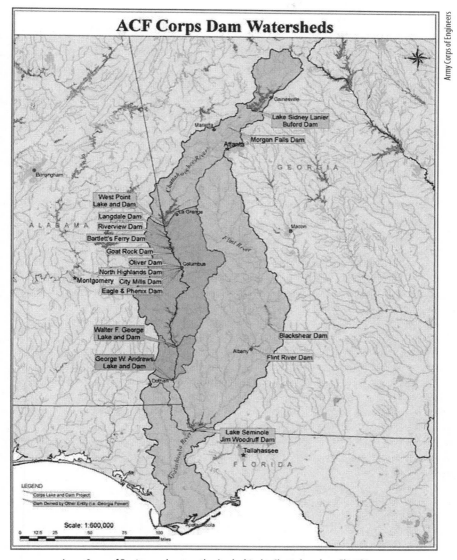

Army Corps of Engineers dams on the Apalachicola-Chattahoochee-Flint Rivers.

THE RIVER NEVER FORGETS

Equinox

I must keep from breaking into the story by force
for if I do I will find myself with a war club in my hand
and the smoke of grief staggering toward the sun,
your nation dead beside you.

I keep walking away though it has been an eternity
and from each drop of blood
springs up sons and daughters, trees,
a mountain of sorrows, of songs.

—Joy Harjo, Muskogee Creek

The Apalachicola-Chattahoochee-Flint watershed, here for millennia, sustained the people who first lived in its embrace, from a time before the waters were polluted. It witnessed dispossession of the Cherokee after the first American gold rush on the Chattahoochee in 1829, 20 years before the California gold rush. At the time, the Cherokee thought they had successfully fought forcible removal with a Supreme Court finding in their favor. However, the ruling was overturned by a margin of one vote in Congress and Andrew Jackson ordered removal of nearly all the Cherokee and other eastern tribes. The Cherokee Trail of Tears alone brought the deaths of over one quarter of the 16,000 people forced to walk or ride out of Georgia to Oklahoma.

Not long ago, the descendants of the Cherokee, Creek and other Native nations who evaded removal or who returned to this watershed, created an event to raise awareness of the river. They walked from the headwaters of the Chattahoochee in the Blue Ridge, past the impounded waters behind Lake Buford's dam, to Atlanta and on downriver. They blessed the river that still carries its ancestral name.

In Native ceremony, the ancestors live on. Ceremony leaders say the songs open the door between living and dead, and the ghosts slip quietly into the watershed to dance. In ceremonies, songs of the people join the songs of the river going back to a time before Jeep Grand Cherokees and Ocmulgee Creek Village strip malls. Those who died from smallpox, cholera, yellow fever, and malaria also return whole. They join hands with descendants of Africans brought to the watershed against their will. Following them are all the others who lived and died in this watershed for whatever life circumstances brought them here.

We thank those who eradicated smallpox, those who contained cholera and malaria epidemics, ended slavery, marched for civil rights, and fought for clean water. Where the river is not degraded, the waters reflect multi-colored rocks while dappled sunlight reveals fish leaping for insects. Racing down rocks, then changing form into filigreed splashes, the water gains momentum to wash over the next flat boulder. Hickory and beech curl down to spy their own wavy forms within the river's changing palette. In bright yellow-orange above and below the waterline, rocks show their forms surrounded by sky reflections carried on the water's surface. This Apalachicola-Chattahoochee-Flint watershed lives on. It needs our protection.

CHAPTER SEVEN

THE RIO GRANDE NUCLEAR RIFT BETWEEN US

Rio Grande/Rio Bravo

BEGINNING WITH THE 1945 Trinity bomb test at White Sands in the Rio Grande watershed of New Mexico, the nuclear age still leaves its marks in the land, water, and people of the watershed. Throughout the drainage of the Upper Rio Grande down to the border with Mexico, weapons manufacture debris, dismantled nuclear weaponry, plutonium from fallout, and all forms of nuclear waste wash through the watershed basins, leaving a trail of radioactive materials in the land.

Mushroom clouds of fear inhabit back corners of consciousness of all those able to understand the image. Until all nuclear weapons are banned, the shadow remains. The movement to stop military and commercial nuclear industries and their toxic products burdens one generation to the next, now over three generations and counting. In Colorado down through New Mexico, the Rio Grande carves the Rio Grande Rift, a geologic crack in the earth from the fracturing of the North American tectonic plate. The Rio Grande also marks the rift in the world brought on by nuclear bombs born at Los Alamos National Laboratory (LANL) in the river's Española Basin near Santa Fe in the Rift zone.

Since the first bomb named Trinity detonated in the New Mexico desert in July 1945, followed by the bombings of Hiroshima and Nagasaki in Japan one month later, the atomic age casts its shadow over the entire lifespan of the majority of people now living on earth. In 2010, a full 87 percent of the US population had been born after 1945; that percentage will be 97.5 percent in 2030. Born in 1950, I fully inhabit this nuclear age. Bomb drills in grade school heightened our fears of shattered buildings falling on our desks as we crouched beneath them. Over time, between the far more noisy youth culture and commercial jingles of our world, we saw brief glimpses of the intense suffering of those killed by the Hiroshima and Nagasaki bombs in blinding fireballs and intense radiation.

In 1957, during the time my family lived in the Texas-Mexico Lower Rio Grande borderlands at a military testing and bombardier training air base, I saw a *Life Magazine* article with a riveting photo of a 37-megaton bomb named Priscilla. This bomb's double mushroom cloud and lightning-like streaks above the Nevada desert were but a short display during Operation Plumbbob. Priscilla came as one in series of 29 nuclear tests in a period of four months, exposing 18,000 US military soldiers in ground maneuvers. Hundreds of animals were placed in various structures near the bomb hypocenter. One could see the mushroom clouds in Las Vegas, but at the time, no one spoke of the fallout near the blast site as black rain or traveling on the winds of the west. No one spoke of the short-lived radioactive iodine, or the long-lived radioactive strontium and cesium reaching bodies unseen, traveling over and into the lands of the Rio Grande and beyond.

Ten years later, in my high school art class, I painted Priscilla in smoky black-tinged greys, burnt oranges and gold streaks against a deep cobalt sky. Prominently displayed for months in the high school stairwell, no one spoke of it. This occurred just a few short years after the Cuban missile crisis when the words "mutual annihilation" had forcefully entered our lives. Perhaps potential mass erasure as a species along with most of the living beings on the earth could be ended if we did not acknowledge it. But the image remained, a silent reminder above our heads every time we used those stairs.

Tracing this long shadow in my life and the lives of everyone on earth, I turn to the Upper Rio Grande watershed to visit the birthplace and nursery of the nuclear age. This story lives on in each of the four basins of the Upper Rio Grande as its waters flows into and through the Rio Grande rift basins, from its Colorado headwaters to Mexico. And at every turn, river guardians and protectors speak up.

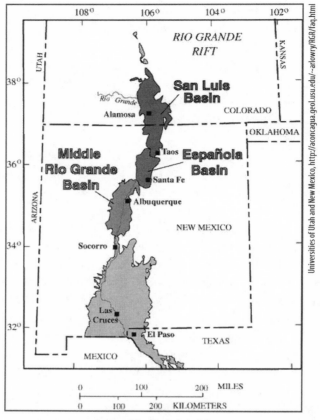

Basins of the Rio Grande Rift

Universities of Utah and New Mexico, http://aconcagua.geol.usu.edu/~arlowry/RGR/faq.html

SAN LUIS BASIN

We didn't know the word "aquifer."
We didn't know the phrase "perched water zone."
We didn't know the meaning of "ephemeral stream,"
        in relation to precipitation or melting snow.
We didn't know about "impairment," (the available
options). The list:
        where we could no longer swim,
        where and what we could no longer drink.

—Sawnie Morris, Her, Infinite,
"Cochiti Lake, 1989"

The San Luis Basin, just below the river's headwaters in the San Juan Mountains of southwest Colorado, marks the beginning of the Rio Grande's journey through the Rio Grande Rift. Along the western edge of the San Luis Basin, the Colorado Plateau imperceptibly turns clockwise toward the eastern continental *craton*, the basement rock of the North American continental plate. As if opening a door, this clockwise movement joins in the widening of the Rio Grande Rift. In 200 million years, a new sea will appear along the Rio Grande Rift from the Gulf of Mexico up through the San Luis Basin as far north as Leadville, Colorado. That period, eight times longer than the time span of our species, constitutes but a fraction of the 4.5 billion-year half-life of U-238, the most common radioactive isotope of uranium. Natural uranium deposits in the region discharge particles that wash through the volcanic field of the Taos Plateau, especially in unconfined ground water. In 0.72 percent of uranium can be found the naturally occurring U-235. Once separated and purified, this isotope is the only natural fissionable substance in existence. Other fissionable elements, such as plutonium, are man-made.

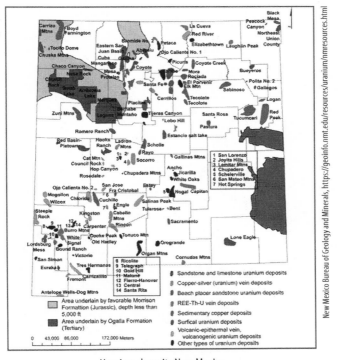

Uranium deposits New Mexico

New Mexico Bureau of Geology and Minerals, https://geoinfo.nmt.edu/resources/uranium/nmresources.html

In the upper basin of the Rio Grande, mining leaves its marks on the land in active and defunct hard rock mines. Flanked by the San Juan Mountains to the west and the Sangre de Christos to the east, the heavily agricultural San Luis Valley hosts ancient irrigation networks of *Acequias*, a Moorish term brought here by early Spaniards. Throughout the valley, contemporary irrigation overtakes traditional and ancient indigenous irrigation, along with livestock ponds, and wells that can contain and carry toxic heavy metals, including uranium. This human-made network of water exists alongside the natural water arteries above and below ground in open aquifers of the Rio Grande watershed. Ancient closed aquifers, with water older than 27,000 years, quietly hold their fossil waters unless wells and deep mines are drilled into them.

Thousands of uranium mines of all sizes dot the Rio Grande watershed, most unregistered open pit mines, sometimes called "dog holes." Active uranium mining in this uppermost Rio Grande Rift basin ceased in the 1980s, with preference for far larger deposits in the Grants Mineral Belt to the south and west. Other hard rock mining operations, active here and throughout New Mexico, remove ore inevitably mixed with uranium, thorium, lead, and other heavy metals especially in copper, coal, and shale deposits. All find their way into irrigation ditches, streams, and rivers, wildlife, livestock, food, crops, and people.

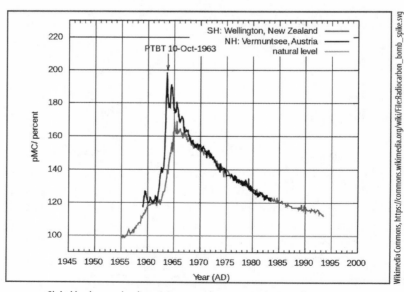

Global background radioactivity pre and post atmospheric nuclear testing

Life in the San Luis basin in New Mexico on the Taos Plateau brings relatively high background radiation exposures. Background radiation would be the level before one is exposed as a uranium miner, or from a series of nuclear medicine imaging, or from working in nuclear weapons labs. The background itself is not entirely natural, as the atomic age of atmospheric testing nearly doubles the pre-atomic age total. The graph below shows the change in general radiation exposure through the years of atmospheric nuclear bomb testing compared to the straight line for pre-testing at the bottom of the chart. Peaking in the 1960s, the levels have still not returned to pre-testing baseline.

For the United States on average, total background ionizing radiation exposures reach 3.1 milli-Sieverts (mSv), which is roughly one-third of a typical computed tomography (CT) scan. Three-quarters of that estimated 3.1 mSv US average background radiation occurs through inhalation of radon gas and its radioactive decay progeny, typically in buildings. The rest are from food, water, ground, and extra-terrestrial sources. In the uranium and radioactive thorium-rich lands of New Mexico, background exposures average two or more times the background for the country as a whole since ancient times. Archeologists studying Taos Pueblo, a 1,000-year-old village of Tewa people, hypothesize that radioactivity caused disease in human remains dating from as long ago as the late thirteenth or early fourteenth century. New Mexico has long been radioactive, but background levels here rose far higher after the early 1940s from uranium mining and atmospheric testing.

One cannot see these hazards in the streams, irrigation trenches, wells, or in glasses of water without a Geiger counter. And until the waters enter the Española Basin downstream of Los Alamos, radioactivity remains close to the relatively high background for New Mexico as a whole. The Rio Grande in the San Luis basin remains wild, with no dams or manmade channels. In this valley, once a vast ancient lake-bed, the river cuts through the Rio Grande Gorge, a 68-mile stretch. The gorge, seeming to appear out of nowhere in the flat country around it, quickly drops 800 feet from the rim to the river in some sections. Now part of the Rio Grande Del Norte National Monument, piñon and juniper forests still support 500-year-old trees. Mule deer, red-tailed hawk, mountain bluebird, prairie dog, and big horn sheep inhabit the gorge beside petroglyphs, hot springs, and ruins.

Starting in March through July, depending on melt-water and rain, the gorge provides the wildest ride on the river in a 16-mile stretch called the Taos Box, so named for its steep-sided canyons. Britt Huggins and his partner CJ McCue of New Wave river outfitters offer to guide a group of us. My only experience before this trip is solo kayaking in class II-III rapids, but I do not hesitate to go. Maybe I should have read the description on the New Wave website: "Difficult. Challenging rapids (Class 4+), in the top rank of one-day wilderness whitewater trips in the country."

CJ called me to make sure I could handle it.

"Can you swim?" she asked.

"I can dog paddle," I say.

After a long pause, she asks, "Would you panic in situations of rapids with high drops and a density of boulders?"

"I trust you guys. I'm not prone to panic."

One sunny but chilly day in early March 2015, after learning of promising river flows, we set out to run the river from Dunn's Bridge near Taos to the end of the wilderness section of the gorge, a minimum six-hour rafting trip. In the beginning the river runs moderately fast and calm by turns. We could count bighorn sheep groups along the gorge, soar with eagle sightings, and look for elusive otters. On the river bank at lunch, Britt carries on his personal war against Bud Lite cans and trash. After lunch, the run becomes fully engrossing, especially the last four miles. As the New Wave literature puts it, this last section starts with: "the notorious Powerline Falls, where the river drops rapidly down between large basalt boulders . . . with rapids called Rock Garden, Boat Reamer, Screaming Left-hand Turn." Smacked by drenching, foaming waves capable of ejecting us from the raft, all ears tune above the roar of the river to our guide's commands. Britt calls out, "Left forward, stop, back, forward." We waste no time following Britt's commands, until we could not. I clear the water from my eyes to learn that our raft is "broached" but not "tacoed"—stuck at an angle, wedged against rocks, but not folded like a taco. For an eternity of perhaps five minutes we rock the raft on Powerline Falls, using our paddles to free it. It turns out water withdrawals upriver had lowered the river height and flow that day. We became free to head further into a continuously challenging ride. By the end, after the Sunset Falls rapids, we reach calm water and the take-out. Yes, "worth the price of admission," as Britt puts it.

We have other river guides to call out our safe passage directions for watershed protection. One river guide turned environmental advocate, Brian Shields, heads a major environmental action organization. This watershed conservation organization for the Rio Grande serves as a hub for opposition to mining waste and radioactive pollution throughout the watershed. It operates from a modest white adobe building in the center of Taos as the office of *Amigos Bravos*. A painting of the Rio Grande Gorge in thick brush strokes of sage, orange, burnt sienna, dark greens, indigo, amethyst, and cobalt blue claims the back wall. Brian Shields created the gorge painting and *Amigos Bravos*.

I arrive in the organization's Taos office from a long drive, reeking of sweat and oily road dust. Brian Shields, wavy dark hair heavily streaked with grey, clad in crimson shirt and black jeans, stands to greet me. As we sit down to begin our discussion, he moves away from me. I fear offending him with my disheveled state, but I care more about learning his views on the Rio Grande, and I move closer. He moves away again, this time pinching his hand in some kind of mechanism under the long table where we sit. I resist the urge to bolt in embarrassment.

Yet, even with this awkward start, he patiently tells me he is originally from Barcelona, Spain, living in Taos since 1976. Brian's work history encompasses diverse people and places in all social classes. He spoke Spanish until eight, then went to a British boarding school, studied Euro-centric art history, then, as a young man, lived in Harlem during the time of the early Black Panther movement. He paid close attention to this movement, and realized he needed to work with Spanish speakers. His work list goes on: selling dumpster treasures in flea markets in Oakland, skiing instructor in Colorado, teaching art in Spanish (for which he was fired), and river guide. Hauling in fishnets on the Mediterranean as a boy brought his earliest awareness of the boundless beauty of bodies of water.

Brian Shields confides that he "was often out of place, between cultures." It made him sensitive to others, especially those suffering social injustices. From its inception, *Amigos Bravos* put social justice at the top of its mission. "In New Mexico, the land is colonized, we are colonizers, and this permeates society. People see environmentalists as just another colonizer, taking land and now water," Brian explains. In order to truly protect the watershed of the Rio Grande for all people and wildlife, a strong and cooperative coalition across groups had to form.

As we are speaking, Sawnie Morris enters the office, taking up the story from Brian. She fills the room with exuberant observations from under her wide brimmed straw hat, tendrils of unraveling hat ribbon mixing with her endless fall of brown hair. I half expect a small bird to appear on her shoulder as if emerging from a thicket. Her frank eyes, slightly knit brows, and engaging words quickly carry one into her world, one that closely binds her to her husband, Brian, and to the hundreds of people ready to protect and defend the Rio Grande watershed. She tells me she became the founding executive director of Amigos Bravos in 1989. "I got into this when interviewed by Brian; sparks flew unacknowledged for some time," she admits. The river united them from the start. "When I saw the Rio Grande Gorge for the first time, a profound experience of the female quality of the river came over me." She has been its ally and protector ever since.

As a poet and non-conformist Texan, Sawnie says she felt like an outsider in the beginning. In 1989, when they started, she recalls "words like carbon footprint did not exist, and there was little environmental knowledge in the general public. People are more conscious now that it is becoming clear our survival is threatened." They held listening sessions without an agenda in diverse communities to learn from people directly. The result is that Amigos Bravos now cooperates and partners with environmental and social justice groups in over 400 other organizations including: the Citizens Agenda for Rivers, Westerners for Responsible Mining, the New Mexico Mining Act Network, NM-SEES (New Mexicans for Safe and Sustainable Energy), Communities for Clean Water, Alliance for Rio Grande Heritage, the Coalition for the Valle Vidal, and an unnamed network of individuals representing organizations working on water-related issues impacting poor and indigenous communities.

One of the earliest actions of *Amigos Bravos* formed around the irresponsible mining practices of Molycorp Mine owned by Chevron in Questa. Beginning in 1920, these open pit and underground molybdenum mining operations had been heavily polluting the Red River east of Questa and the Rio Grande west of Questa, along with groundwater and wells. Local opposition to the mine began before *Amigos Bravos* entered the fight. Esther Garcia, an 11th-generation resident of Questa, speaking for many in Questa, replied to my questions about the views of locals. "Initially people didn't trust *Amigos Bravos*, and some are still angry.

But people are changing. They don't want polluting jobs, and now we work together in ways that were not possible in the past."

The growing coalition included scientists allied in Molycorp opposition. Research scientists have repeatedly shown widespread seepage of acid mine drainage through hydrologic connections between the mountains of waste rock piles at the mine and the river. And the ultra-fine particles of mining waste blow throughout the region. Hazardous levels of toxic metals including aluminum, copper, zinc, lead, cadmium, and silver have been recorded in the twenty-mile reach between the Red River's confluence with Placer Creek and its confluence with the Río Grande, a reach which includes the Molycorp mine. In 1995, *Amigos Bravos*, under the leadership of Brian Shields, sued Molycorp for Clean Water Act violations. In 2010, the EPA designated the mine a superfund site and shut down its operations.

Amigos Bravos watershed advocates carry their experience with the Molycorp Mine forward as an on-going Molycorp watch group. Added to this are multiple projects down the drainage basins of the Rio Grande, including Los Alamos downriver. From the San Luis Basin and the Taos Plateau, the river ends its untamed rush at the Española Basin a few short miles below Taos. There the nuclear age story has a far heavier hand on the Rio Grande watershed and the world.

ESPAÑOLA BASIN

A bronze statue occupies a shadowy corner next to the movie theater in the DeVargas Mall in Santa Fe. At the bottom of the statue, a Native man gazes straight ahead. Above him, Onate, the Last Spanish Conquistador, squints into the distance. Atop Onate's helmet sits the head of a cowboy, one of the rough men who wrested the land from the Spanish. To this totem we could add the head of Robert Oppenheimer who led his secret team of brilliant young men at Los Alamos, in cycles of hard work and hard play, to create the first nuclear bombs in the 1940s.

After an engine-straining climb through hairpin switchbacks up the steep canyons of the 7000-foot Parajito Plain, the quiet town of Los Alamos comes into view. The town and its laboratories occupy land on four mesas overlooking the Rio Grande on the edge of the Rio Grande Rift. Oppenheimer's portrait as a young man flutters gaily from flags on every lamppost in the town of Los Alamos. Homes near the laboratory resemble military base family housing everywhere. Their drab and fairly uniform appearance contrasts with traditional adobe homes of the Pueblos at the foot of the plateau.

Tent Rocks National Monument near the pueblos below Los Alamos marks an important geologic feature of the land. The capped spire hoodoos of Tent Rocks result from erosion of 1000 foot-deep pumice, tuff, and ash deposits of volcanic pyroclastic flows six to seven million years ago. The spires point upward toward the Valles/Toledo Caldera, a complex volcano capable of super-eruptions connected to a series of smaller volcanoes of the Jemez Volcanic Field. This caldera, formed around 1.2 million years ago, remains active, the last flow only 40,000 years ago from one of the smaller volcanoes within the main caldera. Remnants of air-fall ash and pumice from its last major eruption can be found throughout New Mexico and into Kansas.

The Valles/Toledo super-volcano occurs in a line of volcanoes, the Jemez lineament, from northeast New Mexico near Raton on a diagonal line through the Valles Caldera, through Mount Taylor, and ending in the San Carlos volcanic field of southeast Arizona. It includes up to nine related volcanic fields in a line that intersects the Rio Grande Rift at the Valles Caldera. This intersection with its volcanic activity related to the tectonic movements of these intersecting faults, creates a bull's eye shape when seen from space next to Los Alamos. Second only to Yellowstone's volcanoes in the US, the current caldera was created with 150 times the volcanic ash production of Mount St. Helen's eruption in 1980. A super-eruption would equal the force of 1,000 Hiroshima atomic bombs exploding every second as long as the eruption lasted. Super-eruptions can go on for weeks and months. The national lab plays with nuclear fire right next door to a potential super-eruption that could redden the nights and block the sun for a very long time.

Which form of annihilation will reach us first, the volcano's ash umbrella cloud or the nuclear products of Los Alamos, accidental or manufactured? We can place sure bets on both the volcano and on nuclear accidents in our future although we do not know the timing and magnitudes of any of these events. The volcano's 50,000 year average cycle is due any time. If we could see a graph of all human-made nuclear accidents, we would also see those are just as likely but with far shorter cycles of occurrence counted in months rather than in centuries.

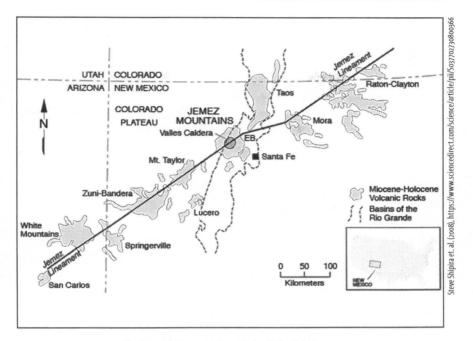

The Jemez Lineament through the Valles Caldera

Five months after the meltdowns of the Japanese Fukushima nuclear reactors in March 2011, an accidental near chain reaction took place at Los Alamos National Laboratory. Lab staff had placed eight rods of plutonium close together for a photo to proudly display their work. Any closer, and the rods would have started a spontaneous chain reaction. Fortunately, a supervisor noticed, and stopped the photo session. A series of protocol violations followed, including failure to evacuate the lab. Any closer placement of those rods, and it would have joined the list of 60 known criticality accidents in the world. But it was a close call. That same August in 2011, Sandia Laboratories in Albuquerque had an accident when a liquefied lithium experiment exploded. It broke the vacuum seal on the Plasma Materials Lab, lifted the roof and split the wall. These accidents did not make headlines. The Los Alamos event tipped the scales to closure of the Los Alamos nuclear core lab, PF4, for a list of safety violations over which most of its nuclear safety staff resigned. In 2013, the lab's plutonium handling operations were closed down in order to hire and train staff but the lab has not yet met safety standards. The Department of Energy gave the Los Alamos plutonium handling facilities a failing grade in its 2016 inspection report, citing 24 instances of noncompliance. As the only lab in the US licensed to create new nuclear core pits, and to share responsibility for testing existing weapons with two other national laboratories (Sandia in New Mexico and Livermore in California) the nuclear weapons program of the United States has been seriously crippled since 2013.

No one really knows all the nuclear hazard safety violations and near misses in the nuclear weapons and nuclear reactor world. People make mistakes, ignore regulations and safety in every industry, but accidents with unstable nuclear materials used in the nation's weapons arsenal constitute problems of the highest consequences. The Center for Public Integrity details the safety violations, contamination, personnel exposures, deaths, failures of regulation and fines, and the excessive profits of industries under contract to the federal government to run the US nuclear weapons complex. It's a harrowing read, and doesn't come close to assessing the entire industry, including the nation's 100 nuclear reactors, their risky fuel manufacture, complex management, and problematic waste storage.

In these desert basins rain can be scant then appear suddenly. A hard downpour creates gullies of fast moving water, and in this water unstable radioactive substances, by-products of the work at Los Alamos remain in the land, wash into streams, through the Pueblos, and into Cochiti Lake that impounds the waters of the Rio Grande to supply drinking water to everyone in the basin. In San Ildefonso Pueblo, a reservation straddling the Rio Grande below Los Alamos, lives Kathy Sanchez, a potter in a multi-generational lineage of artists. She is known for her traditional blackware pottery and for co-founding *Tewa Women United*, an organization active on environmental and social justice fronts. Sanchez and her husband, working with *Amigos Bravos*, and ten other river and *acequias* traditional irrigation advocacy groups, won a 2011 court case against Los Alamos National Lab for the lab's decades-long violations of the Clean Water Act. These days the Sanchez family and their collaborators, along with lab staff assigned to the job, act as guardians for clean up of the 405 identified toxic sites on LANL's 36 square miles. The site includes Area G, the 63-acre radioactive materials dumping ground. No one really knows how long the cleanup will take or how safe the storage of the lab's radioactive waste removed in this process.

NUCLEAR WEAPONS LEGACY IN HUMAN LIVES

Nuclear weapons products and materials processing are written in human lives. At the Los Alamos museum, I stand aside as a middle-aged Japanese couple snaps pictures of one another in front of exhibits labeled Little Boy and Fat Man. These are full-size reproductions of the bombs dropped on Hiroshima and Nagasaki in August 1945. In the museum, there are no images or words devoted to the Japanese wounded and dead except for a single poster. There is a guest book for commentary in a back corner with comments split between those appalled by what happened and those defending the dropping of atomic bombs on Japan. Nowhere does it say that on August 6, 1945, the atomic bomb created at the Los Alamos Laboratory reduced the population of Hiroshima from 340,000 to less than 250,000 in a single blinding flash.

For decades there were no images of the mothers, infants, schoolchildren, grocers, artisans, shopkeepers, and office workers who were incinerated, melted, and mutilated by the 3000-degree fire and 800 mph winds when the bombs were detonated in the skies over their heads. Sickness and death followed not only in the following days and months after, but for decades thereafter with elevated cancers, immune dysfunction, liver, endocrine, and cardiovascular diseases among survivors. The world saw the mushroom cloud photos taken from the air by the bombing crew, the blackened land below, and a twisted building dome. But we did not see the dead—only an empty plain of debris crossed by seven debris-filled rivers in black and white photos.

Images of bomb victims slowly began to appear from archives. Photos of the dead and dying Japanese were first seen by the world when *Life* released a small series in September 1952. The photos and accompanying article were printed in an issue with a cover of television showgirls in fishnet stockings, ads for new cars, televisions, high heel shoes, and a Regina vacuum cleaner. The black and white images of massive burns, demolished buildings, and a girl drinking water moments before her death were buried many pages deep in the issue. These Japanese photographers later said they had wet their lenses with tears and felt intense conflict in recording the dying. Yoshito Matsushige reported young girls with plate sized burns and skin hanging down "like a rug." Hiroshima A-bomb archives list 59 Japanese photographers and filmmakers who witnessed the destruction and suffering in Hiroshima and Nagasaki, but their images were suppressed by the occupying US military.

Japanese news footage and photos that had been confiscated by the US military surfaced later due to a copy hidden in a ceiling, as well as footage returned to Japan by the US government 25 years later. In 1970, some of the Japanese footage was aired on public television in the US. In 2003, survivor drawings were posted on the internet from images now stored at the Atomic Bomb Peace Dome. One man, 13 years old in 1945, drew the contours of women and children crawling toward a river, their skin hanging in strips. In 2004, the first color film images from US military footage of the dead and injured in Hiroshima and Nagasaki appeared in a short documentary called *Original Child Bomb*. A US military crew sent into Hiroshima the day after the bombs had gathered 90,000 feet of raw color film taken by skilled cinematographers of Hollywood studio quality. The footage was classed top secret, never shown in full, even after it was quietly declassified decades later.

And then there were the US military's experiments to study "survivability" in nuclear war. In a secret program, US citizens were injected with plutonium and exposed to other radioactive materials in varied ways starting in 1945, not ending until 1977, after they became public. In a series published by the Albuquerque Tribune and later as a 1999 book, Eileen Welsome details the experiments on hundreds of impoverished, powerless, and sick people as young as age four. At the Nevada Test Site, numerous tests on live animals and buildings were conducted. A 1957 *Life Magazine* article on Survival City, a town built just for the nuclear detonations at what was then called the Nevada Proving Grounds, offered surreal dioramas. Elegantly dressed manikins from JC Penney's placed in cottages hosted dinner parties while their manikin children played nearby. Unseen were the live sheep, dogs and pigs injured or killed as they were strapped into bomb shelters and chained in buildings to study the effects of blasts.

ALBUQUERQUE BASIN

Church Rock, west of Albuquerque and east of Gallup, New Mexico, raises supplicant stone fingers to the sky. It marks the 1979 uranium mine tailings breach, an event that exceeded the radioactive release at Three Mile Island four months earlier. A break in an earthen dam, known to be unstable at the time, sent 1100 tons of milled uranium ore and 94 million gallons of heavy metal effluent into the Puerco River.

On I-40, as I pass the flashy façade of Fire Rock Casino, a Navajo boy climbs up from the river just as children have always done in this place in Navajo country. But in 1979, children came away with burnt feet from the radioactive river while whole herds of cattle and sheep died. Wherever the acidic wall of water penetrated, the radioactive metals uranium, thorium, radium, polonium, and nonradioactive toxic heavy metals were left in its wake. Tests of water sources regularly used by the people for drinking, bathing, irrigation, and livestock in the area show it remains radioactive, well beyond tribal or US government drinking water standards.

Running 133 miles through the Grants Mineral Belt in Navajo, Zuni, and Acoma lands, the Rio Puerco, starting just over the continental divide from its sister river, the Puerco River, joins the Rio Grande at Albuquerque. When uranium mining for what the Navajo call *leetso* or yellow dirt, began in the 1940s, miner health and safety were criminally neglected. It was not until 1984 that the first complete study of lung cancer in Navajo miners appeared in spite of the fact that the hazards had been known since 1942. Today, there are radionuclides on the ground, in the air, and in local water sources from uranium mining especially after 1948 when the federal government committed to buying uranium mined in the US. On reservation land, private companies ran mining and milling operations that paid below minimum wage in this poverty belt. Mining in the Grant's Mining District lasted into the late 1990s, providing raw materials for defense research, for weapons manufacture and maintenance, and other nuclear age purposes. Despite this history, there is an attempt to reopen mines on Mount Taylor, the most sacred site for indigenous people in the area. But people here, all of whom have family members or know someone harmed or killed by uranium mining, have not forgotten. Opposition to the mine is strong and comes from the Multicultural Alliance for a Safe Environment and Amigos Bravos.

Mining took the lives of fathers and sons. It killed women and children who milled uranium and lived in homes built from mine tailings. For Native miners, their families, and their communities, the total burden of cancer and other diseases related to uranium mining, such as neurological and kidney diseases from heavy metals, cannot be fully quantified. Diseases and deaths due to radiation are routinely undercounted as many lived and died outside of record-keeping medical centers. Those whose illnesses and deaths did make it into the records were often in advanced stages of disease when diagnosed. Despite the undercounts, records show appalling rates of lung cancer in Native uranium miners, 29 times that of non-miners in the same areas.

Activism on the part of Native communities resulted in their inclusion in the compensation program under the Radiation Exposure Compensation Act (RECA) passed in 1990. Thirty years or more too late for those who had already died from radiation-induced conditions, there are billboards in New Mexico, just down the highway and along the river from Fire Rock Casino asking those who worked in the mines to come forward for possible compensation.

As the river moves through the ravaged land of the Albuquerque Basin, it enters a set of sub-basins that together comprise the fourth basin in which a Los Alamos bomb named Trinity was set off from a wooden tower at Alamogordo, White Sands, on July 1945 as the world's first full nuclear test just weeks before the bombings of Hiroshima and Nagasaki.

WHITE SANDS

Winter at White Sands is a blaze of crystallized gypsum, a sulfate mineral used in fertilizer and in plaster. It looks like an endless beach of sugar. A tarantula moves atop the glittering sand, but beyond the slight movement of the wind, there is nothing else to be seen. The bomb site itself, a destroyed patch of the desert, is closed to the public except once a year. Very little *Trinitite* remains there. This radioactive light green glass formed in the heat of the Trinity explosion has been nearly completely scavenged by tourists before it became illegal to pick it up.

The DNA in all our cells contains radioactive markers from Trinity that will continue to mark us. Carbon-14 (C-14) has been elevated since 1945 to a degree sufficient for scientific studies of the natural history of our cells. Because of it, we know the heart turns over its cells every ten years while other cells turn over every seven years. Carbon-14 literally marks each living being in our nuclear age along with other long-lived radionuclides from nuclear testing and fuel reprocessing such as Iodine-129 at a half-life of 15.7 millions years.

White Sands still contains a 3200 square mile missile range, but nuclear testing shifted to Nevada in 1951 with a test called "Dog," a yield of 21 kT. It was the first US nuclear field exercise conducted with live troops maneuvering on land six miles from the blast. One hundred atmospheric and 828 underground nuclear bomb tests occurred within the 400 miles of the Nevada Test Site. Borne on the winds, the heaviest concentrations of fallout from atmospheric tests can be found in people and dust and water-borne sediments between the Cascades and the western Rockies, and it can be found in New Mexico.

Altogether, the US government conducted 228 atmospheric nuclear bomb tests, each of which exceeded the firepower of the bombs dropped on Japan. Highest exposures occurred for those downwind in the fallout plume. Now referred to as "Downwinders," they and soldiers exposed in testing may apply for compensation. The final US atmospheric test in 1962 came just as a global test ban was enacted. Not every country signed the ban. France continued atmospheric tests until 1974 and China until 1980. Los Alamos and its affiliated Sandia Labs in Albuquerque, first established to oversee Trinity, still handle nuclear materials in a new world of nuclear testing with computer models, materials testing, and contained miniature sub-critical tests. The most recent UN treaty to completely ban nuclear weapons, signed in 2017 by non-nuclear arms holding countries but not by those holding weapons or under the nuclear "umbrella" of those countries. The US and Russia still have over 90 percent of the world's active nuclear weapons, 6,800 and 7000 respectively. The graph below shows the change in weapons numbers after the Cuban Missile Crisis in 1962 from a peak of 30,000 to current levels with each international treaty.

As for the land of the Rio Grande, a large-scale study of plutonium, an element that is extremely rare in nature, and thus marks manmade manufacture, found that 90 percent of plutonium in the Rio Grande watershed derives from past atmospheric nuclear tests. The remainder is from weapons development and nuclear waste. The Stockholm International Peace Research Institute estimates 500 tons of plutonium in the world, equally divided between military and civilian stocks as of 2007. Nuclear materials handling and potential mishandling accompany all nuclear technology in every step of the process.

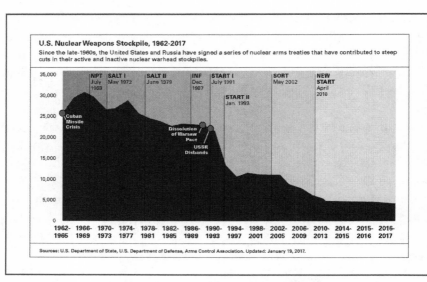

US Nuclear weapons stockpile since Cuban missile crisis

CARLSBAD

There is still no completely safe method for disposing of nuclear waste like plutonium-239 with its half-life of 24,000 years. Weapons grade nuclear waste and lower-level nuclear power spent fuel rods were once destined for Yucca Mountain, Nevada, until 2010 when its funding and licensing ended. Congress is now debating the continued evaluation of the site. Even if Yucca Mountain, located near the Nevada Test Site, had not been judged unsafe due to the mountain's permeable volcanic rock known as tuff, its lifetime expected capacity was already exceeded in its last permitted year for existing nuclear waste. Meanwhile, after 25 years of evaluations and construction, the Waste Isolation Pilot Plant (WIPP) near Carlsbad, NM, accepted its first shipment of nuclear waste from Los Alamos in 1999.

On Valentine's Day, 2014, a drum of waste from Los Alamos that was improperly packaged and mislabeled exploded at the WIPP. It resulted in exposure of 21 workers to inhaled internal low-dose radiation likely to cause cancer. It also led to the shut down of the nation's only repository for radioactive nuclear weapon waste, reopened in 2017. Since 2012 alone, Los Alamos was responsible for 11 of 25 shipping mistakes involving radioactive materials, most of them plutonium.

WIPP occupies a salt mine created 250 million years ago from evaporated Permian age seas. Cavernous carved rooms host nuclear waste four-tenths of a mile below ground. Sited in the sparsely populated "nuclear corridor," its neighbors include a uranium enrichment facility for nuclear reactors in Eunice, NM, and a low-level nuclear waste plant near Andrews, Texas. Prior to the 2014 Valentine's Day explosion, the WIPP received over 11,223 shipments from facilities all over the country coming via 13,435,681 highway and rail miles. Eventually, the waste will fill the fifty-six 100-yard long chambers during the next 25 to 35 years. And there will no doubt be transportation and mishandling incidents over that period and beyond into its extremely long storage life. What will our species be in the thousands of years these stored radioactive clocks keeps ticking?

FAR WEST TEXAS

In Andrews, Texas, a few miles away from the WIPP, a company named Waste Control Specialists began accepting nuclear power plant waste in 2009. As of 2011, thirty-one states had 71,862 tons of commercial nuclear waste, increasing by 2200 tons a year. On-site storage pools at most nuclear plants are filled beyond their capacity and the majority have moved to dry cask storage once the waste is cooled for five years. Most are looking to ship it elsewhere, and "elsewhere" usually means New Mexico and Texas.

Before the Andrews Texas nuclear waste plant, a nuclear waste dump was planned for the Rio Grande watershed in Far West Texas in 1991. It was to accept nuclear waste from New England and Texas plants via rail to Sierra Blanca. Contractors praised the site location for the low education of its 533 inhabitants, who are 90 percent Hispanic. But the policy makers did not count on the presence of Bill Guerra Addington, who founded the Sierra Blanca Legal Defense Fund, a bi-national organization that defeated the dump.

~

Bill Guerra Addington's family ranch first came into being in 1919. It stretches back to the Rio Grande with a natural land bridge connecting the two sides of the river. The family holds 380 acre-feet per year of prime river rights. In October 2009, I wait two days in Sierra Blanca,

90 miles downriver from El Paso, for Bill to show up at his family ranch to speak with me about toxic dumps here. When I finally find a fairly weak but adequate cell signal, his lengthy apologies play in voicemail. He says he is helping Heather McMurray with her car. I had sensed their complicated relationship, her vulnerability and his attempts to please her, when we had all sat down together in an El Paso cantina to talk about Bill's anti-nuclear waste dump actions. Heather's personal relationship aside, she possesses a passionate and strong voice for the environment, and I feel great affection for her. In fact, I don't mind waiting. I roam the area to view the border fence with its abrupt end a few miles past Fort Bliss. And I wander the town of Sierra Blanca with its horse motel, 1950s defunct gas station, and steak house open only at night in what appears, by day, to be an abandoned shack.

Bill finally arrives, rushing down the low rise from his mother's stone house wearing a ragged t-shirt from his Sierra Blanca Legal Defense days. He created the bi-national legal defense nonprofit to stop the radioactive waste coming by train from the New England Yankee nuclear plant to his back yard in the Rio Grande watershed. At La Familia restaurant, we fill up on huevos rancheros for breakfast followed by a substantial lunch of enchiladas, all the while detailed and knowledgeable stories pour non-stop from Bill.

Fortunately for my aching backside, he suggests we go out to visit some sites before our third meal at La Familia. As we stand, the town sheriff fills the doorway, keys in hand, badge on his pink shirt pocket. Partially concealed by his pink shirt, a holstered pistol rests on his thigh. With a backward turn, he takes a look at the decals on my car, shaking his head at "Undam the Klamath, Save Pacific Salmon" and nodding in agreement with "No Farms No Food." "Hello, Bill" he says softly and joins his deputy to drink tea. I wonder what the sheriff thinks of his long-time neighbor Bill. No doubt they are accustomed to his ways. And he did save the land for everyone here. The border is the real issue for people here now. I overhear the sheriff commenting on the incompetence of the border patrols, saying he could protect this section of the border himself with just a few deputies and a fraction of the border patrol's budget.

Outside the restaurant, tiny red flowers bloom on the cactus. We walk energetically away from the restaurant and back up the hill. When we drop Bill's battered hard-shell briefcase at his home, at least six dogs jump with excitement. They move too fast to get a good count. Outside a dozen bony cats make their restless sinewy rounds drooling in anticipation of a meal. Bill obliges and feeds them all. Animal rights occupy much of Bill's time when he isn't defending the river. In addition to the nuclear waste dump, Bill successfully fended off two other dumps in the course of over 30 years of local activism. The second dump was NYC sewage sludge, highly toxic waste passed off as organic fertilizer via contracts held by the Luchesse crime family. When that action successfully ended, another attempted dump for the PCB-contaminated dredge from the Hudson River was also blocked. "But, the most recent construction on the land, a new border patrol prison, could not be stopped," says Bill, shaking his head.

Half-Latino, Bill jokes about how he will have to be buried under the dividing fence between the Mexican and white settler sides of the local cemetery. We walk up the hill behind his home. He stiffly clasps his arms against his lanky frame, and tells me how his fight against the first dump cost him his wife and his young son who left when death threats mounted. Bill's saucer-shaped eyes well up with tears. The death threats were the least of it. Arsonists torched the Guerra family lumberyard, the charred frame still visible on the town's main street. Later the Guerra family grocery store closed when Bill and his mother used all their resources to fight the dump. When the conflict was at its greatest, riflemen in the hills shot the rear panel of Bill's car but he would not back down. He went on a hunger strike for 56 days, living on electrolytes in water. It brought national attention to Sierra Blanca's plight. As we stand on the hill, Bill points out Eagle Mountain. "My orders came from the mountain. The mountain screamed to do something. This land of Sierra Blanca is inseparable from my own body and I had to act."

Bill firmly believes that "If you know in your heart what is right and do it, you will be given special strength." He and his compatriots drew upon that extraordinary strength and the dump was stopped in 1998. The Sierra Blanca dump was to have held up to 1.8 billion cubic feet of low-level radioactive waste, such as filters, curtains and other nuclear power-plant waste as well as gloves and boots used in medical facilities. The evidence against the dump included studies of water tables at the proposed site hydrologically connected to the Rio Grande. In the end, the dump was judged to be in violation of the 1983 La Paz Agreement between the United States and Mexico, which prohibits toxic installations within 60 miles of the border. In this case, the border is the Rio Grande itself.

BEYOND THE RIFT

We do not yet know the future of the Andrews Texas waste disposal site or how the WIPP will contain the dismantled nuclear weapons and other radioactive materials within its salt mine chambers. It is not clear whether a nuclear power "renaissance" with newer nuclear power technology will take place as part of the effort to curb the mounting green house gases of climate disruption. And we still hope for an end to nuclear weapons and all forms of nuclear waste new and old. We know Bill Addington in West Texas and Kathy Sanchez in San Idelfonso continue to work for the end of nuclear contamination. We know that *Amigos Bravos* with its over 400 partner groups active in the lands of the Rio Grande watershed will continue to be the watershed's watchdog now and for generations into the future.

～

From Navajo and Pueblos lands, the ghosts of relatives working without safety equipment who died of exposure to radiation well above the average 20 mSv per year limit for workplaces of the present, with exposures close to the dosages of the Hiroshima hypocenter, are heard by the present generation. They urge their descendants' activism against the proposed Mount Taylor uranium mine. From all of them, we know that we must create a collective shift to a safer world. We know that amidst the noise of everyday life, we need to hear the urgent call that arises daily from the Rio Grande to protect the watershed.

CHAPTER EIGHT

THE GREAT RIVER DOES NOT DIVIDE

Rio Grande/Rio Bravo

FOR WILDLIFE IN THE RIO Grande watershed, there is no New Mexico, no Texas, no Chihuahua, no Coahuila, and no US-Mexico international border. For free animals, natural ecologies of rivers and streams, snowy mountaintop forests called sky islands, ephemeral washes, pockets of pooled water, and open aquifers that feed springs define life. In the Pueblo indigenous way of seeing, the entire hydrologic cycle, including clouds and rain, defines the watershed along with the community of plants and animals. It would include humans, but contemporary humans, disregarding these relations, continue to unbalance the watershed in too many engineered water projects, fragmented wildlife habitat, polluting industries, unsustainable agriculture, and wild species extinctions. In the Chihuahuan Desert eco-region through which the Rio Grande flows, the greatest threat to wildlife habitat destruction arises from domestic animal grazing. But it also comes from making the river serve as a heavily militarized border, through which wildlife passage becomes impossible.

The Rio Grange changes its name to the Rio Bravo, the Great River, in Mexico. It is here in the Mexican side of the desert where its longest tributary, the Rio Conchos, joins at the sister cities of Ojinaga and Presidio. This eco-region still bears the title of one of the world's most biologically diverse deserts, although it also suffers heavy abuses.

The Mexican Gray Wolf calls the mesas and uplands of the Chihuahuan Desert home. El lobo, as he is usually known (ba'cho in Apache), lived here long before any human. This subspecies of gray wolf goes back 800,000 years in this region until its disappearance from the United States by the mid-1900s, leaving just a handful in zoos. In 1976, when it was placed on the endangered species list, captive breeding programs arose and the captive population reached about 300. In 1998, 11 captive-reared Lobos were released into the wild and lived to reproduce. The wild population currently numbers about 110, and programs such as at Sevilleta Wolf Management Facility, 20 miles north of Socorro in New Mexico, continue to breed and monitor them in the wild. This smallest of all the wolves, Lobo stands about 28 to 32 inches at the shoulder, and weighs 50 to 80 pounds. Its richly colored coat distinguishes it from all other wolves: buff, gray, rust, and black. Its long legs relative to its overall size make it a fast runner and the region's top dog.

When Aldo Leopold witnessed the dying fierce green fire in the eye of a wolf he had shot, it led to his understanding of the rightful place of wolves. "The cowman who cleans his range of wolves does not realize that he is taking over the wolf's job of trimming the herd to fit the range. He has not learned to think like a mountain. Hence we have dustbowls, and rivers washing the future into the sea." The killing of wolves resulting in an increase of herbivores overgrazing with attendant environmental degradation led to the concept of "trophic cascade." Hairston and colleagues, who first coined the term, echoed Leopold stating that the land is green because grazers are controlled by their predators, rather than simply by the quality of forage. Research since has examined the issue in many ecosystems, finding that runaway consumption of vegetation tends toward lowered biodiversity and potentially unnatural desertification.

Restoration of wild apex predators like the wolf, known as keystone species in a trophic cascade, can bring restoration of an entire ecosystem. First-hand knowledge comes from restoration of wolves to Yellowstone National Park. Doug Smith, who reintroduced 31 gray (timber) wolves into the park in 1995 and 1996, says there are now roughly 100 wolves—down from a peak of 174 in 2004. Many have left the park to start packs of their own, and, of those, many have been shot and killed. Since the wolf re-introduction, numerous indicators of the healthy balance of Yellowstone have appeared such as no over-population by elk, the return of beavers, and increases in aspen groves, healthy grasslands, and renewed wetlands. Rangers believe at the moment the park is in a long-term equilibrium, although that may be upset with climate change bringing earlier thaws and throwing vegetation cycles out of sync.

El Lobo has its admirers. In Las Cruces, I went to meet Kevin Bixby, head of the Southwest Environmental Center. Dressed in loose blue shirt, comfortable black jeans, sunglasses, and well-worn walking shoes, Kevin carries himself with a relaxed air. In his 50s, no gray in his sandy brown hair and mustache, I sense long hours of hard work in his slightly stooped shoulders. Time in New Mexican wild places shows in his leathery tanned skin and body language, especially in his steady watchful gaze.

His organization is an important one working collaboratively with other groups on wildlife protection and watershed restoration in this part of the Chihuahuan Desert. Protection of the Mexican Gray Wolf tops the list of Kevin's many passions. This work follows a consistent thread in his life, and he believes his interest in the Mexican Gray Wolf is closely linked to his life-long love of dogs. It could be that dog lovers will find Lobo in their hearts as well. This is true for my own sister, who has her "pack" of wolf-like dogs and who supports wolf causes of all kinds.

Kevin's college studies centered on the environment as did organizations he joined, groups like Earth First and Friends of the River (FOR). It was during work with FOR that he met its founder, David Brower. John McPhee recounts the many confrontations between Brower and those who would destroy wild places in his book, *Encounters with the Archdruid*. Kevin carries the lessons of Brower, moderated by his own experience, into the present work.

Kevin Bixby has lived in the Rio Grande watershed since 1996, two years before the release of the first Lobos into the wild. An oral history project here brought him closer to people who grew up nearby, and through it he learned how they view the changes in the land and water. An important experience that surfaces often in local stories stems from the time one could freely fish the river, cook on its banks, and swim in the Rio Grande. Over time, fishermen observed the disappearance of two-thirds of native fish, and the shrinking of natural lands, along with access to the river itself. He found that people love wildlife, but have a hard time changing attitudes toward killing wolves. That attitude has been changing with outreach education to let ranchers and farmworkers know Lobo does not prefer cattle, sheep, and chickens when its own habitat supports sufficient natural prey. Carnivorous by nature, Lobo preys upon elk, deer, javelina, rabbits, and other small mammals.

Kevin Bixby dreams of restoring the natural meanders of the river, of bringing back the local shovel-nosed sturgeon and other native fish populations, restoring the wild habitat of Lobos within the watershed, and helping people reclaim the river as it was before the channel got straightened and the river became a dangerous "no man's land."

What will save the Mexican gray wolf and all the other animals with their rights to the land? Kevin thinks we need some big charismatic leader for biodiversity, someone without the stigma of environmentalism. "Around here, we need ranchers, hunters, and even catholic bishops to help bring us together." In Kevin's own experience, the local landowners, once afraid environmentalists would take away water rights, are now taking steps to protect wetlands and wildlife.

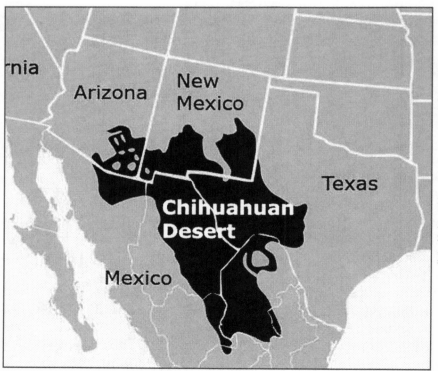

National Park Service, https://www.nps.gov/whsa/learn/nature/chihuahuan-desert.htm

The Chihuahuan Desert

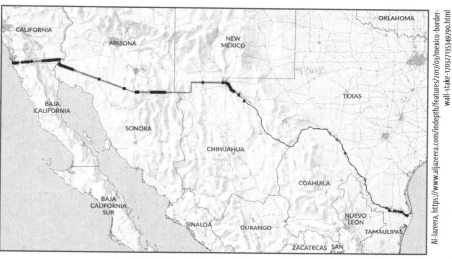

The Mexico-US Border with existing fence marked

Al-Jazeera, https://www.aljazeera.com/indepth/features/2017/03/mexico-border-wall-state-170327135349790.html

Still there are natural wild places. Near Socorro, New Mexico, below White Sands, a stretch of one of the last natural grasslands in a sea of dry desert exists on Otero Mesa. Vegetation in the Chihuahuan Desert includes a singular indicator agave, *lechuguilla*, along with more ordinary desert creosote bush, mesquite, and ocatillo. But Otero Mesa, at a higher elevation than the surrounding desert, flows with grasses, especially black gramma. It is home to mule deer and pronghorn, jackrabbits, cottontails, and reptiles of all kinds. There are peccaries, ringtails, bobcats, elk, mountain lions, coyotes, skunks, foxes, bats and badgers. Golden eagles and other birds of prey hunt the black-tailed prairie dogs, mice, gophers, and other rodents native to it. And this food web owes it life to both the grasses and the top predators. When the apex predators disappear, the mid-trophic animals thrive, vegetation dies, and the web falls apart. The marker of its destruction is the appearance of creosote bush, a change closely watched by protectors of the land.

Poor access to Otero Mesa by rough, largely unmarked roads amid sparse human settlement helps to keep it protected, for now. Its defenders would like it to have official protection status, but so far that remains elusive. From the busy highways of southern New Mexico and El Paso, Otero Mesa slips away unseen, its native ecologies continually re-weaving themselves into being. As Kevin Bixby notes, "The big problem is the trouble down there, where we made the river into a border."

THE TROUBLE DOWN THERE

On Interstate 10 in El Paso, the dust swirls so thick I can barely see the trucks hemming in my white Subaru. A dull brownish glow locates the sun, an eerie beacon. "It's strangely beautiful," I remark to my passenger, Mariana Chew, an environmental engineer currently working with the Sierra Club El Paso. She sighs, "I love my community." This afternoon Mariana's cobalt blue dress complements her warm skin tones and blue-black hair. Her dress also matches the color of her home near the Rio Grande in El Paso to which we travel. That blue replaces the color missing from today's sky and its reflection in the river.

In the evening we join Mariana's family and friends in the local eatery, a high-ceilinged room strung with soft yellow lights over buttery yellow walls. Music of borderlands popular groups like *Intocable,* a mix of traditional Mexican Son and 80s pop, fills the room, rolling over our conversations. Our words become rhythmic along with our feet tapping to the beats, buoying broken-hearted lyrics. In the morning we down soft tacos and coffee while Mariana's two lively girls prepare for school. But first they show me their family album and hand made posters for a cross-border peace event. They will join others to hold hands across the Bridge of the Americas over the Rio Grande. Mariana is passionate about every aspect of her life here, even the dust.

She tells me that before there was an international border, the original city was called Paso del Norte and it occupied both sides of the river. After the 1848 treaty between Mexico and the United States, the one city, existing for hundreds of years, became two cities. Mariana specializes in environmental justice as an environmental engineer. She devotes her time to the higher environmental toxic exposures in low-income neighborhoods of the Juarez/El Paso Rio Grande watershed. It is a complex story set in war-riven borderlands or *la frontera.*

WAR ON THE WATERSHED

Dr. Mariana Chew works on the massive pollution from the metal smelter that operated for 120 years at the north end of El Paso just a short distance to the river. Land on either side of the Great River near El Paso rises below the southernmost tip of the Rocky Mountains, and between them, the impossibly high towers of the smelters that punched holes of poisonous smoke in the sky from 1887 to 2005 at which point the company declared bankruptcy. The river itself, girdled in concrete ever since the upriver Elephant Butte dam opened in 1916, still carries pollution from the defunct American Smelting and Refining Company (ASARCO) plant in El Paso. Once a source of local pride, first as a Guggenheim family multi-national company before its current owner Grupo Mexico, the name stands now as a symbol of cross-border shame. ASARCO's smelter pollution constitutes a massive crime of toxicity against this watershed, its people, and its wildlife.

The divided land means the Mexican side of the river receives the worst of it. The company would increase its emissions every time the wind blew toward Juarez. As early as the 1950s, Joe Pinon, a pharmacist in El Paso, observed physical problems among ASARCO workers from lead, arsenic, cadmium and other byproducts of smelting. Wading across the river to visit the Juarez *colonias*, he found the most impoverished areas nearest to the smelter. Water collected into cisterns from rooftops contained so much metal that residues remained in clothing and anything the water touched. Residents of Smeltertown at the foot of the smelter in El Paso protested the pollution to no avail. Those in Juarez had no voice across the border.

Upon passage of the Clean Air Act in 1970, the City of El Paso sued ASARCO for its sulfur dioxide emissions. Air standards at the time, based on a limited set of contaminants, did not include lead emissions, and the actions against ASARCO required new studies. The court case netted internal ASARCO documents showing that between 1969 and 1971, the plant emitted over 1000 tons of lead particles that landed everywhere the wind blew and the polluted rain fell. The Centers for Disease Control, at the request of local Texas health officials, initiated a study of blood lead levels in children living near the smelter. Phillip Landrigan, an Epidemiology Intelligence Service physician from the Centers for Disease Control (CDC), drew maps with concentric rings around the smelter and sampled the blood of children within each ring in El Paso. They could not sample blood in Juarez citizens for the contaminants generated across the international border. In Smeltertown, the company town at the foot of the smelter, 53 percent of children showed lead levels bordering on acute poisoning. Smeltertown children with the highest blood lead levels, nearly all low-income Latino under five, underwent extremely painful chelation therapy in medical centers as far away as Chicago. The conditions of the children devastated this tight-knit community.

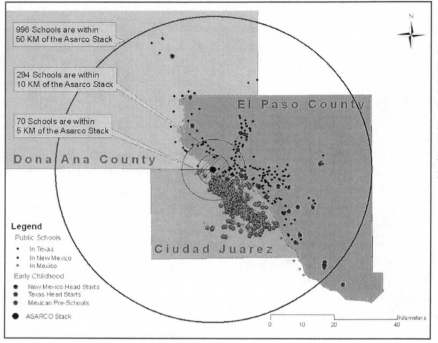

P. Landrigan et. al., 1975, New England J Medicine, 292: 123-129

Schools in El Paso and Ciudad Juarez shown in lead exposure circles.

All people within at least four miles of the smelter, which includes the river itself, had been exposed for decades, but for most of its period of operation, no opposition to ASARCO materialized. Understanding the discrimination against impoverished Smeltertown and Mexican residents, Landrigan conducted an additional study of lead levels in nursery school children in Kern Place, a prosperous neighborhood near the University of Texas, a mile from the smelter. White residents lived there in greater numbers than the rest of El Paso. Three-quarters of the children tested showed lead levels in their blood exceeding what was at the time considered the safe limit of 40 ug/dl. With decades of medical progress since, allowable limits decreased to 10 ug/dl. Some scientists now say there is no safe level. After the shocking results hit the papers, residents later learned smelter metals had contaminated entire neighborhoods, nearby areas, the river itself, and anything living. A meticulously executed study published in the New England Journal of Medicine in 1975 by Landrigan and his colleagues presented conclusive evidence of the plant's culpability in the lead poisoning epidemic.

Further, reductions in scores on Wexlar intelligence tests and lowered rates of finger-tapping responses, both markers of neurological dysfunction, coincided with higher blood lead levels. We now know that lead exposures affect every system in the body in children: development of bones, decreases in kidney and liver function, along with damage to the nervous system. The other toxins spewing daily from the smelter made things worse: cadmium, copper sulfate, zinc, arsenic, sulfur dioxide, dioxins, furans, and radon—all above safe limits depending on proximity to the smelter.

ASARCO officials undertook their own studies, finding no harmful levels, to counter the findings of Landrigan and colleagues. And they blocked remediation, taking no responsibility at every turn until forced to do so. The company findings were refuted and the series of investigations by Landrigan became a major contributor to the scientific basis for EPA's 1975 phasing out of lead products including gasoline additives and the ban on lead paint in 1978. At present, lead-containing products are under federal regulation with the exception of lead in bullets. This major fight and turning point in environmental action represented a victory for the nation, but it did little for those directly impacted by the smelter that disproportionately harmed low-income Latino, particularly those in Ciudad Juarez over the border.

ASARCO filed for Chapter 11 Bankruptcy in 2005 to shed liability for the costs of its dirty history, but new violations surfaced. Heather McMurray of the Sierra Club obtained a copy of an EPA confidential memo about ASARCO's illegal burning of industrial waste in the name of recycling. The document showed that the EPA official in charge had covered it up. She and Bill Guerra Addington, both co-workers of Mariana Chew, released the evidence to the New York Times and ASARCOs history of violations aired nationally. Bi-national protests ensued resulting in the development of Mexico-US environmental protection programs.

In 2013, the two remaining dormant smelter stacks of ASARCO came down in a blast of billowing smoke. In a meeting following the demolition, Dr. Mariana Chew showed data from the plume exiting the collapsing stack. The smoke was rife with lead, cadmium, dioxins, furans, and other substances. Environmental testing and remediation efforts continue though the land and water will likely never be fully free of the pervasive ASARCO contaminants. ASARCO poisons mix with other toxins from a Cemex cement plant, and the growing number of poorly regulated *maquiladoras*, small manufacturing companies mostly American-owned on the Mexican side of the border. All of these toxins find their way into the Rio Grande/Rio Bravo.

Only the cemetery remains where Smeltertown once stood. The Spanish-speaking families of workers had built their own homes, set up water and sewer themselves, but ASARCO owned the land and razed the town. Since the residents did not own the land, they were not eligible for relocation benefits. Those who remember life in Smeltertown knew its long-standing strong community ties in spite of criminal treatment by the company. No one would dare suggest razing Kern Place, still undergoing remediation. Organizations in the watershed, both sides of the river, work ceaselessly to address the environmental injustices, seek remediation and compensation for all affected communities.

All these efforts face a uniquely heavy complication in working to protect and unite the Rio Grande watershed on the Mexico-US border. Mariana says it is necessary to see the interrelated destruction of human lives when the river is forced to serve as a border. Mitigation of environmental problems are hampered given the wars between cartels to distribute marijuana, crack, cocaine, methamphetamine, and heroin to drug users in the United States. She asks me to attend a meeting with a friend of just released from the local Immigration and Customs Enforcement (ICE) prison. She says, "This will show you what life is like here for so many, and why it is hard to work together even when most people want that."

The next day is Wednesday October 21, 2009. I pull in to Annunciation House, a Catholic human rights organization housed in an aging brick building ten blocks from the border in downtown El Paso. Mariana, in a festive red dress with matching high heels and lipstick, makes her appearance shortly after my arrival. She and the people inside eagerly await Mariana's friend, Gustavo Delarosa Hickerson. We join the others happily gathered around a table of warm tamales from the food vendor across the street. Delarosa prosecutes cases against the Mexican military in Ciudad Juarez as the ombudsman for the Human Rights Commission of the Mexican State of Chihuahua just south of the Rio Bravo/Rio Grande.

When he reached the border in a routine crossing one week earlier, he was handling over 170 cases of threats, beatings, torture, kidnapping, and murder of Mexican citizens. We had gathered to meet him upon his release. The door flies open and Delarosa, dressed all in white, bounces into the room to a burst of congratulations, hugs, and handshakes. His wavy white hair and beard encircle his face, matching his clothes and his smile. He invites us to drink tequila and celebrate his release after the press conference that will take place later that day. Clasping my hand in his, he says, "Any friend of Mariana is a friend of mine."

Gustavo had been facing death threats for some time in Ciudad Juarez. One of his body guards was murdered, and another beaten prompting Delarosa to move his family to El Paso. Before his arrest by ICE, a stranger had pulled up in traffic and made his fingers in the shape of a gun. "Tone it down or we will kill you," the man said and drove off. But Gustavo Delarosa continued his Juarez casework mostly from El Paso although frequent crossings to Juarez were necessary as part of the work. On his last border crossing from Juarez to return home to El Paso, the immigration officer asked if he was afraid. "Yes," he replied and then said no when asked if he was seeking asylum. Instead of letting him cross, the officer put him in detention. That was followed by placement in prison "for your own protection" and Gustavo was caught in the bureaucratic labyrinth. For the week of his imprisonment, not allowed to speak with his lawyer, he was constantly pushed to sign asylum papers which he repeatedly refused as it would effectively end his work in Juarez. During the press conference, Delarosa's lawyer, Carlos Spector, assured us it was not an American plot, just a screw up. He and Gustavo were most of all concerned for ordinary citizens who would be trapped into signing asylum papers out of fear. Such action would instantly cut them off from their immediate families, homes, and jobs.

The Annunciation House meeting with Gustavo Delarosa Hickerson came in what we now know to be the second year of the war for control of drug trafficking routes to the US between the Juarez Cartel and the Sinaloa Cartel headed by "el Chapo" Guzman. Now incarcerated, Guzman's power surpasses Pablo Escobar, deceased head of the Medellin cartel in Columbia. The US Drug Enforcement Agency (DEA) designates Guzman "the godfather of the drug world." The peak of violence in Juarez occurred in 2010 with 3,766 known murders.

For a time, the violence nearly stopped in 2012 with the purging of corrupt police and officials, but also with the demise of the Juarez cartel. When the cartel violence abated, the people took stock. Juarez peak violence left 14,000 children orphaned, homes and businesses destroyed, and every family mourning their dead. Just across the border, El Paso enjoys a relatively low rate of violent crime now and over the entire period of the cartel war. But grieving crosses the border, both cities populated with entwined networks of families and friends, workers, and cross-border businesses. "These are my people, both sides of this river," says Mariana. Her voice drops, eyes lower, and sadness overtakes her usually cheerful mien. In the past year, murders in Juarez began to rise again. The Jemez and the current heads of the Sinoloa cartels fight in the power vacuum left by el Chapo. And now border crossing for everyday needs and for relocation or asylum has become far more risky in the era of Donald Trump anti-immigration racist policies.

Mariana and so many others continue their work to protect the Rio Grande/Rio Bravo environment on both sides of the international border. They work tirelessly to raise awareness of the watershed amidst the din of violence centered on drug cartels.

DUMPING AND DIVISION OF THE GREAT RIVER

Demoted from its true calling to gather waters from headwaters in Colorado to the Gulf of Mexico, the shallow muddy stretch below Elephant Butte dam to the Rio Conchos tributary in Presidio has turned into the gathering of toxins. What happened to the water would take decades to tell in real time. It involves dams and reservoirs, a tangle of river rights tied to treaties and Spanish land grants, international agreements and disagreements, wars, increasing industry and toxic dumping, water-hogging invasive salt cedar and giant cane. Climate instability, the most recent to enter the mix, could be the sum of all wars on this local hydrosphere. The headwaters of the Rio Grande in the mountains of southern Colorado, many natural thin trickles joining one another, bear no resemblance to the trickle of water below El Paso. The urban diversions of water run the river dry. Farmland irrigation runs it even drier.

HOW WE MADE THE RIVER DIVIDE

Until recent times on the Rio Grande, long after the 1848 treaty creating the international border, the river did not divide and people passed over to shop, attend school, work, and hang out in the now abandoned cantinas that still dot the local roadways off the interstate. There are still inviting signs advertising local music groups. These cantinas once filled with Texans and Mexicans drinking and swapping stories while local musicians sweated out lively songs in the summer heat. I am repeatedly told that September 11 dealt the final blow to local border-town life. The potential increase in the border "wall" will just make matters worse for everyone, human and wild. Before that 9/11 dividing date in our early twenty-first century world, when the border patrol forces suddenly bulged with military support personnel, people found each other's cows, showed up to build or re-build one another's corrals, and married one another. Animals, including rare jaguars and a re-introduced pure strain bison herd, could cross the river in their migrations. For a very long time, the border was a fiction created by people who did not live along this river.

For over 12,000 years Native American tribes held the water as sacred, for cleansing and ceremony as well as drinking. Later on the Spanish brought horses, cattle, pigs, and donkeys; the French supplied guns. All of these have proliferated since that time, displacing and killing local people and wildlife. Alvar Nunez Cabeza de Vaca, one of four survivors of a failed Spanish exploration, crossed the Great River in 1535, then traveled the land first as captive and later as healer among the Karankara and other tribes in the 1530s. In 1540 Don Juan de Onate y Salazar crossed the river at Paso del Norte with 600 soldiers and colonists. As they moved upriver, Onate's soldiers killed more than two-thirds of the Acoma tribe. The survivors were enslaved and the right foot of the remaining warriors severed. Yet the Acoma's Sky City at the top of a high bluff of the lower Colorado Plateau that borders the Rio Grande watershed remains inhabited to this day. The people remember. In 1998 for the quadri-centennial anniversary of Onate's conquest, the right foot of a statue of Onate near Española, New Mexico was severed with a message attached to the leg: "Fair is fair."

Other Spaniards followed Onate and after 1548 crude maps appeared showing the first Spanish missions and forts along the river. Over time, six different flags and the wars in their names came to the Great River's watershed here: France, Spain, Mexico, the Republic of Texas, the Confederacy, and the United States. In the early 1830s, after decades of relative peace, northern Mexicans and the independent Native nations descended into a cycle of violence. For the next fifteen years, owing to changes unleashed by American expansion, the Comanche and their allies mounted raids on Mexican settlers from the Llano Estacado or Staked Plain near present-day Odessa. The raids claimed thousands of lives and depopulated the countryside. The Comanche were the most skilled light horse warriors the world has ever known, and retaliations from the Mexican army proved futile.

The US saw this northern Mexico situation as an opportunity to push forward arguments in favor of seizing Mexican territory while northern Mexicans were too divided and exhausted to resist the American invasion. The relatively new Mexican Republic, upon defeat in the Mexican-American War, ceded nearly half of its territory to the United States including California and parts of six other states. And, importantly, Article 11 of the 1848 Treaty of Guadalupe Hidalgo stipulated that the US control the "independent Indians" as part of the agreement. Americans stepped up the genocide of Native people in the newly ceded lands shortly thereafter, particularly at the conclusion of the Civil War. The Comanche, a name conferred by the Ute and Spanish for the Nermernuh, encompassing six major bands linked by language and culture, saw their numbers plummet from 30-40 thousand people and two million horses in the early nineteenth century. As in other indigenous nations, the first strike came from infectious diseases, followed by loss of the great buffalo herds, and war with soldiers and settlers. The last free band of Nermernuh/Comanche chief, led by Quannah Parker, surrendered in 1875. The Comanche Nation numbers 15,100 members, most living in Oklahoma. Quannah Parker, son of a captured white woman and a band leader, later became a wealthy rancher who spoke for the rights of his people including traditional religion and medicine, the most controversial of which was use of peyote.

The Rio Grande as *La Frontera*, the border, is currently at its most severe and restrictive in this first part of the twenty-first century. The US military, providing support for law enforcement along the US-Mexico border for 150 years, remains ready to supply assistance to the border patrol. Military support of civilian operations on the border escalated with the war on drugs during the Nixon administration, expanding in the Reagan and the George W. Bush administrations. By 1990, the combined Army and Marine border force, under the Department of Defense, received $450 million for drug interdiction and counterdrug activity. Additional troops and funds came from the National Guard. After September 11, 2001 attacks on the World Trade Center and the Pentagon, border patrol agents numbered 21,000 with most in the southwest Mexico-US border. An estimated 1.2 to 2.4 undocumented immigrants each year changed status from families and workers to suspected terrorists.

BRING BACK THE WORKERS

In Ruidosa, Texas, with a population 16 people outnumbered 20 to 1 by cattle and horses, the once great river becomes "the forgotten river." This part of the river extends from below El Paso to Presidio where the Rio Conchos enters from Ojinaja, Mexico, bringing the Rio Bravo/Rio Grande back to life. Ruidosa itself started out as a penal colony for the Mexican government long before farming took root. It was a fast moving river then, true to the meaning of the town's name, "wild and rushing."

Now the river in this stretch would barely get you wet if you crossed it on foot. But It is not always quiet. Signs of flood exist everywhere on the roadways with tall marker rods in the arroyos. What might look like a flat stretch with a puddle could drown you. Each hilltop hosts small cemeteries to keep the entombed bodies safe from sudden deluge. For this part of West Texas, climate change means longer periods of drought punctuated by more frequent flash floods filling arroyos and breaching levees. In 2008, the sister border towns of Presidio/Ojinaga experienced a major flood exacerbated by river engineering that created high powerful flows against the levees. The levees did not hold.

Everyone here knows everyone, most related by blood. My host, Mattie Matthaei, tells me a story of watching two men on horseback ride over the river from the Mexico side. The border patrol happened to be near and called out to them. The men on horseback panicked, jumped off their horses and ran back over the river, cursing the border agents. The agents assured them they could come back to retrieve their horses without arrest, but the men refused. It was then everyone noticed the horses were skinny and sickly. Their saddles were then removed and left by the river for their owners. But the horses were taken into custody to be fed and restored to health. Everyone present felt it was a just solution including Mattie's neighbor, Diana. This wiry, fast-speaking Texan then recounted how the Martinez cow from the Mexico side wandered over to her place. She fed the cow and the calf born on her land for a year even on her hand-to-mouth budget. She said if Martinez ever comes to get his cow, she might keep the calf as payment. Mattie now lives in Alpine in the Big Bend where she is an environmental activist. Such things happen when you fall in love with this watershed; it asks you to defend it.

I travel to Rancho Viejo with Ruidosa friends including Mattie and her neighbor. It is Christmas time and people are stringing lights along the road. We see kids pouring out of the church in town while javelinas rush to safety in the low brush. On the way to the ranch, we stop and look for arrowheads in the scattered multi-colored stones dispersed in the arroyos. We find one intact arrowhead and some fragments. Just before they were forced out, the Lipan Apache, Hasinai, and Caddo tribes would camp along this part of the river. Apart from non-indigenous plant species of salt cedar and mesquite—an invader after the Spanish overgrazed the land—little else has changed. Photos from just after the war with Mexico show the land looking very much the same today.

Things changed for ranching in 1964 when the *braceros*, Mexicans who freely traveled to work in the US, were outlawed. The program had been created in 1942 with the Mexican Farm Labor Agreement. Two decades later, braceros became illegals and workers became "wets." Maybe they are really "waders" since most times no one can swim the river here—it's too shallow. This region once grew some of the finest pima cotton in the world until the dams and cities upriver ran it dry. But then cotton doesn't belong here; it's too thirsty for this Chihuahuan Desert. Cattle ranches, replacing farms, can stretch for 100 sections, 160 acres per section, and an average of one steer per section. Because cattle chew vegetation completely down to the roots, there is little natural forage left.

At the end of a 12-mile, hour-long drive on unmarked roads from Candelaria, we approach the entry gate to Rancho Viejo appearing like a mirage through the dust. The owner and ranch hands come out to meet us. As we speak, Tommy who manages Rancho Viejo tells us, "Prices for steer are really low these days, same for horses," A wide-brimmed hat hides his face down to his nose and mustache. His honest appraising eyes periodically peer under the shadow of the brim when he tilts his face upward. Years of squinting in the sun have left deep furrowed lines like ditches in his rugged face. He tells me he "went to Nam for 62 days and got blown up." After recovering, he went back into ranching and stayed with it ever since.

Not long ago, Tommy hired on to play himself, as did the ranch's horses and cattle, in the film *There Will Be Blood*. We agree no redeeming characters inhabit that film, which diverges a great deal from Upton Sinclair's book *Oil!* Tommy notes the irony of making the film here. The oil boom began in Texas in 1901 but never touched the lands of the "forgotten river," although drilling for shale oil and gas occurs north of here in the Pecos watershed. Tommy says the work paid well but he found fault with the film crew who made the animals wait for hours of technical tinkering. "That just isn't the way to treat animals."

We enjoy a barbecue lunch at the ranch to celebrate the birthday of a friend of Johnnie Chambers, our local hostess and driver on this trip. On the way back to Candelaria, we skirt one of the many dry buttes to stop at an imposing stone house astride two terraces. Close to the roof, wavy lines of light and dark rocks adorn the building, a sort of rough-hewn West Texas Art Deco style. "It was built by an Easterner for his alcoholic son," explains Johnnie Chambers. "It was supposed to keep him from liquor during Prohibition, but it turned out it was even easier to get Mexican liquor out here." On this lonely desert ranch, it is hard to imagine any thirst could ever be quenched. I later learned "the Easterner" was the chief of the Burroughs adding machine company, and an ancestor of William Burroughs, the writer.

At one time, Johnnie Chambers lived in the house with her husband Boyd and daughter Theresa. At 80, Johnnie's stance is still solid in her pale blue sweatpants with matching purple-trimmed knit top. Johnnie's grey-brown hair pulled up in a bun pokes from the back of her white visor. Hands on hips supporting a full round belly, her chin juts over a full neck. The long folds in her neck resemble those I've seen in young calves. The sole teacher here for years, she tells me, "I called myself Johnnie as women were not allowed to teach school in this rough district." This isolated place kept people from meeting her in person, "so I got away with it." Johnnie's Jeep flies over rocks and sudden drops in the road, and we risk crashing heads on the jeep roof. She interrupts her flow of stories to point out three-foot piles of adobe bricks and stones. "That was a school house," she tells us. "I used to teach there." Everything seems to be crumbling in these dry lands.

A life-long member of the NRA, Johnnie recounts shooting cougar and coyotes to stop them from feeding on their ranch cattle and goats. "We just killed 'em and tossed 'em," she says, when I asked if they did anything with the meat and pelts. It was as if she were talking about housework or taking out the garbage. She reminisces about the old days when people would come from miles around, some flying private planes, to butcher steer at her ranch. They used a table saw in the end room of the bunkhouse. "Everyone helped cut and pack. When the freezers were full we had a BBQ with what didn't fit." She insists that this whole area below the rim of the Llano Estacado and the tablelands of Marfa is one land, including both sides of the river to the nearest mountains in Mexico. She wishes it were still easy to get good labor from across the river. Along the "forgotten river," people on both sides of the river wish the restrictions would disappear. And nearly everyone opposes the border fence.

THE BIG BEND: RIVER AS RIVER

I travel from Presidio to Big Bend to meet Marcos Paredes, a ranger with the Big Bend National Park. He suggests I stop at a place called Closed Canyon for a walk through a dark grey, rose, and ochre slot canyon ending in a steep descent to the Rio Grande. At the bottom of the vertical canyon walls, water-carved igneous rock verifies the reality of posted flash flood warnings. I feel entranced by this walled walk with its narrow sliver of sky high above, but my hiking skills could not manage the precipitous descent to the river at the end of Closed Canyon. Out of the canyon and down the road, I find another spot with easy access to dip my toes into the Rio. Stopping for directions at a ranger station, I am told the area attracts herpetologists from all over the world. The snakes must have been sleeping. Or I didn't see them. Or they avoided me upon hearing the loose dry pebbles under my feet. Seen or not, snakes always have the right of way. And I wonder how they see the river in this thirsty land.

The day is coming to a close, so I stop for the night before meeting Marcos Paredes. Coyotes set up an exuberant howl. They are close. On the other side of flimsy faux wood wallboard, the owner of a black pickup joins in and keeps going long after the coyotes cease. I boil noodles to which I add carrots, spring onions, and tempeh with garlic chili paste in a pot on my camp stove inside the motel room. Door gaps, thin walls, and open windows mean cooking without peril of asphyxiation. Outdoor cooking would surely bring the wildlife, and possibly my drunken neighbor to dinner, though I doubt Mr. Black Pickup would stay once I tell him tempeh comes from fermented soy. Sleep rapidly overtakes me in the cool December night as I lay my head on a pillow used by uncounted restless heads before me. By morning a worn-out pale version of the full moon remains visible outside. Deep red streaks paint the sky so wide you have to spin slowly around to see them all. At breakfast in the nearby Terlingua Ghost Town cafe, locals talk about the eerie sky. Big fires nearby, they say, too close. Like most of the west, the land here dries up and burns with increasing frequency.

Marcos Paredes, the Chief Ranger for Big Bend, greets me from the porch of the adobe home he and his wife built next to corrals for their horses. We first speak of people we know in common. When I ask if he knows Johnnie Carlson, he says he does. "She calls me 'boy' though her daughter Theresa is not like her." When I tell him she doesn't remember him, he says, "ask her about the time I saved her brother." I leave that story to them to discuss some other time.

Son of migrant workers, Paredes spent his 35-year career involved in preservation and restoration of the river, working closely with his counterparts in US and Mexican states. Like so many river defenders, Marcos Paredes started out as a river guide. One of his earliest mentors was Steve Harris of Far Flung Adventures river guiding. Steve's own river defense career began when he lived on the Stanislaus in California. He was involved in the early days of Friends of the River when Mark Dubois chained himself to a rock for seven days to block the filling of the New Melones reservoir. A general called off the action because he realized DuBois would die rather than back down. Harris now devotes his time to building coalitions of scientists and activists, especially in northern New Mexico. Marcos calls him Uncle Steve as do the other activists of this river.

Before he became a park ranger, Marcos traveled the region by river and by horse on both sides of the river. He took the ranger job as he wanted to "return the benefits he received from the river." He has seen and been instrumental in many improvements in the Big Bend with innovative tamarisk (salt cedar) abatement techniques, fish and wildlife recovery, substantially reduced pollution levels, and improved instream flow. Instream flows, sources of water rights conflicts, are important to aquatic and riparian wildlife. Nearly all surface water rights are based on the principle of use-it-or-lose-it which means those with rights must make withdrawals, whether they need them or not. On the Rio Grande one conservation group purchased water rights in order to give them back to the river. That was followed with an unsuccessful backlash lawsuit.

In Oregon, followed by other states, a system of water credits allows one to leave the water in the river yet retain one's water rights. In this way, irrigators may give the river that year's unused share. This system is under consideration on the Rio Grande/Rio Bravo but complexities mount when dealing with two different countries with an uneasy history for which the river forms part of the international border.

Marcos Paredes eyes light up and his face relaxes with contentment when re-telling the work that brought about protection of three million acres of wildlands in this region. The protected watershed lands comprise a continuous stretch starting just below Ojinaga/Presidio with Big Bend State Park, Parque Nacional Cañón de Santa Elena, Big Bend National Park, and Area Natural Protegida Maderas del Carmen. Together, they constitute a bi-lateral conservation project called the El Carmen—Big Bend Conservation Corridor Initiative, which includes contiguous land designated for conservation on both sides of the border. Wildlife protection of black bears, cougars, bighorn sheep and other animals allows them to thrive on both sides of the river. And bi-national cooperation affords restoration of the scrublands, grasslands, and sky island ecosystems here. Paredes and others hope it will eventually become a bi-national park like Glacier National Park. But it may have to await an eco-friendly change in US national government policies.

These magnificent changes often go unnoticed, as Marcos puts it, since there are no murders, no massive drug confiscations, no deaths among those crossing the boundary, and no lost ranches. This part of the river has a particularly rugged terrain, and it is rare for anyone to successfully cross it for any reason. Of the current 700 miles of border barriers, these natural barriers remain the most difficult to breach. Marcos asks, "do you want a live river or a dead ditch?" that could be the outcome of fencing the entire border down through Texas to the Gulf.

Paredes recounts how those involved in this massive wildlife corridor and watershed protection would get together informally, telling stories, laughing, and drinking tequila that forged lifelong friendships. He conducted *Maderas del Carmen* trips on horseback to understand the land and river. And in his own sustained dedication to the plans, declined promotion up the hierarchy of the US National Park Service as it would impede his work here. When asked about sources of inspiration, he mentioned two; the first was Julio Carrera. "Everyone knows and learns from Julio Carrera," says Marcos. He could accomplish more than everyone on a tenth of the budget of US projects. He is now in the *Comision Nacional de Areas Naturales Protegidas,* heading projects to protect grassland and scrubland ecosystems. People on both sides of the border also learned from Paredes, who conducted training programs in Big Bend for most of the environmental protection rangers on both sides of the border.

The second source of inspiration may come as a surprise. As we are speaking, Marcos fishes around for his dog-eared and well-thumbed copy of the Treaty of Guadalupe Hidalgo/*Tratado de Guadalupe Hidalgo,* named after the place of its signing in 1848. From behind wire rim glasses, his eyes sparkle as he reads the first lines of the treaty. "The United States of America and the United Mexican States animated by a sincere desire to put an end to the calamities of the war which unhappily exists between the two Republics and to establish upon a solid basis relations of peace and friendship, which shall confer reciprocal benefits upon the citizens of both, and assure the concord, harmony, and mutual confidence wherein the two people should live, as good neighbors." As enshrined in an international treaty, these words supersede all others regarding the two nations. Marcos takes these words to heart in his life, through his work, and in bi-national environmental protection "as good neighbors."

As I ready to depart, Marcos again stands on his porch while his wife prepares her horse for the day's ride. He leaves me with one last story, practically dancing his way through the telling. Years ago, everyone gathered for a bi-national conference to give testimony for watershed protection. Bill Guerra Addington especially was on a spirited roll. The chairman indicated Bill's testimony time was up, but Marcos conceded his minutes to him. As Bill used up the minutes, every person in line conceded minutes to Bill. It may be a very long river, but the river defenders do not divide its defense.

FROM BIG BEND TO THE GULF

Little did I know at the time and for many years after that my family was part of the military occupation of *la frontera.* My father joined the Army Air Corps later the US Air Force when he was 18, leaving his family's farm in Buffalo, NY. He met my mother in Sacramento and married in Las Vegas within three months, and I was born fifteen months later. Like most military families, we moved from place to place. Two of our assignments were in Texas, one in Laredo, sister city to Nuevo Laredo in Mexico, the other at College Station not far from Houston. Laredo Air Force Base at that time was a munitions and test pilot training base and my father's services were needed there. Dad worked an essential Air Force job as a meteorologist most of his career, retiring when he received his first conflict zone assignment for Viet Nam. By then my anti-war activism and our conversations had changed his views of that war, and he retired rather than go to Vietnam.

We lived in a dusty rose stucco house with a pink fence and matching Chevy station wagon in the carport. Next door, to the right as you face the front door, an empty lot lay between our house and our neighbors. That is, adults thought it empty. Pathways of fine light brown dirt, anthills, sticker bushes, lizards, little white flowers, and walking stick insects beckoned from the lot. I thought the mantises in it holy, praying for their victims. My friend Teresa lived at the other end of the dirt path. We played together nearly every day after school and untold weekend hours.

I was in awe of Teresa's older sister Maria who had her own tiny room with a light blue curtain door. Inside the room hung so many pretty dresses, some with floral patterns and lace trim. Twirling skirts we called them; dancing skirts Maria called them. Teresa taught me some Spanish but I did not have to teach her English, as she was bilingual. Every birthday party included a piñata to hit while blindfolded. The blindfold was annoying but scrambling for candy could be fun. There was a bridge not far from our house that we could cross to shop in Nuevo Laredo. I did not know the bridge had one end in Texas, the other in Mexico. For us, like most people of *la frontera*, there was no border.

We attended school at Ursuline Academy which is still there. Ursuline Academy's imposing façade and heavy wooden front door still hide a courtyard. On our first visit, my mother, sister, and I walked nervously into the courtyard. The space held no sounds but the soft clicking of long wooden rosary beads and firm footsteps of nuns. A starched rounded bib topping black robes held smells of talcum powder and soap. "The nuns live here," my mother said, trying to ease her own anxiety. I imagined that life, so close to God, a bride of Jesus. But my religious fervor could not erase the knot in my belly. The academy with its black robed nuns, showing only their faces like pale flowers inside their bibs and under a long black veil, terrified me.

My walk to school brought me past a whitewash adobe house with rounded arches for doors and a garden bursting with flowering shrubs and fruit trees. This is where I wanted to live and wear dresses like Maria's. But we lived in the little ranch-style box house instead, and we wore pink-checked skirts my mother made. Nearly everyone in our neighborhood and at Ursuline Academy, the local Catholic school, spoke Spanish. The cafeteria served enchiladas and tacos with beans and rice most days except for Friday when we ate baked fish to remember Christ's death on Good Friday.

The First Communion rite, when I was finally allowed to receive the little wafer consecrated by the priest said to be the actual body of Christ, came closer to my dreams. Though I avoided contemplation of the inferred act of cannibalism, I could see myself as a holy bride in the lacy white dress and matching veil. Maybe I could be a twirling dancer of Jesus, I thought, but quickly banished the idea. Already I knew this idea could be blasphemy, and surely not good behavior in a good Catholic girl.

Meanwhile Dad went to work at Laredo Air Force Base every day. He took qualifying tests in marksmanship and for the first time I saw a pistol at home though it quickly disappeared from our curious eyes. We did not really know what our dad did when he went off in his uniform. One day the pink phone on the kitchen wall rang. Carrying my youngest sister in her arms, my mother herded us into the yard. She told us dad would fly over the house. Much as we craned our necks toward the sky, we did not see him though a small plane flew overhead. As we danced from one foot to the other wanting to go in, my mother said in her flat far Northern California mountain accent, "Well, that's it, girls." That statement underlined our collective lack of enthusiasm. I remember it to this day more for its empty than its full. And it shed no light on what Dad did in his uniform.

Later I learned the base at Laredo served intermediate and advanced flight training for jet pilots including trainees from 24 countries of NATO nations. The base also trained tail gunners for the heavy bomber, the B-24 Liberator. Lumbering with low air speeds, the B-24 made by the Ford Motor Company was not the first choice for pilots who preferred the B-17 Flying Fortress. But the B-24 became the most deployed plane of WWII and remained in service during the Korean Conflict. These training planes were replaced by the T-33 Shooting Star and the T-38 Trojan jets in Laredo for the Vietnam War in the 1960s. It was during this period that the US Air Force Strategic Air Command kept B-52 Stratofortresses on 24/7 flights with active nuclear weapons on board.

In 1961, a SAC bomber broke up in the air above Goldsboro, NC. Its payload of two nuclear bombs fell to earth at 700 mph, one with its parachute caught in a tree, and the other buried in a muddy field. Decades later, the details of the incident, referred to in Air Force parlance as a Broken Arrow and one of many to follow, became public. A nuclear detonation would have completely changed much of eastern North Carolina. Lt. Jack Revelle, the bomb disposal expert responsible for disarming the device said, "we came damn close." As of 1991, the US no longer has a continuously flying nuclear defense. Most likely my father and the majority of the US Air Force military personnel were unaware of this incident at the time, but their work supported the program nonetheless.

WE CARRY WATER FOR THE RIVER

Given my military brat history and my subsequent anti-war and pro-environment work, my present time in this watershed unites my childhood life here. It reinvigorates my dedication to the watershed, to all of its communities—plant and animal, and to its people. The horrifying prospect of more miles of border fence calls me to action along with the rest of the people of the borderlands. The next section slated for building would cut through an important butterfly and bird sanctuary as well as the last habitat of the endangered Ocelot at the southernmost end of the Rio Bravo/Rio Grande. What if we embraced an ethic in which we do not steal the water from the fish, the air from the birds, or the grasslands and forests from el Lobo and the ocelot? What if we espouse an ethics of only taking what we really need as part of the integrated whole web of being? In these watersheds I see such ethics coming into being.

Upriver, in the Rio Grande Gorge, I first met Basia Irland, water artist. A tall, cheerful woman of generous disposition, she immediately tells me how much she appreciates epidemiology. How many people can say that? Working with epidemiologists, she has created international art projects for important waterborne infections. But my interest that first day of meeting centers on her multi-level, five-year project for the Rio Grande called *Gathering Waters: from headwaters to sea*. She loves the Rio Bravo/Rio Grande, and is dismayed by how we see only little segments of it, how we do not comprehend its vast webs of connected flowing life.

Basia Irland made small canteens from river mud, a reliquary backpack from very old water-smoothed wood, a river map from river stones. And she connected a river of people carrying water. In the center of this project was a canteen she and her son used on river runs. In 1995 at the river's headwaters near Creede Colorado, she dipped the canteen in water in a lush green alpine meadow, to pass it person to person through every mile of the river, along with a log book for each person to sign. It passed down through the San Luis Valley, Questa, the Rio Grande gorge near Taos Pueblo, down through pueblos near Española, Los Alamos, Albuquerque, Elephant Butte reservoir, el Bosque del Apache and Sevilleta wildlife preserves, down near White Sands and Otero Mesa, through Ciudad Juarez/El Paso in the vast Chihuahuan Desert. The canteen met people along the "forgotten" river, through the Big Bend/Maderas del Carmen, past the five dams and reservoirs of the International Boundaries and Water Commission including Amistad by Ciudad Acuna/Del Rio and Falcon below the heavily fenced and guarded border of Nuevo Laredo/Laredo, eventually finding the Gulf of Mexico by a palm grove below Matamoros/Brownsville. Some years the river does not reach the gulf. And so we carry water for the river, for its restoration and our own relations.

"Water is LIVING," says Basia Irland as we gaze into the magnificent aquarium in Albuquerque, even in this tank with its stingrays and sharks." If we think of bodies of water as living, we would treat them differently." She continues, "As an artist I can say things others cannot, as they would have to prove it to a skeptical public. It makes me free to speak for the river. I see the problems we face are huge, but I'm optimistic by nature, and I will continue to speak out." And so shall so many others, in growing numbers by the day.

CHAPTER NINE

WE CONTINUE

WRITING THE FIVE WATERSHED STORIES evolved over time through a series of travels in five major regions of the US. In general, my journeys had meager funds, and required personal stamina and determination. People donated here and there, hosted me, packed me sandwiches, let me park in their driveways, bought gas, replenished my water and food supplies, gave me books and articles, and taught me what they know. One person bought new tires for my old Subaru; another paid for a new exhaust system. And a young man who came to replace the car's broken window after a St. Louis break-in, cheerily departed with the words, "I hope to hear you on NPR someday." He never charged me for the window.

So why did a middle-aged woman resign her position in an elite eastern university long before retirement age, forgoing a pension, to take this on? It began with loss. In 2003, my Japanese mother-in-law lay dying in the Bay Area and I traveled west to see her and my elderly parents. I took a cross-country trip with a good friend to catch up with my estranged daughter and to see the family elders who were dying or in decline. When I left my job and home, I could not be sure if I would return, where I would live, or how I would earn money. And I stayed out west near my parents, sometimes working as a consultant writing reports and analyzing epidemiologic data. While there, I founded an arts and environment organization, Madrona Arts, through which I could initiate social and environmental community activist projects.

The losses continued when my ex-husband died in Japan in 2006 from emphysema. My daughter attended the funeral in Japan, and I was visiting with her in Los Angeles when she returned. There, we received a call from my sister and parents who were hiding out in my house in Ashland, Oregon from my sister's ex-husband. He was in a full-blown bipolar hypomanic phase, and had physically threatened them. He was paranoid, delusional, and verbally abusive with his 19 firearms, crossbow, and two Tasers, some displayed on the front lawn of my sister's house. It was a Sunday, and they were going to the county office to file a restraining and no contact order the next day. They were too late. Early Monday morning, my sister's home was ablaze, a fire so hot it melted the cast iron stove. My former brother-in-law also torched two neighbor's homes, and destroyed one-third of the local community services center. By the end of his reign of fire, there were nine felony counts, one dropped, the remainder to which he pleaded insanity. After seven years in a forensic hospital, the California criminal justice system still monitors him to this day as an out patient.

It would take many years for my family to recover from this period of trauma, and in some ways the trauma remains though everyone has moved on, coping and adapting. I took my own distress and grief to the river. The Klamath held and still holds a special place in my life, my parents residing in the embrace of that watershed for so many years. It always brightened my day as I traveled its length, camping, painting, and writing. I found my self drawn to the history of the river's own losses: stream bank erosion, depleted upland forests, yellow-green cyanobactera-clogged stretches of water, dams reducing flows, and most of all, the over 95 percent loss of wild Pacific salmon. From past activism, I knew working to restore the river would help heal me, and, by extension, my family. Healing occurs in subtle and not so subtle, mostly non-linear ways, and continues to the present.

After an art event in Ashland for the Klamath River called "Freeing the Waters," I set out for St Louis to learn about the Upper Mississippi. I wanted to know how watershed, floodplain, and river restoration worked on such an enormous river, one with more concrete structures than any other in the country. And I wanted to know how protecting the watershed affected people who do this work. I was gathering information, setting up interviews, when I attended an Illinois Water Conference in September 2008 in which Richard Sparks was the keynote speaker. Rip Sparks assented to an interview, and others followed. He referred me to Calvin Fremling, zoologist and author of *Immortal River: the Upper*

Mississippi in Ancient and Modern Times, who had spent a lifetime protecting the Upper Mississippi. It went on from there, referral to referral, and stories that moved me.

And what of the title, *Watershed Redemption?*

The word "redemption" sounds like a savior may be or should be on the way. By acting in harmony with all life, especially caring for lives and places without representation or voice, and by keeping a strong ethical center, we can save life. Water figures in nearly every religious or spiritual tradition to cleanse our hearts and minds. By restoring the waters, we cleanse and restore ourselves. Martin Luther King, Jr. called on justice to roll down like waters and righteousness like a mighty stream. We need the rain of justice to turn around the collective ignorance that harms wild beings, forests, meadows, rocks, soil, and water, and our own health. Redemption occurs together in one interconnected body, each action rippling through the whole. This is how spiritual ecology works.

When I was eight, a Catholic teacher used the words "Mystical body of Christ." At the time, I partly misunderstood this to mean the transformed Christ as universal love in all creation. I still favor my version, as it is natural to me. It accords with ecology that sees the known and unknown interconnections in all. There are physico-chemical processes, true. Beyond our conceptions, analyses, and biases, existence holds more than any philosophy or science can or ever will map or describe. And in it our hearts beat, compassion flows, and wisdom enters through the still quiet voice within. I only ask that we work for the benefit of all beings in this our only earth. You do not need to believe as I believe, but simply act together for the good of all.

Below is the chronicle of my journeys with the names of people audio recorded in conversations as semi-structured interviews. Most interviews were completed before 2010. In that year, completely out of money, I went to live with friends on Denman Island, off Vancouver Island, in Canada. During that time I began to write, applied for, and attended an Orion Magazine writing workshop in Vermont. I didn't get a whole lot written, however, as much-needed jobs came my way in environmental air pollution, childhood obesity, a teaching position in Australia for a semester, and more, in a dizzying patchwork of paid work. At one point I had four different research projects to juggle. Then my father's health entered a steep decline, and I returned to Oregon. My father died in 2013, and I moved across the country to the Catskills with the promise of steady work. The *Watershed Redemption* book lay in boxes gathering dust until early in 2016 when I turned down all work, and cleared my time as best I could. The recorded interviews are stored and backed up.

~

TIMELINE INTERVIEWS AND EXPLORATIONS

2008—TRIP 1 AND 2

Drive from Ashland Oregon to Klamath California, boat trip up the Klamath to where it meets Trinity, hosted by a former Yurok Tribe research scientist.

Oregon To St. Louis, Mo

> Ron Yarborough, St Louis audio, incomplete recording
> 11-04-08
> Chad Pegracke, East Moline, IL audio and video
> Roger Smith, Midland, OR—audio, photos by David Winston
> Mark Van Patten, St Louis, MO—audio
> Rip Sparks, St Louis, MO—audio
> Calvin Fremling, Winona, MN—audio, transcribed, copy to wife
> after his death

Forks of The Salmon, Ca

> Petey Brucker, Forks of the Salmon, CA—audio, David Winston
> photography
> Geba Greenberg, Forks of the Salmon, CA audio, David
> Winston photography
> Hendrickson—audio
> David Wilson—audio
> Bruce Hannon—audio
> David Conrad—audio, multiple interviews

Oregon to Chattahoochee watershed in Georgia via LA,
Phoenix, Tucson.

> Greg Addington, Klamath, OR—audio

2009—CONTINUE TRIP 2, START TRIP 3

Tucson to Belmont, TX then on to Whitesburg, GA

Bob Williams, Belmont, TX environmental educator

Sally Bethea, Atlanta, GA Chattahoochee Riverkeeper

Jerry Stober, Carrolton, GA retired EPA

Bill Eisenhauer, Atlanta, GA activist involved in Atlanta sewer protests

Jenny Hoffner, Atlanta, GA Bronx River and American Rivers Southeast

James Hathorn, Mobile, AL Army Corps of Engineers

Howard Marshall, Villa Rica, GA retired zoologist

Bruce Morton, Atlanta, West Atlanta Watershed Alliance and City of Atlanta

Sherrill Marcus, Atlanta, Civil Rights and Environmental Justice activist

Naataki Osborn, Atlanta, National Wildlife Federation

Jim Kulstad, Atlanta

N. Carolina, Virginia, to Washington DC

David Conrad, Washington DC, Feb 20 and 23

Catskills and NYC

Dart Westphal, Bronx NY

Ruth Anderberg, Bronx, NY 1st Bronx River restoration

Linda Cox, Bronx, head of Bronx River Alliance, now retired

Harry Jameson, Phoenicia, NY Mar 27

Jack Issacs, DEC offices NY, April 1

Nancy Wallace, Bronx, successor to Ruth Anderberg Apr 7

Dan Davis, Shandaken, NYC Dept of Env Protection Apr 8

Catskills to headwaters of the Chattahoochee

Jackie Echols, Atlanta, environmental justice advocate

Ron Warnken, A-C-F headwaters, Wildlife Federation, Apr 14,

Mark Williams, Army Corps of Engineers at Lake Lanier, Apr 21,

Howard Marshall, Villa Rica, GA zoologist Apr 22,

Mississippi to Missouri to California

Jeff Barrow, Columbia, Missouri River Relief May 14,

Vicki Richmond, Kansas City, Missouri River Relief KC Apr 15, Kansas City

Melissa Samet, San Anselmo, CA, American Rivers May 26,

Kristian Gustafson, Libertyville, IL by phone May 29,

Hoopa, CA

August 24-26 Hoopa, Boat Dance, World Renewal, September Jump Dance

John Ward, Ashland OR Sept 27

Anita Ward, Klamath River Sept 27,

Merv George Jr, Sept 28, 2009

Oregon to Great Basin National Park to Taos, NM 2009

Brian Shields, Taos Oct 6

Sawnie Morris, Taos Oct 6

Steve Harris, Santa Fe Oct 13

CJ McCue, Santa Fe Oct 15,

Esther Gonzales, Questa Oct 20

Kevin Bixby, October 24

Mariana Chew, El Paso Sierra Club, Oct 22 and 26

Bill Guerra Addington, Sierra Blanca Defense Fund, Sierra Blanca, TX

Basia Irland, Albuquerque, Oct 27,

Dave Groenfeldt, Santa Fe Oct 30,

Lucy Moore, Santa Fe, conflict resolution Klamath and Rio Grande October 31

Back in NY

Marilyn Gelber, Brooklyn, Nov 9

Diane Galusha, Mt Tremper, Nov 24, meeting, later oral hx of Catskills MOA

Santa Fe to El Paso, Presidio, Big Bend

Johnnie Carlson, Ruidosa ranch, Dec 13,

Marcos Paredes, River guide, and National Parks Service, Big Bend, Dec 14,

2010—PARTIAL YEAR IN BRITISH COLUMBIA, CANADA, BACK TO OREGON

Steve Kandra, farmer Klamath River Settlement, photos David Winston

2011—AUSTRALIA TEACHING, MOVED PARENTS TO ASSISTED LIVING, SHORT TRIP 4

Becky Hyde, Yainix Ranch, photos only David Winston

Gunnison, Headwaters Conference, Winona LaDuke speaker, Estevan Arrellano, explore headwaters of Rio Grande

Felice Pace, activist Klamath River, June 25

2012—TRAVEL TO NEW MEXICO SHORT TRIP 5
Taos to Santa Fe, Los Alamos, Sky City, Church Rock

Estevan Arrellano, *acequias* and Native harvest, Mar 9, 2012

2013—BYRDCLIFFE RESIDENCY IN THE CATSKILLS

Fly STL from NY, River Rally May 13-17, out on the Missouri and Mississippi river

Steve Schnarr, follow-up talk

Chad Pregracke, follow-up talk

2014—ENERGY FEST ROGUE CLIMATE EVENT MEDFORD, MOVE TO CATSKILLS

Explore Hudson River and the Catskills Aqueduct down to NYC

2015—TRIP 6

Explore Rio Grande watershed, Taos Box rafting March 6

2016—STANDING ROCK TRIP, TRIP 7

Final Trip: Oregon to Malheur to Yellowstone, Standing Rock, Duluth, Mankato, Colorado, end Taos.

∼

During this time, Calvin Fremling, Ruth Anderberg, and Estevan Arellano walked on from life. They gave treasured time and wisdom, and they remain in my heart. My hope is this book serves to honor their monumental life works and the work of so many, named and unnamed on every river and watershed of this nation.

On the Madrona Arts website, you can read archived newsletters and descriptions of environmental art projects, view some of the photos and short bios from my project that I first called "Over the River." www.madronaarts.org

Madrona Arts was a 501(c) organization that I founded in Oregon. It still exists on the web, but the burdens of seeking grants, government paperwork, and meetings became more than I could manage. Its nonprofit status was discontinued in 2017. It still hosts the projects on which this book is based. And it is now the site of Madrona Arts Press.

STUDY METHODS

After first contacts on each watershed, I used a chain referral process for the stories of river and watershed protectors. This is a method used when one does not have a sampling frame or any kind of pre-determined list. From initial contacts, I would ask, "Who would you interview?" And interviewees contacted their colleagues and co-workers for me or told me to mention them when I called the next person. This method is often used to generate meetings with people one would not ordinarily find. It isn't representative sampling, but it is interesting sampling.

At first I reached out through environmental activists on watersheds I already knew: the Hudson and the Bronx River where I had spent so much of my adult life, the Klamath watershed where my parents lived, and the Upper Mississippi where my maternal grandfather was born in Mankato and where I attended high school downriver neat East St. Louis. My connection to the Rio Grande began in childhood in Laredo Texas and later again through an HIV prevention program in Ciudad Juarez when I worked for the National Institute on Drug Abuse. The Chattahoochee watershed hosts the Centers for Disease Control and Prevention that figured heavily in my career as an epidemiologist.

Starting from activist work on the Klamath, I realized how localized actions often barely reach locals, much less the people of other watersheds. Could we share lessons from each place? I wanted to learn from veteran river defenders and water protectors of each region. Some people welcomed me, hosted me in their homes, others would not answer me at all, or rapidly canceled. Some were too busy or too important, didn't know me, or didn't care for or believe in my project. Majora Carter canceled after agreeing to an interview. Her husband, James, who managed her meetings and her public image after she had won a MacArthur "genius" award for her work on the Bronx River and her organization, Sustainable South Bronx, canceled via email. She was and remains a powerhouse of activism in the Bronx. I get it. Even though her Bronx River colleagues referred me, she did not know me, and did not know if I would waste her time.

I make no judgments on those who declined or canceled or funders who rejected my grant applications. Still, there was great generosity that came from love of rivers and the desire to protect and restore watersheds. Many opened their lives to me, even though I would sometimes turn up in dirty clothes, straight from sleeping on the ground in a campsite and a long dusty drive to their clean home or office. Many of them took me out on the river, told me of their favorite places and how to get there. Some spots were so remote the GPS did not show them. It turned out to be a truly amazing set of journeys, and I'm filled with gratitude for it. Throughout my many travels, I considered this work as a circumambulatory prayer cycle for the watersheds of this country.

At the outset I wanted to collect oral histories, especially from those defending watersheds most of their lives. Some told me the watershed project was overly ambitious, covering too many river miles and watershed square miles. But I remained undaunted, the result being the long-form essays of this book. When giving talks on the fight to remove four dams on the Klamath, I found sharing river stories from other places helped to drop the entrenched positions of locals. Listeners could be more objective and sympathetic, and I could then follow up with the local watershed in a more thoughtful discussion.

Story-telling gatherings occur on rivers throughout the country. My friend, Sybil Rosen, has been holding gatherings on Chattahoochee River stories in Georgia since 2012. Bronx River friends do the same, among them Gerry Segal, who grew up on the Bronx River. Gerry wrote a song about it referring to a photo from 1957 when he was a young boy standing by the river with his Schwinn bike and wearing his cowboy hat. He sings of his delight in the river's restoration, the return of fish and beaver. Petey Brucker composes river songs and writes plays about the restoration of salmon runs on the Klamath. Stories and songs of one watershed become the stories of many watersheds, all having common elements even with their unique issues, history, and people. Everyone I met spoke of their love of the rivers where they live.

I began with stories, personal spoken histories, funded by a small pilot grant and donations for stories on the Klamath.

My first stop after the Klamath River was St. Louis and the Upper Mississippi. Most people I encountered were happy to share their lives with me, some spending hours recounting their work, background, and inspiration sources. But some did not. Annie Hoagland, an activist living near St Louis who had spent over 30 years successfully fighting floodplain development on the Upper Mississippi at the river's triple confluence with the Missouri and Illinois Rivers. Over the phone, her terse voice informed me she would no longer speak with me, "because you are not doing what you say you are doing." There was no further explanation from her. Since she stopped with the survey, I'm assuming she did not see that as connected to oral history. I would have recorded Annie's stories firsthand, but that was not to be. Fortunately, a documentarian, Boyd Pickup, covered her work around the same time.

Since my knowledge of the Upper Mississippi was still forming, I started with a listserve notice of my project from the Southern Illinois University library. I followed up with email and phone contact, collected a short written background, had people sign a release form, and recorded their words according to a semi-structured format. Then I followed a chain of referrals from the initial contacts. My interviews make up a few squares in a vast American quilt of stories of people defending and restoring the watersheds of the entire country.

Some oral history projects are much more structured than mine, focused on a particular event or related events, and many seek opposing views of the issue in the process. One such excellent oral history by Nancy Burnett centers on the struggle between New York City and the Catskills over Catskills water, a fight that made headlines for over a decade. My interviews for the Hudson, in fact, included Marilyn Gelber, a key figure in the agreement made between upstate Catskills towns and New York City. Nancy Burnett's oral history tapped Marilyn and all the major players in that negotiation for avoidance of a massive filtration plant on Catskills waters funneled to New York City. My project, starting as an exploratory piece, traces a broad arc from pre-European contact to the present. The people I interviewed taught me to see the overall watershed issues as they see them.

In a way, Annie was right. I never got to transcribe all the interviews or fill in enough voices of water defenders on specific issues for each of the five watersheds. If it were a full-funded research project, it would have been. I still have an archive and a database of all the individual histories I collected. The small amount of pilot money for the oral history project did not go far enough, and new funding did not materialize in sufficient amounts. Still there were those who had spent time telling me their stories, their struggles, and what inspired them to act for the rivers and watersheds in which they lived. I kept going, but the project necessarily changed. It turned into this book and archives on the Madrona Arts website.

Over a period from Fall 2009 to the last interview in March, 2012, I gathered 65 full-length recorded interviews lasting from one hour to 12 hours each, the longest interviews spread out over several days. Although I am highly trained in careful and rigorous data collection due to graduate studies and research projects at Columbia University, my methods for this book were not scientific. I was following the people, the fish, the pollution, riverbank restorations, my nose, or "just having fun" as a couple I met in far West Texas declared. And I truly enjoyed the seven trips I made, the people I met whether recorded interview, written notes or surveys, casual encounters. I loved getting out on each river, walking the land to follow the water, observing, writing, and painting the landscape from watershed to watershed.

AUTHOR'S NOTE

THIS BOOK GREW FROM A set of writings based on journeys to speak with water protectors, an excerpt of which appeared in an article entitled "Doctor's Orders: Undam the Klamath" published in 2011 by *High Country News*. Research began before and continued after that time for the watershed case studies of this book: the Klamath, Upper Mississippi, Lower Hudson, Chattahoochee, and Rio Grande/Rio Bravo. Selected literature sources are included at the end of the book under the heading "Chapter Notes." Although I have spent decades publishing in academic research, this book is not an academic work. It is my wish for the reader to take it in without the encumbrance of embedded and detailed footnotes or lengthy critical reviews. Nonetheless, scholarly research underlies the book's content.

Environmental justice, a movement for equal rights to be free of toxins and to live in an ecologically sound environment, runs through all of these essays. I write about people and communities subject to environmental racism as described by writers such as Robert D. Bullard, an early leader of environmental justice (See *Dumping in Dixie*, 3rd Edition, 2000). Harmful environmental contamination and destruction have far greater frequency and impact on any group deemed "other" and" less than" in the United States, typically based on skin color, religion, social class, gender identity, and sexual preference. To present each case, I use the language and terms individuals or groups subjected to environmental injustice espouse. When I do not have specific information, I use the terms deemed respectful at present by responsible writer groups such as the Society of Environmental Journalists.

Those who laid claim to the "new world" from Europe conducted a war on its indigenous inhabitants in the name of colonization. They further attempted erasure of the over 500 Native nations and assigned new names for places, animals, plants, rivers, and the people themselves. This re-naming along with forced diaspora and mixing of so many indigenous cultures renders writing on the issues inordinately complex. For this book, I follow the nomenclature of Roxanne Dunbar-Ortiz, author of *An Indigenous People's History of the United States*. First, she states it is important to emphasize that Native peoples were colonized and deposed of their territories as distinct peoples and that the nations are still here.

To reflect these facts and their tangled history, Dunbar-Ortiz uses "indigenous," "Indian," and "Native" interchangeably as preferred by the people themselves. Since all citizens of Native nations much prefer their own language names (autonyms) be used such as Tsalagi (Cherokee), Anishinaabe (Ojibway, Chippewa), pre-Columbian names are combined with more familiar usages such as "Navajo." Instead of "tribe," preference is for "community" "people" and "nation" used interchangeably, but "tribe" often appears due to official titles or use by Native speakers. "America" or "American" is not used when referring only to the United States and its citizens, instead "United States" as a noun, "US" as an adjective.

When necessary, federally designated Nation names are used such as "The Standing Rock Sioux Tribe" although people from various nations live at the reservation, most calling themselves "Lakota." Another example is "The Hoopa Valley Tribe " as the federal designation for the Natinixwe (People of the Place Where the Trails Return), also called the Hupa, a name given to them by the coastal Yurok people for the valley in which they lived. It has been in common use for hundreds of years and thus recognizable in Northern California indigenous groups. At times both autonyms and common usage names are given together.

It is a shameful fact of history that the Doctrine of Discovery by Pope Nicholas V gives European Christian nations the so-called right to "capture, vanquish, and subdue the Saracens, pagans, and other enemies of Christ," to "put them into perpetual slavery," and "to take all their possessions and property." This decree, elaborated by Pope Alexander VI for Spain and Portugal in the Age of Discovery, gave permission to enslave people, to sell slaves, and promote acts of genocide and dispossession against the "discovered" people of this continent. It has never been rescinded and remains embedded in US legal code since the John Marshall ruling on Johnson v. M'Intosh in 1823. The ruling asserted the United States had pre-existing rights based on the Doctrine of Discovery via transfer from Great Britain's acquisition of those rights. Cases concerning indigenous land in the United States still fall under this over-arching precedent that gives purchase rights of indigenous land solely to the federal government, although the government can in turn sell these properties to anyone. It further gives the federal government sole right to extinguish indigenous "right to occupancy." Environmental justice takes a complicated hair-pin turn under these convoluted laws upholding institutionalized racism and colonialism.

Beyond the issues of environmental civil rights and Native nation rights, environmental justice extends to all non-human species and their requirements for habitat. This point was made explicit in the *Principles of Environmental Justice* of 1991 (First National People of Color Summit). Along with asserting that acts of environmental injustice are violations of international law, and that environmental policies and actions must be free of discrimination and bias, it asserts the rights of all species to be free from population decimation and ecological destruction.

Over time, many countries have been moving toward greater defense of wildlife, starting in the US with the Endangered Species and the Marine Mammal Protection Acts of 1973, followed by a series of related protective laws regarding habitat. The most recent case concerns protection of jaguar critical habitat in cross-border cooperation and international treaty laws between the US and Mexico. The current and proposed border wall between the US and Mexico upends this work, and action through US American, Mexican, and international courts have become vital to many locally extirpated and at risk threatened and endangered species.

Thus, environmental justice encompasses the rights of all people and all non-human species along with the dynamic health of natural ecosystem habitats. It is a broad but necessary definition of environmental justice thanks to the far-reaching injustices that have been perpetrated here, especially after 1492. Just as a web of hollow tubing filling with poison will later reach all parts, the consequences of harming any human group or nonhuman species reaches the entire living web. The environmental justice path for us now is to specify and act on the most pressing triage issues for the health, resilience, and sustainability for all species and of the entire ecosystem. We are no longer in the position of addressing local emergencies, but have entered into a crisis that encompasses at least half of all beings on earth. These points underlie the work on the most vital of places, the watersheds in which we live and the water sustaining us all.

NOTES ON SOURCES

AUTHOR'S NOTE CITATIONS

An Indigenous People's History of the United States, Four Hundred Years of Native American History from the Bottom Up Perspective, (ReVisioning American History), Roxanne Dunbar-Ortiz, (2015), Beacon Press, Boston.

The introduction to Dunbar-Ortiz's history of Indigenous people explains her method of naming for people and places. The book works from the Indigenous perspective to cover the full range of genocidal policies, corruption and greed as witnessed through historic documents and known events throughout the United States from its beginning to the present. It also examines the rise of Native resistance movements such as the American Indian Movement (AIM).

Dumping in Dixie: Race, Class, and Environmental Quality. Robert D. Bullard, (2000, 3rd Edition) Westview Press.

Principles of Environmental Justice 1991.https://www.ejnet.org/ej/principles.html

Pagans in the Promised Land: Decoding the Doctrine of Discovery. Steven Newcomb, (2008, 3rd Edition), Fulcrum Publishing.

Pagans in the Promised Land provides a unique, well-researched challenge to the US historical and current federal Indian law and policy. It dissects and challenges the presumption that Indigenous nations are legitimately subject to the plenary power of the United States.

CHAPTER NOTES

The references with short descriptions and commentary for each chapter represent books and articles I find knowledgeable, interesting, and appropriate to general audience readers. There are some scientific papers that are exceptions, although their basic findings will be clear. The references are not a comprehensive list; however, everything in this book can be verified or updated from verifiable sources if necessary.

1 WE BEGIN IN WATER

Water Library, Basia Irland (2007) University of New Mexico Press.
   Water Library consists of nine interconnected sections focusing on projects that artist Basia Irland has created over the last thirty years in Africa, Canada, Europe, South America, Southeast Asia, and the United States. This book describes the years-long Rio Grande project from headwaters to gulf to bring water to the gulf where the Rio Grande mouth normally exists. Given years when the river did not reach the gulf, Basia Irland and groups all down the mainstem river carried water for the depleted Great River. http://www.basiairland.com/projects/book/waterlibrary.html

Reading the River, the Ecological Activist Art of Basia Irland, Museum de Domignan and Basia Irland, (2017), Museum de Domijnen.
   This book continues where *Water Library* left off. It contains descriptions of Irland's Receding/Reseeding project and many others. http://www.basiairland.com/projects/book/readingtheriver.html

Antarctic CO2 Hits 400 PPM for the First Time in 400 Million Years, Brian Kahn, (2016) *Scientific American*, Climate Central. https://www.scientificamerican.com/article/antarctic-co2-hit-400-ppm-for-first-time-in-4-million-years/

How did water come to earth? Brian Greene, (2013) *Smithsonian Magazine*.
   There are many theories and sources of evidence for the earth's water, including water locked in rocks deep in the earth reaching the surface through volcanism, but the cosmic source is considered a likely majority contributor. https://www.smithsonianmag.com/science-nature/how-did-water-come-to-earth-72037248/

Sky Islands of North America, a Globally Unique and Threatened Archipelago. Matt Skroch, (2003), *Terrain, a Journal of the Built and Natural Environments.* https://www.terrain.org/articles/21/skroch.htm

Recovering the Sacred: the Power of Naming and Claiming. Winona LaDuke (2005), *South End Press.*

Only Sixty Years of Farming Left If Soil Degradation Continues, Chris Arsenault (2017), *Scientific American.* https://www.scientificamerican.com/article/only-60-years-of-farming-left-if-soil-degradation-continues/

The World Without Us. Alan Weisman (2007), Macmillan.

Harvesting the Biosphere. What We Have Taken from Nature. Vaclav Smil (2013), *MIT Press.*

The biomass distribution on Earth. Yinon M. Bar-On, Rob Phillips, and Ron Milo, *Proceedings of the National Academy of Sciences*, May 21, 2018. 201711842; http://www.pnas.org/content/early/2018/05/15/1711842115

The biomass of humans is an order of magnitude greater than for all species of wild animals.

Population Clock. US Census Bureau https://www.census.gov/popclock/world

World Population Prospects: the 2017 Revision. United Nations, Dept. of Economic and Social Affairs. https://www.un.org/development/desa/publications/world-population-prospects-the-2017-revision.html

Countdown: Our Last, Best Hope for a Future on Earth? Alan Weisman. (2013) Hachette Book Group.

Weisman's book and its predecessor by Fred Pearce cited below demonstrate how population projections are already showing a decline in populations, especially where women are educated and empowered to make decisions on reproduction. This is happening in the wealthier nations of the world.

The Coming Population Crash: And Our Planet's Surprising Future. Fred Pearce. (2010), Beacon Press, Boston.

A great deal of demographic detail populates this book, overall and by nation. As his fellow population writer Weisman details, the empowerment and education of women is crucial to curbing world overpopulation, a process well underway. Once the downward population trends become more clearly manifest after 2050, the population has the potential to return to early twentieth century or before levels. Pearce examines a number of intersecting trends in environmental degradation, social, and economic issues and posits cities may be key to global sustainable living as they leave more open spaces.

Population Bottlenecks and Pleistocene Human Evolution, Hawks, John et.al, *Molecular Biology and Evolution,* Vol. 17, Jan 2000, pp2-22. https://academic.oup.com/mbe/article/17/1/2/975516

The Dawn of Human Matrilineal Diversity. Behar, DM, et. al and The Genographic Consortium. *Am. J. Human Genetics* 82:1-11.

A credible critique of the long bottleneck estimates was made by John Hawks in his online blog of May 2008: http://johnhawks.net/weblog/reviews/genetics/mtdna_migrations/sub-saharan-africa-population-size-behar-2008.html.

The field of human evolutionary genetics in regard to population bottlenecks relies heavily on sparse observational data, statistical and mathematical models including computation intensive simulations. There is a great deal of controversy; nonetheless, the existence of severe narrowing of the human population and subsequent great expansion is plausible, regardless of lack of consensus on time span and population size estimates. And all population growth, whether post-bottleneck or current, depends on sufficient food, water, mating success, relatively low rates of diseases, especially those limiting the birth and survival of offspring to reproduce.

Water withdrawal by Sector Around 2010. United Nations, Food and Agriculture

Organization. Update Nov. 2016. http://www.fao.org/nr/water/aquastat/tables/WorldData-Withdrawal_eng.pdf

Agriculture is 80 percent of water use in California. Why aren't farmers being forced to cut back? Jeff Guo. *The Washington Post,* April 2015. https://www.washingtonpost.com/blogs/govbeat/wp/2015/04/03/agriculture-is-80-percent-of-water-use-in-california-why-arent-farmers-being-forced-to-cut-back/?noredirect=on&utm_term=.90193f5f2757

Drawdown: the Most Comprehensive Plan to Reverse Global Warming. Paul Hawken (Editor). *Penguin.* 2017.

Why bother? Michael Pollan. *New York Times,* April 20, 2008. https://www.nytimes.com/2008/04/20/magazine/20wwln-lede-t.html

The Sixth Extinction: an Unnatural History. Elizabeth Kolbert. Henry Holt and Co. 2015.

Why E O Wilson is wrong about how to save the earth. Bram Buscher and Robert Fletcher, Aeon, June 2018. https://aeon.co/ideas/why-e-o-wilson-is-wrong-about-how-to-save-the-earth
    Author's summary: In viewing the world, we also construct it, and the world Wilson's offers us in *Half-Earth* is a truly bizarre one. For all his zeal, (misplaced) righteousness and passion, his vision is disturbing and dangerous, and would have profoundly negative 'consequences if played out'. It would entail forcibly herding a drastically reduced human population into increasingly crowded urban areas to be managed in oppressively technocratic ways. How such a global programme of conservation *Lebensraum* would be accomplished is left to the reader's imagination. We therefore hope readers will not take Wilson's proposal seriously. Addressing biodiversity loss and other environmental problems must proceed by confronting the world's obscene inequality, not by blaming the poor and trusting the 'free market' to save them.

An ecosystem approach to protecting half the terrestrial realm. Dinerstein et. al. *Bioscience* (2017), Vol 67, 6: 534-545. https://academic.oup.com/bioscience/article/67/6/534/3102935
    Authors' abstract: We assess progress toward the protection of 50% of the terrestrial biosphere to address the species-extinction crisis and conserve a global ecological heritage for future generations. Using a map of Earth's 846 terrestrial eco-regions, we show that 98 eco-regions (12%) exceed Half Protected; 313 eco-regions (37%) fall short of Half Protected but have sufficient unaltered habitat remaining to reach the target; and 207 eco-regions (24%) are in peril, where an average of only 4% of natural habitat remains. We propose a Global Deal for Nature—a companion to the Paris Climate Deal—to promote increased habitat protection and restoration, national- and eco-region-scale conservation strategies, and the empowerment of indigenous peoples to protect their sovereign lands. The goal of such an

accord would be to protect half the terrestrial realm by 2050 to halt the extinction crisis while sustaining human livelihoods.

Scientists call for a Paris-style agreement to save life on earth. Jeremy Hance. June 28, 2018, The Guardian. https://www.theguardian.com/environment/radical-conservation/2018/jun/28/scientists-call-for-a-paris-style-agreement-to-save-life-on-earth

This article summarizes the issues of global conservation, the Aichi Biodiversity Targets of 2010 aimed for 2020, most of which have not been reached. It is missing a major signatory even though Bill Clinton signed on but Congress failed to ratify it and the US is notably absent as a signer. New proposals include enlisting corporations in addition to all nations for a new international agreement.

E.O. Wilson Biodiversity Foundation. The link below provides a comprehensive listing of articles by and about E.O. Wilson's controversial proposal for conservation of the earth's land and water. https://eowilsonfoundation.org/half-earth-our-planet-s-fight-for-life/

Engineering Eden: The True Story of a Violent Death, a Trial, and the Fight Over Controlling Nature. Jordan Fisher-Smith, (2016), Crown Publishing.

In this environmental history, nature writer and former park ranger Jordan Fisher-Smith uses the story of Harry Walker, killed by a grizzly in Yellowstone, to tell the larger narrative of the futile, sometimes fatal, attempts to remake wilderness in the name of preserving it. Tracing a course from the founding of the national parks through the tangled twentieth-century growth of the conservationist movement, Fisher-Smith shows how virtually every attempt to manage nature in the parks has only created cascading effects that require even more management. Moving across time and between Yellowstone, Yosemite, and Glacier national parks, *Engineering Eden* shows how efforts at wilderness management have always been undone by one fundamental problem—that the idea of what is "wild" dissolves as soon as we begin to examine it, leaving us with little framework to say what wilderness should look like and which human interventions are acceptable in trying to preserve it. Harry Eugene Walker's family won the case against Yellowstone for abruptly ending rather than phasing out garbage dumps and providing alternate food for grizzlies habituated to the dumps for part of their diet. Furthermore, they had not warned Harry about recent bear attacks near closed dump sites. This book speaks to present-day efforts to halt the sixth extinction of wildlife not through museum-like parks but in a far greater effort for connected wilderness and wildlife corridors.

The Myth of Human Supremacy. Derrick Jensen, (2016), Seven Stories Press.

In this impassioned polemic, Derrick Jensen debunks the near-universal belief in a hierarchy of nature and the superiority of humans. Vast and under appreciated complexities of nonhuman life are explored in detail—from the cultures of pigs and prairie dogs, to the creative use of tools by elephants and fish, to the acumen of caterpillars and fungi. The paralysis of the scientific establishment on moral and ethical issues is confronted and a radical new framework for assessing the intelligence and sentience of nonhuman life is put forth. Jensen also attacks mainstream environmental journalism, which too often limits discussions to how ecological changes affect humans or the economy—with little or no regard for nonhuman life. With his signature compassionate logic, he argues that when we separate ourselves from the rest of nature, we in fact orient ourselves against nature, taking an unjust and, in the long run, impossible position.

2 UNDAM THE KLAMATH

Cadillac Desert: the American West and its Disappearing Water. Marc Reisner. (1986), revised 1993. *Viking Press.*

   This book is a must-read for anyone interested in dams and western water. It includes a segment on water-rich Georgia rivers in a chapter devoted to Jimmy Carter's efforts to save rivers but comes up against heavy opposition. Overall, it gives the history of the Bureau of Reclamation and US Army Corps of Engineers, and their struggle to remake the American West. The book's main conclusion is that development-driven policies, formed when settling the West was the country's main concern, are having serious long-term negative effects on the environment and water quantity. The book was revised and updated in 1993.

Klamath Dam Public Comments, YouTube, Diana Hartel public comment included in this excerpts video. https://www.youtube.com/watch?v=U7TppqQoDz4&feature=youtu.be

A Continuing Legacy: Institutional Racism, Hunger, and Nutritional Justice on the Klamath, Chapter 2, Norgaard, Kari M; Reed, Ron; Van Horn, Carolina, In: **Cultivating Food Justice: Race, Class, and Sustainability**, Alkon, Allison H. and Agyeman, Julian, Editors, (2011), MIT Press.

   This book chapter is an excellent piece on the effects of forced assimilation of Native people, loss of culture and traditional livelihood resulting in poverty, malnutrition, and disease of survivors of the Karuk Tribe. It includes the basis of tribal activism to remove dams on the Klamath. See also, *The Effects of Altered Diet on the Health of the Karuk People*, Norgaard, Kari M. Submitted to Federal Energy Regulatory Commission, Docket P-2082, on behalf of the Karuk Tribe of California, November 2005.

An American Genocide: the United States and the California Indian Disaster 1846-1873. The Lamar Series in Western History. Benjamin Madley, Yale University Press, 2016.

   This book is a definitive, thoroughly researched account of genocide in California within the larger context of the Spanish treatment of Native people and of US government policies. *"An American Genocide* provides one of the most detailed and stunning narratives of violence, murder, and state-sponsored genocide in North America, making this book a major achievement in the fields of both Native American history and Genocide Studies."—Ned Blackhawk (Yale University), author of *Violence Over the Land: Indians and Empires in the Early American West*

An Indigenous People's History of the United States, Four Hundred Years of Native American History from the Bottom Up Perspective, (ReVisioning American History), Roxanne Dunbar-Ortiz, Beacon Press (Boston), 2015

A broad perspective on the fate of the California and Oregon Native people of the Klamath and other west coast indigenous lands can be found in Chapter Seven: From Sea to Shining Sea. Dunbar-Ortiz challenges the founding myth of the United States and shows how policy against the Indigenous peoples was colonialist and designed to seize the territories of indigenous nations, displacing or eliminating them since the nation's inception starting with George Washington. As Dunbar-Ortiz shows, this policy was praised in popular culture, through writers like James Fenimore Cooper and Walt Whitman. Walt Whitman was essentially a white supremacist, racist, and believer in social Darwinism calling for the elimination of African-Americans, Indians, and Mexicans. In Song of Myself Whitman asks, "Do I contradict myself? I am large, I contain the multitudes." Apparently his multitudes included only Euro-descended whites. The book encompasses the full range of genocidal policies, corruption and greed as witnessed through historic documents and known events throughout the United States from its beginning to the present. It also examines the rise of Native resistance movements such as the American Indian Movement (AIM).

River of Renewal. Myth and History in the Klamath Basin. Stephen Most, University of Washington Press and the Oregon Historical Society, 2006.

Stephen Most chronicles the complex history of the Klamath River and its many people, especially indigenous nations. It also contains a particularly poignant story of Geneva Mattz who opposed armed federal agents who attacked her people in their traditional fishing place. According to the editor of *Orion Magazine*, "Most tells these stories in the voices of the protagonists, who give the basin's complex history an illuminating immediacy that infuses the entire book. It is a mark of his achievement that he has been able to make these historical, cultural, and environmental pieces into a comprehensive whole. *River of Renewal* is the best source available for those wishing to think clearly about this cumulative tragedy, as well as a first-rate model for regional land use anywhere in the American West." Most and others also produced a film of the same title. http://www.cultureunplugged.com/documentary/watch-online/festival/play/7457/River-of-Renewal

Water War in the Klamath Basin. Macho Law, Combat Biology, and Dirty Politics. Holly D. Doremus and A. Dan Tarlock. Island Press, 2008.

In *Water War in the Klamath Basin*, legal scholars Holly Doremus and A. Dan Tarlock examine the genesis of the crisis and its fallout, offering a comprehensive review of the event and its history. The authors focus primarily on the legal institutions that contributed to the conflict—what they call "the accretion of unintegrated resource management and environmental laws" that make environmental protection challenging, especially in politically divided regions with a long-standing history of entitlement-based resource allocation.

King of Fish: the Thousand Year Run of Salmon. David Montgomery, Basic Books, 2004.

In studying the natural and human forces that shape the rivers and mountains of the Pacific Northwest, geologist David Montgomery has learned to see the evolution and near-extinction of the salmon as a story of changing landscapes. Montgomery shows how a succession of historical experiences -first in the United Kingdom, then in New England, and now in the Pacific Northwest -repeat a disheartening story in which overfishing and sweeping changes to rivers and seas are driving the salmon toward extinction. In *King of Fish*, Montgomery traces the human impacts on salmon over the last thousand years and examines the implications both for salmon recovery efforts and for the more general problem of human impacts on the natural world. Montgomery offers recommendations for reinventing the ways in which we make environmental decisions about land, water, and fish.

The persistence and characteristics of Chinook salmon migrations to the Upper Klamath River prior to exclusion by dams, John B. Hamilton et. al. (2016), *Oregon Historical Society*, 117, no. 3, 327-377.

This article contains historic photos and detailed records from multiple sources of changes in Chinook populations including salmon runs upriver to Klamath and beyond to the headwaters, a fact that is frequently disputed by those opposed to dam removal.

Maps of Trends in Diagnosed Diabetes. CDC Division of Diabetes Translation. US Surveillance System, April 2017.

Data are based on US adults 18 years or older who reported a diabetes diagnosis (apart from gestational diabetes) by a physician. Rates are age-adjusted to the 2000 US population. In 1994, the majority of states had rates of <4.5% and only one state, South Carolina, with 6-7.4% prevalence of diabetes. Each successive year, the prevalence of diabetes rose throughout the entire country. By 2000, statewide diabetes prevalence of 7.5-8.9% appeared for the first time in Mississippi, with only two states showing rates of <4.5%. In 2002, West Virginia reached a prevalence of 9+% and no states were under 4.5%. In 2011, no states were less than 6% and 15 states were in the 9+% group, most from the south. https://www.cdc.gov/diabetes/statistics/slides/maps_diabetes_trends.pdf

National Diabetes Statistics Report, 2017. Centers for Disease Control and Prevention, web accessed in 2018. https://www.cdc.gov/diabetes/pdfs/data/statistics/national-diabetes-statistics-report.pdf

Since prevalence (existing cases at a given time) and incidence (new cases) are shifting rapidly with some evidence of leveling off, these data at the time of publication may be the most useful. It is worthwhile to check updates in on-going and rapidly changing epidemics such as diabetes in the US and worldwide. The report draws on multiple sources including the Indian Health Service, national surveys, and medical studies. Overall 9.4% of the population had diabetes in 2015, of which 23.8% were unaware they met the criteria for diabetes. Diabetes increases with age, reaching its highest percent of 25.2% in those 65 years or older. Pre-diabetes based on fasting glucose or A1C level occurred in 33.9% of adults with nearly half in those 65 or older. Only 11.6% with pre-diabetes knew they had the condition. As with most survey, rates for indigenous people are not shown.

Native American adults have more diabetes than any other race or ethnicity. National Health Interview Survey and Indian Health Services Report, 2010-2012. https://www.cdc.gov/vitalsigns/aian-diabetes/infographic.html#graphic

The overall prevalence of diabetes for Native Americans was 16% compared with 13% for both Blacks and Hispanics, 9% for Asians, and 8% for non-Hispanic Whites. The good news in this report is that the rates are dropping faster than all other groups due to team-based and community-based prevention and care programs. The original data for this very short report can be obtained from the larger databases or the institutions conducting the surveys. However, there are no specific links for this search, further evidence of the underreporting if not outright neglect of health statistics on indigenous populations.

Adult Obesity Maps, 2017. Centers for Disease Control and Prevention,

In 2016, all states had an obesity prevalence of 20% or greater with obesity higher with age and lower with years of education, higher in non-whites. The highest prevalence states (35% or more) were in the south, followed by the Midwest, northeast, and the west. https://www.cdc.gov/obesity/data/prevalence-maps.html

Education, income, employment and prevalence of chronic disease among American Indian/Alaska Native Elders, Collette Anderson et. al. *Prev Chronic Dis* (2018) vol. 15.

Authors' introduction and summary of results: Chronic disease studies have omitted analyses of the American Indian/Alaska Native (AI/AN) population, relied on small samples of AI/ANs, or focused on a single disease among AI/ANs. We measured the influence of income, employment status, and education level on the prevalence of chronic disease among 14,632 AI/AN elders [>=55] from 2011 through 2014. Most AI/AN elders (89.7%) had been diagnosed with at least one chronic disease. AI/AN elders with middle-to-low income levels and who were unemployed were more likely to have a chronic disease than were high-income and employed AI/AN elders. The frequency of hypertension among AI/AN elders (58.9%) nearly mirrored the national average (58%) [Comparison to other elders]. However, other chronic conditions among AI/AN elders occurred at double the national average. Specifically, 54% of the AI/AN elders reported diabetes, compared with only 27% of the US population aged 65 years or older. Roughly 31% of all US adults aged 65 or older were diagnosed with arthritis in 2015, compared with 47.2% of AI/AN elders.

Note: This study is not particularly thorough but there are so few studies of indigenous health issues on a national scale that it provides a rough indicator. We know that poverty, healthful food scarcity, access to health care, and stresses of historical and current trauma of indigenous people play a role in making diabetes and obesity, shortened lifespan, and chronic diseases such as of the kidney disease highest of all racial/ethnic groups in the US Refer to Norgaard et. al. book chapter cited above for more detail. https://www.cdc.gov/pcd/issues/2018/17_0387.htm

Native American embodiment of the chronicities of modernity: reservation food, diabetes, and the metabolic syndrome among the Kiowa, Comanche, and Apache. D. Weidman. *Med Anthropol Q.* (2012) Dec;26(4):595-612.

Author abstract. As a physical embodiment of modernity, the prevalence of obesity, diabetes, and the metabolic syndrome (MetS) among Native Americans reflects their body's biological response to social and cultural structures that routinize daily behaviors and contain their physical body. This article explains why Native Americans were one of the earliest populations* manifesting this epidemic. Ethno-historical methods identify the conjuncture of chronic behaviors among Kiowa, Comanche, and Apache of Oklahoma that promote inactivity, over-nutrition, and psychosocial stresses. Correspondence and primary documents of Federal Indian Agents who managed the reservation food rations and annuity systems beginning in the 1860s, details a culture history of nutrition and food technologies that standardized and established the unhealthy modern diet that continues among Native Americans today. By identifying structural chronicities affecting specific populations and life situations, policies and interventions can be more effective in promoting positive changes for reducing the global pandemic of diabetes and MetS.

* "earliest" needs further elucidation. Pre-European contact, diabetes was extremely rare in North American indigenous people even though it was well-known in Europe and North Africa from at least 1552 BCE. Henry the VIII of England, born in 1491, suffered from uncontrolled diabetes as did many others in Europe.

Endocrine-disrupting chemicals, risk of type 2 diabetes, and diabetes-related metabolic traits: a systematic review and meta-analysis. Y Song et. al. J Diabetes. 2016 Jul;8(4):516-32.

This review shows a doubling or greater risk for type 2 diabetes and diabetes-related metabolic traits with dioxins, PCBs, and chlorinated pesticides. Environmental exposures effects investigations are typically difficult to conduct with results far lower than found in this meta-analysis (mathematical summary statistics based on data from several published study findings, in this case 49 studies). There is a growing body of research showing endocrine disrupting chemicals play a role in diabetes, metabolic syndrome, and in obesity, an important strong risk factor for diabetes. Author summary. **Background:** Elevated blood or urinary concentrations of endocrine-disrupting chemicals (EDCs) may be related to increased risk of type 2 diabetes (T2D). The aim of the present study was to assess the role of EDCs in affecting risk of T2D and related metabolic traits. **Methods:** MEDLINE was searched for cross-sectional and prospective studies published before 8 March 2014 into the association between EDCs (dioxin, polychlorinated biphenyl [PCB], chlorinated pesticide, bisphenol A [BPA], phthalate) and T2D and related metabolic traits. Three investigators independently extracted information on study design, participant characteristics, EDC types and concentrations, and association measures. **Results:** Forty-one cross-sectional and eight prospective studies from ethnically diverse populations were included in the analysis. Serum concentrations of dioxins, PCBs, and chlorinated pesticides were significantly associated with T2D risk; comparing the highest to lowest concentration category, the pooled relative risks (RR) were 1.91 (95% confidence interval [CI] 1.44—2.54) for dioxins, 2.39 (95% CI 1.86-3.08) for total PCBs, and 2.30 (95% CI 1.81-2.93) for chlorinated pesticides. Urinary concentrations of BPA and phthalates were also associated with T2D risk; comparing the highest to lowest concentration categories, the pooled RR were 1.45 (95% CI 1.13-1.87) for BPA and 1.48 (95% CI 0.98-2.25) for phthalates. Further, EDC concentrations were associated with indicators of impaired fasting glucose and insulin resistance. **Conclusions:** Persistent and non-persistent EDCs may affect the risk of T2D. There is an urgent need for further investigation of EDCs, especially non-persistent ones, and T2D risk in large prospective studies.

Disparities in diabetes: the nexus of race, poverty, and place. Darrell Gaskin et. al. (2014), *American Journal of Public Health,* 104(11): 2147–2155.

Author Summary *Results.* We found a race–poverty–place gradient for diabetes prevalence for Blacks and poor Whites. The odds of having diabetes were higher for Blacks than for Whites. Individual poverty increased the odds of having diabetes for both Whites and Blacks. Living in a poor neighborhood increased the odds of having diabetes for Blacks and poor Whites. *Conclusions.* To address race disparities in diabetes, policymakers should address problems created by concentrated poverty (e.g., lack of access to reasonably priced fruits and vegetables, recreational facilities, and health care services; high crime rates; and greater exposures to environmental toxins). Housing and development policies in urban areas should avoid creating high-poverty neighborhoods. https://www.ncbi.nlm.nih.gov/pmc/articles/PMC4021012/

Stress and diabetes: a review of the links. Cathy Lloyd et. al. (2005) *Diabetes Spectrum,* Apr; 18(2): 121-127

Author Abstract (excerpt): Evidence suggests that stressful experiences might affect diabetes, in terms of both its onset and its exacerbation. In recent years, the complexities of the relationship between stress and diabetes have become well known but have been less well researched. Some studies have suggested that stressful experiences might affect the onset and/or the metabolic control of diabetes, but findings have often been inconclusive. In this article, we review some of this research before going on to consider how stress might affect diabetes control and the physiological mechanisms through which this may occur. Finally, we discuss the implications for clinical practice and care. Before going any further, however, the meaning of the term *stress* must be clarified because it can be used in different ways. Stress may be thought of as *a)* a physiological response to an external stimulus, or *b)* a psychological response to external stimuli, or *c)* stressful events themselves, which can be negative or positive or both. In this article, we address all three aspects of stress: stressful events or experiences (sometimes referred to as stressors) and the physiological and psychological/behavioral responses to these. Results: Stress may play a role in the onset of diabetes, it can have a deleterious effect on glycemic control and can affect lifestyle. Emerging evidence strongly suggests, however, that interventions that help individuals prevent or cope with stress can have an important positive effect on quality of life and glycemic control.

This review is a fairly typical clinical perspective although it gathers existing evidence. It does not deal with the forms of chronic distress of indigenous populations with multi-generational trauma and on-going pervasive discrimination, poverty well below federal guidelines, food scarcity and more. It is clear that the stresses indigenous people face can play a very big role in the elevated diabetes epidemic among them. http://spectrum.diabetesjournals.org/content/18/2/121

Why living in a poor neighborhood can change your biology: the sheer stress of an environment contributes to obesity and diabetes. Andrew Curry, (2018) *Nautilus* 61.

A summary of research results and issues on chronic stressors of poverty environments contribute to obesity and diabetes. This is not a scientific piece but it gives a good glimpse into environmental distress factors in obesity and diabetes. http://nautil.us/issue/61/coordinates/why-living-in-a-poor-neighborhood-can-change-your-biology-rp

Canaries in the coal mine: a cross-species analysis of the plurality of obesity epidemics, Yann C. Klimentidis et. al., *Proceedings of the Royal Society B* (2011) 278, 1626-1632

Examination of changes in weight and obesity in non-human species including lab animals shows a definite trend toward weight gain independent of changes in diet. Lab animals in particular are given a restricted diet of the same feed over time with careful weight and size measurements. This report is part of the growing evidence of widespread chemicals in the environment entering multiple food chains and contributing to the human epidemics of obesity and diabetes likely through endocrine disrupting chemicals.

In the Land of the Grasshopper Song. Two Women in the Klamath River Indian Country in 1908-1909. Mary Ellicot Arnold and Mabel Reed (2nd edition 2011) Bison Books.

In the Land of the Grasshopper Song, we find a personal and vibrant view into life on the Klamath River a half century after the gold rush. In 1908 easterners Mary Ellicott Arnold and Mabel Reed accepted appointments as field matrons in Karuk tribal communities in the Klamath and Salmon River country of northern California. Hired to promote the federal government's "assimilation" or cultural destruction and colonization of American Indians, Arnold and Reed instead found themselves adapting to the world they entered, a complex and contentious territory of Anglo miners and Karuk families. Arnold and Reed's account shows their irreverence towards Victorian ideals of womanhood (they were lifelong partners and social justice activists), and recounts their respect toward and friendship with Karuks. *In the Land of the Grasshopper Song* also documents Karuk resilience under horrendous pressures.

Standing Ground: Yurok Spirituality 1850-1990. Thomas Buckley. (2002), University of California Press.

This account of spiritual training and practice within an American Indian social network emphasizes narrative over analysis. Thomas Buckley's foregrounding of Yurok narratives creates one major level of dialogue in an innovative ethnography that features dialogue as its central theoretical trope. Buckley places himself in conversation with contemporary Yurok friends and elders, with written texts, and with twentieth-century anthropology as well. He describes Yurok Indian spirituality as "a significant field in which individual and society meet in dialogue—cooperating, resisting, negotiating, changing each other in manifold ways. 'Culture,' here, is not a thing but a process, an emergence through time." While not written from the Native perspective, this book provides a great deal of documentation and insight. "Its description of Yurok religious practice in recent times is both sympathetic and insightful, providing an interweaving series of narratives and interpretations . . . . The author makes an eloquent case for cultural continuity." —Michael Harkin, author of *The Heiltsuks.*

To the American Indian: Reminiscences of a Yurok Woman. Lucy Thompson, (1991), Heyday Books.

Lucy Thompson published *To the American Indian* in 1916, when the world of the Yurok of the Klamath River in northern California seemed on the edge of collapse. Concerned about the survival of her people and their customs, and concerned also that the true story of the Yurok was not being told—not by the popular press, not by the anthropologists—she took it upon herself to write this book. It is written in a form she thought would reach nonindigenous people using biblical and euro-American perspectives and stories with which she was familiar. A Yurok initiate into the exclusive priestly society known as Talth, Lucy Thompson gives a unique insider's view of her culture.

California's Salmon and Steelhead. The Struggle to Restore an Imperiled Resource. Alan Lufkin, Editor (1990), University of California Press.

Millions upon millions of salmon and steelhead once filled California streams, providing a plentiful and sustainable food resource for the original peoples of the region. But over the years, dams and irrigation diversions have reduced natural spawning habitat from an estimated 6,000 miles to fewer than 300. River pollution has also hit hard at fish populations, which within recent decades have diminished by 80 percent. One species, the San Joaquin River spring Chinook, became extinct soon after World War II. Other species are nearly extinct. No comparable work has ever been published, although some of the material has been available for half a century. In the richly varied contributions in this volume, the reader meets Indigenous people whose culture centers on the salmon and steelhead upon which they depend; commercial fishers who see their livelihood and unique lifestyle vanishing; biologists and fishery managers alarmed at the loss of river water habitable by fish and at the effects of hatcheries on native gene pools. Women who fish, conservation-minded citizens, foresters, economists, outdoor writers, engineers, politicians, city youth restoring streambeds—all are represented. Their lives—and the lives of all Californians—are affected in myriad ways by the fate of California's salmon and steelhead. This book remains a valuable source of history, and hopefully not part of the eulogy for extinct species of California and other west coast rivers.

Finding new ground. Robert Chadwick. (2013). CreateSpace Independent Publishing Platform.

Robert Chadwick (Bob) pioneered the development of consensus building techniques which foster creative solutions to old conflicts. With 29 years experience as a professional, manager, executive and internal organizational development consultant in a major Federal Agency, and 25 years as a private consultant, Bob has accumulated a comprehensive education and experience in managerial and conflict resolution strategies. He has a proven ability to help groups and communities successfully in mission development, organizational change, team building, labor negotiations, and conflict resolution. His management development and consensus activities have involved people at all levels of the public and private sectors and had a crucial role in the long-standing Klamath conflicts between multiple government agencies, environmental groups, tribes, agricultural organizations, Native and commercial fisheries and others.

Common Ground on Hostile Turf. Lucy Moore, (2013), Island Press.

Moore has worked on wide-ranging issues—from radioactive waste storage to loss of traditional grazing lands. More importantly, she has worked with diverse groups and individuals: ranchers, environmental activists, government agencies, corporations, tribal groups, and many more. After decades spent at the negotiating table, she has learned that a case does not turn on facts, legal merit, or moral superiority. It turns on people. Through stories, she shows how issues of culture, personality, history, and power affect negotiations. And she illustrates that equitable solutions depend on a healthy group dynamic. Both the mediator and opposing parties must be honest, vulnerable, open, and respectful. Easier said than done, but Moore proves that subtle shifts can break the logjam and reconcile even the most fiercely warring factions.

Balancing Water: Restoring the Klamath Basin. Tupper Ansel Blake et. al., (2000), University of California Press.

This book contains fine photos of the Upper Klamath before the water shut-off, massive farmer and rancher protests, and catastrophic fish kill of 2001-2. It makes a case for good stewardship and carries a sentiment that does not touch what was and is actually happening on the river. The photos are worth viewing to have an appreciation for the land so many, human and wild, call home.

3 UPPER MISSISSIPPI RIVER: IMMORTAL RIVER, MORTAL SOIL

Immortal River: the Upper Mississippi in Ancient and Modern Times, Calvin Fremling, (2003), University of Wisconsin Press.

Immortal River Covers geology, zoology, botany, changes of the river after arrival of settlers, eutrophication of river side channels and pools of Army Corps of Engineers, effects of locks and dams, and issues in restoration of wetlands and river's natural floodplain. The writing is science-based, yet accessible to general readers.

Agriculture and Soil Erosion in the Upper Mississippi Valley Hill Country, Stanley Trimble, (2012), CRC Press.

This book comes from a strong scientific knowledge base and first-hand studies by the author, written in an accessible and folksy manner.

Where the Sky Begins: Land of the Tallgrass Prairie, James Madson, (2004, 1st edition 1982), Bur Oak Press.

Where the Sky Begins celebrates the prairies in poetic prose. The author, a knowledgeable naturalist, also filled many of its pages with his own sensitive and accurate sketches of plants, animals, landscapes of the lands he wandered and loved. This book sparked strong interest in prairie restoration beyond a few dedicated conservationists to the point that upper Mississippi farmers now often incorporate restored plots into their properties.

The Year the Stars Fell: Lakota Winter Counts at the Smithsonian. Candace S. Greene and Russell Thornton, Editors, (2007), University of Nebraska Press. The selected winter counts of Batiste Goode were drawn from this book. Winter counts—pictorial calendars by which Plains bands kept track of their past—marked each year with a picture of a memorable event. The Lakota recorded many different events in their winter counts, but all include "the year the stars fell," the spectacular Leonid meteor shower of 1833-34. This volume is an unprecedented assemblage of information on the important collection of Lakota winter counts at the Smithsonian, a core resource for the study of Lakota history and culture. Fourteen winter counts are presented in detail, with a chapter devoted to the newly discovered Rosebud Winter Count. Together these counts constitute a visual chronicle over hundreds of years, prior to and during the arrival of Europeans as recorded by Lakota historians. The book provides ready access to primary source material and reproduced images.

Ledger Narratives: The Plains Indians Drawings in the Mark Lansburgh Collection at Dartmouth College (New Directions in Native American Studies Series). Colin G. Galloway et. al., (2012), University of Oklahoma Press.
   Ledger Narratives contains historical drawings and contemporary essays by scholars. The Cheyenne, Crow, Kiowa, Lakota, and other Plains peoples created the genre known as ledger art in the mid-nineteenth century. Before that time, people had chronicled important events of their tribe or band, lives of warriors and chiefs on rock, buffalo robes, and tipi covers. These ledger narrative drawings of events and stories are distinct from the Winter Count yearly chronicles. As they came into increasing contact with American traders, the artists recorded their experiences in pencil and crayon drawings on paper bound in ledger or account books. The drawings became known as ledger art. Dates of ledger narratives overlap periods of Winter Counts and can augment understanding of that history.

Mni Sota Makoce: Land of the Dakota. Gwen Westerman and Bruce White, (2012), Minnesota Historical Society Press.
   Much of the focus on the Dakota people in Minnesota rests on the tragic events of the 1862 US-Dakota War and the resulting exile that sent the majority of the surviving Dakota to prisons and reservations beyond the state's boundaries. But the true depth of the devastation of removal cannot be understood without a closer examination of the history of the Dakota people and their deep cultural connection to the land that is Minnesota. Drawing on oral history interviews, archival work, and painstaking comparisons of Dakota, French, and English sources, *Mni Sota Makoce* tells the detailed history of the Dakota people in their traditional homelands for hundreds of years prior to exile. Authors Gwen Westerman and Bruce White examine narratives of the people's origins, their associations with the land, and the

seasonal round through key players and place names. They examine Dakota interactions with Europeans and offer an in-depth "reading between the lines" of historical documents—some of them virtually unknown—and treaties made with the United States, uncovering misunderstandings and outright deceptions that led to war in 1862. Gwen Westerman is an enrolled member of the Sisseton-Whapeton Dakota Oyate, speaker of Dakota language, professor of English, and Director of the Humanities Program at University of Minnesota, Mankato. Bruce White is an award-winning historian specializing in Minnesota history.

The New York Times 1862 article on the Dakota hangings at Mankato has been reproduced in its entirety in the this link. http://www.startribune.com/ dec-26-1862-38-dakota-men-executed-in-mankato/138273909/

Inheriting the Trade: a Northern Family Confronts its Legacy as the Largest Slave-Trading Dynasty in the US Thomas Norman DeWolf, (2008), Beacon Press, Boston.

In the summer of 2001, Katrina Browne led nine distant family members on their own triangular passage as she made a documentary film (Traces of the Trade: A Story from the Deep North) about their DeWolf ancestors, the largest slave-trading dynasty in early America—who transported 10,000 Africans to America and the Caribbean between 1769 and 1820. DeWolf, one of Browne's cousins, traces the journey in this soul-searching memoir, beginning in Bristol, RI, the hub of the late–18th-century trade, and continuing to Ghana, Cuba and back to New England. At each station of the trip, the Family of Ten visits historic sites, and distinguished historians address the group about aspects of the slave trade. DeWolf's account gains immediacy as he reports these presentations and the ensuing group discussions, along with their personal struggles to come to terms with an ignominious family history.

Fortunately, this is not my grandfather DeWolf's line, but it could have been. Just as this family was thrust into the history of slavery and their role in it, we as a nation and as individuals need to examine how race and slavery shaped what we sometimes superficially know as the United States.

The Essential Charles Eastman (Ohiyesa): Light on the Indian World. Charles Eastman, (2007, revised and updated edition), World Wisdom.

Ohiyesa Charles Eastman authored eleven books published from 1902 until 1918 as he lived simultaneously in both the traditional world of the Santee Dakota and the modern civilization of the white man. He was also of French and English descent. An intelligent, thoughtful man, he set out to explain the philosophy and moral code of the Dakota to the dominant white culture. Eastman attended the injured at the infamous Battle of Wounded Knee, and knew first hand the plight of Native nations seeking a spiritual way for themselves while having to live increasingly under white culture dominated by materialism and industrial technology. He received his medical degree from Boston College and became the government physician on the Pine Ridge reservation in South Dakota. Until his life ended in 1939 at age 80, Eastman had witnessed and chronicled the period of greatest change in the lives of Indigenous people since his birth in 1858 near Redwood Falls, Minnesota.

John Trudell (1946-2015). The biography, discography, poetry, and other archives for John Trudell Santee Sioux/Dakota activist, actor, writer, musician and more can be found on the John Trudell website below. He was the spokesperson of the All Tribes' takeover of Alcatraz starting in 1969, broadcasting as Radio Free Alcatraz. During the 1970s, he served as chair of the American Indian Movement, head-quartered in Minneapolis. The documentary *Trudell* depicts the important events of his life, including the deaths of his pregnant wife, three children, and mother-in-law in a suspicious fire after he burned the American flag in an act of protest against US racism and classism. His father-in-law who survived the fire had been working on tribal treaty rights. https://www.johntrudell.com/biography/

Red Bird, Red Power: The Life and Legacy of Zitkala-Ša. Tadeusz Lewandowski, (2016), University of Oklahoma Press.

Red Bird, Red Power traces the story of one of the most influential—and controversial—Native activists of the twentieth century. Zitkala-Ša (1876–1938), also known as Gertrude Simmons Bonnin, was a writer, editor, and musician who dedicated her life to achieving justice for Native peoples. This is the first full-scale biography of the woman whose passionate commitment to improving the lives of her people propelled her to the forefront of Progressive-era reform movements. Zitkala-Ša's life encompassed events such as the Battle of Little Bighorn, the Dawes Severalty Act, and the Wounded Knee massacre, Indian military service during World War One, the Women's Suffrage Movement, the impact of the Great Depression, and the establishment of the Indian New Deal. Accused by some current activists of being an assimilationist, Zitkala-Ša can be seen here as a brilliant thinker working with the conditions of her time. It's worth considering how one woman responded in her times and conditions and led the way to later, more progressive activists. She was a younger though less known contemporary of Charles Eastman (1858-1939).

Coyote warrior: One Man, Three Tribes, and the Trial that Forged a Nation. Paul van Develder, (2004), Little, Brown, and Company.

Raymond Cross, a Yale-educated attorney and the youngest son of Martin Cross, an American Indian tribal chairman, who spent the bulk of his life fighting a losing battle against the construction of a post-WWII Garrison dam near the upper Missouri River that would forcibly remove hundreds of families from their ancestral lands. Van Develder's book uses the Cross family story—and Raymond Cross's eventual transformation into Coyote Warrior, the term given to a growing group of Ivy League–trained lawyers working on Indigenous rights issues—to help trace the century-long struggle of the Mandan, Hidatsa and Arikara tribes to protect their North Dakota homelands. "It doesn't take long with Indian law before you realize you're breathing a different kind of air," notes one attorney who oversaw legislation to terminate federal wardship over tribes. When Martin Cross, the great-grandson of the Mandan chief who befriended Lewis and Clark, brought his passionate protest against the proposed Garrison Dam to the Senate floor in 1945, his argument that the land where three tribes had lived "from time immemorial" would be destroyed was overridden. But then his son, Raymond, a Yale-educated lawyer whose life was shaped by the dam's deleterious effect, took up the fight. Returning to North Dakota as the lawyer for the Three Affiliated Tribes, he successfully argued before the Supreme Court for reparations for those tribes who suffered ill effects caused by the dam's destructive environmental impact. The loss of the homeland, however, could never be compensated.

The Worst Hard Time: The Untold Story of Those Who Survived the Great American Dust Bowl. Timothy Egan, (2005), Houghton Mifflin.

Annie Dillard expresses my take on *The Worst Hard Time.* "Here's a terrific true story—who could put it down? Egan humanizes Dust Bowl history by telling the vivid stories of the families who stayed behind. One loves the people and admires Egan's vigor and sympathy." —Annie Dillard, author of *Pilgrim at Tinker Creek*

Ojibwe in Minnesota. Anton Truer, (2010), Minnesota Historical Society Press.

With insight and candor, noted Ojibwe scholar Anton Treuer traces thousands of years of the complicated history of the Ojibwe people—their economy, culture, and clan system and how these have changed throughout time, perhaps most dramatically with the arrival of Europeans into Minnesota territory. *Ojibwe in Minnesota* covers the fur trade, the Iroquois Wars, and Ojibwe-Dakota relations, the treaty process and creation of reservations, and the systematic push for assimilation as seen in missionary activity, government policy, and boarding schools. Treuer deals with issues of sovereignty as they influence the running of casinos and land management, the need for reform in modern tribal government, poverty, unemployment, and drug abuse, and constitutional and educational reform. He also tackles the complicated issue of identity and details recent efforts and successes in cultural preservation and language revitalization.

All our relations: Native Struggles for Land and Life. Winona Laduke, (2016, 2nd Edition), Haymarket Books.

Winona LaDuke shows us a vital Native environmentalism linking Indigenous people throughout North America and Hawaii in the fight to protect and restore their health, culture, and the ecosystems on their lands. LaDuke is a member of the Anishinaabeg nation, daughter of Vincent LaDuke (Sun Bear) and Betty LaDuke nee Bernstein, an artist from the Bronx. These Native activists take inspiration from their forebears' responsible treatment of natural systems, based on reverence for the interconnectedness of all life forms.

Ricekeepers, Winona LaDuke, (2007), *Orion Magazine.*
This article is a succinct telling of the fight to protect Native foods and seeds against corporate ownership and genetic engineering of traditional food crops. https://orionmagazine.org/article/ricekeepers/

Killers of the Flower Moon: The Osage Murders and the Birth of the FBI.
David Grann, (2017), Doubleday.
Oklahoma hosts dozens of displaced tribes within the watershed of the Arkansas, tributary to the Mississippi. The Osage originally occupied the land in the Ohio and Mississippi River valleys. In the 1920s, the Osage found themselves in a unique position among Indigenous people. As other tribal lands were parceled out in an effort by the government to encourage dissolution and assimilation of both lands and culture, the Osage negotiated to maintain the mineral rights for their corner of Oklahoma, creating a kind of "underground reservation." It proved a savvy move as countless oil rigs filled the landscape, making the Osage very rich. And that's when they started dying. Execution-style shootings, poisonings, and exploding houses drove the body count to over two dozen, while private eyes and undercover operatives scoured the territory for clues. Even as legendary and infamous oil barons vied for the most lucrative leases, J. Edgar Hoover's investigation—which he would leverage to enhance both the prestige and power of his fledgling FBI—began to overtake even the town's most respected leaders. Corruption occurred at all levels of government, including the so-called management of leases and oil royalties. In a follow-up to this history, the Osage Nation filed a suit against the Department of the Interior, alleging that it had not adequately managed the assets and paid people the royalties they were due. The suit was settled in 2011 for $380 million with commitments to improve program management. Hopefully these commitments are enforceable as the current US Interior Department descends into greater corruption.

Rising Tide: The Great Mississippi Flood of 1927 and How It Changed America. John M. Barry, (2007), Simon and Schuster.
In the spring of 1927, America witnessed one of its greatest natural disasters: a flood that profoundly changed race relations, government, and society in the Mississippi River Valley region. Flooding affected the Mississippi River Valley from Missouri and Illinois down to the delta. In Tennessee, the flooding river was 60 miles wide. More than 30 feet of water stood over land inhabited by nearly one million people prior to the flood. Close to 300,000 African Americans were forced to live in refugee camps for months. Many people, both black and white, left the land and never returned. A misguided and unnecessary attempt to protect New Orleans by dynamiting a levee destroyed towns and killed even more people and animals. Using an impressive array of primary and secondary sources, Barry traces and analyzes how the changes produced by the flood came into conflict and

ultimately changed the old planter aristocracy, accelerated black migration to the North, and foreshadowed federal government intervention in the region's social and economic life during the New Deal.

1000 Year Flood: Destruction, Loss, Rescue, And Redemption Along the Mississippi River. Stephen Lyons, (2010), Globe Pequot.

When the Mississippi River crested 30 feet above its banks in June 2008, tens of thousands of Midwesterners lost their homes, their crops and all their possessions; eventually, the disaster would cost the region tens of billions in damages and trigger incalculable psychological trauma. The Midwest flood was especially hard on Cedar Rapids, Iowa, where journalist Stephen Lyons describes a city of growing frustration with the slowness of government recovery efforts. This story may have been different if the Mississippi River were still connected to its floodplain and had not been restricted and channelized by Army Corps of Engineers concrete projects. The book does not examine these engineering issues in depth as it primarily the story of suffering compounded by the inept handling of the flood aftermath.

1491: New Revelations of the Americas Before Columbus. Charles Mann, (2006, 2nd Edition), Vintage.

1491 stands for the long-debated question of what human civilization in the Americas was like before Europeans. The history books most Americans were (and still are) raised on describe the continents before Columbus as a vast, underused territory, sparsely populated by primitives whose cultures would inevitably bow before the advanced technologies of the Europeans. For decades, though, among the archaeologists, anthropologists, paleo-linguists, and others whose discoveries Charles C. Mann brings together in *1491*, very different stories have been emerging. Among the revelations: the first people in the Americas may not have come over the Bering land bridge around 12,000 BC but by boat along the Pacific coast 10 or even 20 thousand years earlier; the Americas were a far more urban, more populated, and more technologically advanced region than generally assumed; and the Indigenous people, rather than living in static harmony with nature, radically engineered the landscape to the point that even "timeless" natural features like the Amazon rainforest can be seen as products of human intervention.

1493: Uncovering the New World Columbus Created. Charles Mann, (2011), Vintage.

The follow-up book to *1493* covers the changes post-Columbus starting with the devastating pandemic of smallpox that raced through all the pre-existing and extensive trade routes of the Americas. Smallpox and other European diseases decimated Indigenous people and culture long before the increasing numbers of conquistadors, colonizers, and settlers came to displace, murder, and enslave the Indigenous survivors. We learn how the spread of malaria, cultivation of the potato, tobacco, guano, rubber plants, and sugar cane have disrupted and convulsed the planet and will continue to do so until we make radical changes or live with the consequences of unchecked land exploitation.

The Mississippi River in Maps and Views. Robert Holland, (2008), Rizzoli.

Full-color maps dating from as early as 1524 illustrate the Mississippi River and the cities that grew up on its shores, including New Orleans, Memphis, St. Louis, Minneapolis and St. Paul. Hand drawn maps document the European discovery and exploration of the river (de Soto, Marquette, Jolliet, LaSalle), as well as the subsequent colonization of the Mississippi River valley. Other maps illustrate the many efforts over several centuries to pin down the end points of the Mississippi—its source and mouth. A number of maps present key moments along the Mississippi in times of war (The War of 1812, The Civil War). More recent maps and charts seek a scientific understanding of the river in an attempt to harness and control it.

Disturbing the Mississippi: The Language of Science, Engineering, and River Restoration. Christopher Morris, (2016), *Open Rivers: Rethinking Water, Place, and Community,* Issue 2.

This paper is an excellent review of how we frame river restoration in specialized concept-driven language. Author's Introduction: From top to bottom, projects aimed at restoring the Mississippi River are underway in both deed and word. In the area of the Twin Cities, the U. S. Army Corps of Engineers is dredging pools along the floodplain and using the sediment to construct islands and restore wetland fish and waterfowl habitat. In the area of New Orleans, a coalition of engineers, scientists, and nonprofit organizations is likewise dredging and redirecting sediment in an effort to stem erosion of the Mississippi River delta and the Louisiana coastline. In between the upper- and lower-most portions of the river, conservation groups are restoring a forested floodplain habitat upon the batture, the ribbon of land between the levees and the river. Restoration of river and floodplain habitat in the Mississippi valley is part of a national and international trend. Across the country, decades-old dams are coming down, floodwaters are returning to floodplain, and migratory fish are swimming in streams where they have not been seen in living memory. This discussion includes evolution of the Flood-pulse Concept and gives its primary citations. http://editions. lib.umn.edu/openrivers/article/disturbing-the-mississippi-the-language-of-science-engineering-and-river-restoration/

The Flood Pulse Concept in River-Floodplain Systems. W. Junk, PB Bayley, RE Sparks, (1989), *Canadian Journal of Fisheries and Aquatic Sciences* 106, Conference: International Large River Symposium, At: Honey Harbour, Ontario, Canada

Author's Summary: The flood pulse concept in river-floodplain systems, p. 110-127. In D. P. Dodge [ed.] Proceedings of the International Large River Symposium. Can. Spec. Publ. Fish. Aquat. Sci. 106. The principal driving force responsible for the existence, productivity, and interactions of the major biota in river—floodplain systems is the flood pulse. A spectrum of geomorphological and hydrological conditions produces flood pulses, which range from unpredictable to predictable and from short to long duration. Short and generally unpredictable pulses occur in low-order streams or heavily modified systems with floodplains that have been leveed and drained by man. Because low-order stream pulses are brief and unpredictable, organisms have limited adaptations for directly utilizing the aquatic/terrestrial transition zone (ATTZ), although aquatic organisms benefit indirectly from transport of resources into the lotic environment. Conversely, a predictable pulse of long duration engenders organismic adaptations and strategies that efficiently utilize attributes of the ATTZ. This pulse is coupled with a dynamic edge effect, which extends a "moving littoral" throughout the ATTZ. The moving littoral prevents prolonged stagnation and allows rapid recycling of organic matter and nutrients, thereby resulting in high productivity. Primary production associated with the ATTZ is much higher than that of permanent water bodies in unmodified systems. Fish yields and production are strongly related to the extent of accessible floodplain, whereas the main river is used as a migration route by most of the fishes. In temperate regions, light and/or temperature variations may modify the effects of the pulse, and anthropogenic influences on the flood pulse or floodplain frequently limit production. A local floodplain, however, can develop by sedimentation in a river stretch modified by a low head dam. Borders of slowly flowing rivers turn into floodplain habitats, becoming separated from the main channel by levées. The flood pulse is a "batch" process and is distinct from concepts that emphasize the continuous processes in flowing water environments, such as the river continuum concept. Flood plains are distinct because they do not depend on upstream processing inefficiencies of organic matter, although their nutrient pool is influenced by periodic lateral exchange of water and sediments with the main channel. The pulse concept is distinct because the position of a floodplain within the river network is not a primary determinant of the processes that occur. The pulse concept requires an approach other than the traditional limnological paradigms used in lotic or lentic systems. https://www.researchgate.net/publication/256981220_The_Flood_Pulse_Concept_in_River-Floodplain_Systems

Agricultural Lands: Flooding and Levee Breaches. Kenneth Olson and Lois Morton, (2017), **Encyclopedia of Soil Science, 3rd Edition.** http://www.ngrrec.org/uploadedFiles/Pages/Research_Program/Levee breaches E-ESS3-120053228.pdf

Lewis and Clark through Indian Eyes: Nine Indian Writers on the Legacy of the Expedition. Alvin M. Josephy, (2008), Vintage.

From perspectives as diverse as the Indigenous nations whose lands Meriwether Lewis and William Clark traversed, these nine essays provide a rarely seen view of that colonizing 1803 mission. Josephy had asked the essayists: "What impact, good or bad, immediate or long-range, did the

Indians experience from the Lewis and Clark expedition?" Vine Deloria, Jr., a member of the Standing Rock Sioux Tribe in North Dakota, says that "we often tend to clothe the accounts of Lewis and Clark in more heroic terms than they deserve." Pulitzer Prize-winning Kiowa N. Scott Momaday (*House Made of Dawn*) provides a creative evocation of historic "voices of encounter." Bill Yellowtail, a Crow, sees Lewis and Clark as "envoys for free-trade agreements, long prior to NAFTA and CAFTA and the WTO." Several authors recall oral histories transmitted through older relatives. One such story of the ragged, unwashed, and starving expedition survivors relates their refused offers of Pacific salmon when they reached the west coast holding out for meat including dogs. All along the way they survived on meat, often buying dogs from indigenous people, crashing through village homes uninvited, and being a nuisance to everyone they met. Some fed them only because they felt sorry for them.

4 UPPER MISSISSIPPI RIVER, FERTILITY RITES

Silent Spring, Rachel Carson, (1962, anniversary edition 2002), Houghton Mifflin.
    First serialized in the New Yorker, Carson was vilified for this work by the chemical industry, agri-business, and politicians. The book still stands as an important document that used the best science of her time.

Envisioning Cahokia: a Landscape Perspective. Rinita Dalan et. al., (2003), Northern Illinois University Press.
    The massive earthen mounds of ancient Cahokia in southwestern Illinois form the largest and most complex archaeological site in the United States. Here, at the center of a vibrant Native American culture, a settlement of Mississippian Indians grew, prospered, and declined. Tracing perceptions of the Cahokian landscape from the times of Indians and explorers to the present, *Envisioning Cahokia* details the archaeology of North America›s largest prehistoric urban center. The authors draw on archeology, geography, and natural sciences.

Cahokia Mounds. America's First City. William Ismeninger. (2010, 3rd Edition), The History Press.
    Interpreting the rich heritage of a site like Cahokia Mounds is a balancing act; the interpreter must speak as a scholar to the general public on behalf of an entirely different civilization. William Iseminger's work at the site has given him nearly four decades of on-site practice in interpreting Cahokia to tell the story of the place and its ancient culture as well as its place in contemporary culture.

1491: New Revelations of the Americas Before Columbus. Charles Mann, (2006, 2nd Edition), Vintage
    This book cited in previous chapters has a section devoted to mound builder cultures and Cahokia in particular as the greatest city north of the Rio Grande. Cahokia held a singular mound, now called Monk's Mound, greater than the Great Pyramid of Giza.

Savage Inequalities, Jonathan Kozol, (1991), Crown Publishing.

Kozol visited schools between 1988 and 1990 in burnt-out Camden, NJ, Washington, D.C., New York's South Bronx, Chicago's South Side, San Antonio, Tex., and East St. Louis, Mo. These places were awash in toxins and were 95 to 99 percent nonwhite. Kozol found that racial segregation has intensified since 1954. Even in the suburbs, he charges, the slotting of minority children into lower tracks sets up a differential, two-tier system that diminishes poor children's horizons and aspirations. He lets the pupils and teachers speak for themselves. This important, eye-opening report is a ringing indictment of the shameful neglect that has fostered a ghetto school system in America that exists to this day.

Toxic Wastes and Race at Twenty 1987-2007. Robert Bullard et. al. (2007), Report prepared for the United Church of Christ and Justice and Witness Ministries. https://www.nrdc.org/sites/default/files/toxic-wastes-and-race-at-twenty-1987-2007.pdf

Having Faith: An Ecologist's Journey to Motherhood. Sandra Steingraber, (2012), Decapo Press.

Sandra Steingraber tells the month-by-month story of her own pregnancy, weaving in the new knowledge of embryology, the intricate development of organs, the emerging architecture of the brain, and the transformation of the mother's body to nourish and protect the new life. At the same time, Steingraber shows all the hazards that we are now allowing to threaten each stage of development, including the breast-feeding relationship between mothers and their newborns. In the eyes of an ecologist, the mother's body is the first environment, the mediator between the toxins in our food, water, and air and her unborn child.

DDT and Reproductive Health, J Bonde and G Taft, (2011), *Encyclopedia of Environmental Health.*

This article reviews the evidence up to 2011. Although the research continues and broadens to date, it contains a balanced view of the literature. This article is not free to the public, requires purchase online but the authors can be contacted for a reprint. Authors' Abstract. DDT (dichlorodiphenyltrichloroethane) is an insecticide that was used worldwide in agriculture and for malaria vector control from the 1940s until its ban in many countries in 1970 and in subsequent years, mainly due to its biopersistence and adverse ecological effects. The main components of commercial DDT are its isomers (85%), although dichlorodiphenyldichloroethylene (DDE) and dichlorodiphenyldichloroethane (DDD) are present in small amounts. It has been demonstrated in several *in vitro* and *in vivo* studies that the DDT compounds have the potential to interfere with hormonal homeostasis which has raised concern that the compound impacts human health. o,p'-DDT, which constitutes 15–20% of DDT, and to a lesser extent p,p'-DDT and o,p'-DDE are mimicking the action of the natural ligand, 17-β-estradiol, whereas p,p'-DDE, the main metabolite in living organisms, is antagonizing the natural action of androgens. There have been few studies investigating DDT effects on male reproductive function, but the evidence shows that men living in endemic malaria areas where DDT is still sprayed may have impaired reproductive function. Exposure to DDT has also been linked to early onset of puberty in girls, reduced or increased fertility among daughters, increased risk of spontaneous abortions, premature delivery, small-for-gestational age, and low birth weight, but generally, findings have not been consistent. For instance, an analysis of some 2400 children in the US Collaborative Perinatal Study found a highly significant steadily increasing risk for preterm birth with increasing DDE blood concentration above 10 ppb. Finally, there are reports linking blood DDE or measures of DDT body burden in adults with premature menopause, disturbance of menstrual cycle in terms of reduced luteal cycle length, and delayed conception as a measure of reduced fecundity. https://www.sciencedirect.com/science/article/pii/B9780444522726004049

Persistent Organic Pollutants, World Health Organization, Overview on POPs in food, accessed August 1, 2018. http://www.who.int/foodsafety/areas_work/chemical-risks/pops/en/

Effect of Hormone Disruptor Pesticides: A Review. Wissem Minef, (2011), *International Journal of Environmental Research and Public Health.*

Authors' Abstract. Endocrine disrupting chemicals (EDC) are compounds that alter the normal functioning of the endocrine system of both wildlife and humans. A huge number of chemicals have been identified as endocrine disruptors, among them several pesticides. Pesticides are used to kill unwanted organisms in crops, public areas, homes and gardens, and parasites in medicine. Human are exposed to pesticides due to their occupations or through dietary and environmental exposure (water, soil, air). For several years, there have been enquiries about the impact of environmental factors on the occurrence of human pathologies. This paper reviews the current knowledge of the potential impacts of endocrine disruptor pesticides on human health. https://www.ncbi.nlm.nih.gov/pmc/articles/PMC3138025/

Ch. 2. The History of the Controversy Over the Use of Herbicides. Institute of Medicine Committee to Review the Health Effects in Viet Nam Veterans of Exposure to Herbicides, (1994), National Academies Press.

This chapter reviews the use of herbicides, the early history of the controversy, the concerns that Vietnam veterans have voiced about health problems they believe are related to exposure to herbicides, the Agent Orange product liability litigation, and the response to concerns of Vietnam veterans and the public by the federal government, state governments, veterans organizations, and others. The events and issues surrounding the domestic use of 2,4-D (2,4-dichlorophenoxyacetic acid) and 2,4,5-T (2,4,5-trichlorophenoxyacetic acid) and occupational exposure to 2,4,5-T and its dioxin contaminant are also addressed in this chapter. As a result of several major events relating to dioxin exposure, the public became aware of the potential health effects of exposure to dioxin in tandem with the increased concern over possible health effects of exposure to herbicides sprayed in Vietnam. Researchers studied populations (described in this chapter) that had potential health effects from exposure to herbicides and TCDD, including production workers in chemical plants, agricultural and forestry workers, pulp and paper mill workers, and residents environmentally exposed in specific areas, such as Times Beach, Missouri; Alsea, Oregon; and Seveso, Italy. For the studies introduced in this chapter, the methodological framework is described in Chapter Seven and the results are discussed in the health outcome chapters (8-11). https://www.ncbi.nlm.nih.gov/books/NBK236351/

Fourth National Report on Human Exposure to Environmental Chemicals, (2009), Centers for Disease Control and Prevention. Updated Tables 2018.

This report with its *Updated Tables, March 2018*, presents nationally representative and cumulative biomonitoring data gathered from 1999-2000 through 2015-2016. It also includes all the data from each previous *National Report on Human Exposure to Environmental Chemicals* and each of the previous *Updated Tables*. The *Updated Tables* are represented in two separate volumes: Volume One contains data tables for chemicals measured in the general US population; Volume Two contains data tables for persistent organic pollutants and pesticides measured in pooled samples and adult cigarette smokers and nonsmokers. For additional details, see the Introduction section of the *Updated Tables, Volume One, March 2018*. https://www.cdc.gov/exposurereport/index.html and https://www.cdc.gov/exposurereport/pdf/FourthReport_ExecutiveSummary.pdf

A Plague of Frogs: Unraveling an Environmental Mystery. William Souder, (2002), University of Minnesota Press.

Analyzing the startling 1995 discovery of frog mutations starting in Minnesota and found to occur around the globe, the author discusses the scientific attempt to identify the cause of this problem, an early warning of major environmental catastrophe.

Aquatic Eutrophication Promotes Pathogenic Infection in Amphibians, Peter Johnson et.al., (2007), *Proceedings of the National Academy of Sciences* 104(40):15781-15786.

Authors' Abstract: The widespread emergence of human and wildlife diseases has challenged ecologists to understand how large-scale agents of environmental change affect host–pathogen interactions. Accelerated eutrophication of aquatic ecosystems owing to nitrogen and phosphorus enrichment is a pervasive form of environmental change that has been implicated in the emergence of diseases through direct and indirect pathways. We provide experimental evidence linking eutrophication and disease in a multihost parasite system. The trematode parasite *Ribeiroia ondatrae* sequentially infects birds, snails, and amphibian larvae, frequently causing severe limb deformities and mortality. Eutrophication has been implicated in the emergence of this parasite, but definitive evidence, as well as a mechanistic understanding, have been lacking until now. We show that the effects of eutrophication cascade through the parasite life cycle to promote algal production, the density of snail hosts, and, ultimately, the intensity of infection in amphibians. Infection also negatively affected the survival of developing amphibians. Mechanistically, eutrophication promoted amphibian disease through two distinctive pathways: by increasing the density of infected snail hosts and by enhancing per-snail production of infectious parasites. Given forecasted increases in global eutrophication, amphibian extinctions, and similarities between *Ribeiroia* and important human and wildlife pathogens, our results have broad epidemiological and ecological significance. http://www.pnas.org/content/104/40/15781

Pesticide Mixtures, Endocrine Disruption, and Amphibian Declines: Are We Understanding the Impact?, Hayes, et. al. (2006), *Environmental Health Perspectives, 114 (Supplement 1): 40-50.*

Authors' Abstract: Amphibian populations are declining globally at an alarming rate. Pesticides are among a number of proposed causes for these declines. Although a sizable database examining effects of pesticides on amphibians exists, the vast majority of these studies focus on toxicological effects (lethality, external malformations, etc.) at relatively high doses (parts per million). Very few studies focus on effects such as endocrine disruption at low concentrations. Further, most studies examine exposures to single chemicals only. The present study examined nine pesticides (four herbicides, two fungicides, and three insecticides) used on cornfields in the midwestern United States. Effects of each pesticide alone (0.1 ppb) or in combination were examined. In addition, we also examined atrazine and *S*-metolachlor combined (0.1 or 10 ppb each) and the commercial formulation Bicep II Magnum, which contains both of these herbicides. These two pesticides were examined in combination because they are persistent throughout the year in the wild. We examined larval growth and development, sex differentiation, and immune function in leopard frogs (*Rana pipiens*). In a follow-up study, we also examined the effects of the nine-compound mixture on plasma corticosterone levels in male African clawed frogs (*Xenopus laevis*). Although some of the pesticides individually inhibited larval growth and development, the pesticide mixtures had much greater effects. Larval growth and development were retarded, but most significantly, pesticide mixtures negated or reversed the typically positive correlation between time to metamorphosis and size at metamorphosis observed in controls: exposed larvae that took longer to metamorphose were smaller than their counterparts that metamorphosed earlier. The nine-pesticide mixture also induced damage to the thymus, resulting in immunosuppression and contraction of flavobacterial meningitis. The study in *X. laevis* revealed that these adverse effects may be due to an increase in plasma levels of the stress hormone corticosterone. Although it cannot be determined whether all the pesticides in the mixture contribute to these adverse effects or whether some pesticides are effectors, some are enhancers, and some are neutral, the present study revealed that estimating ecological risk and the impact of pesticides on amphibians using studies that examine only single pesticides at high concentrations may lead to gross underestimations of the role of pesticides in amphibian declines. https://www.ncbi.nlm.nih.gov/pmc/articles/PMC1874187/

Are We In a Male Fertility Death Spiral?, Pete Myers, (2017), *Environmental Health News.*

Article reviews recent evidence of declining male fertility that appears to be amplified over successive generations. https://www.ehn.org/science_are_we_in_a_male_fertility_death_spiral-2497202098.html

Contaminants in the Upper Mississippi, Donald Goolsby and Wilfred Pereira, (1995), USGS Circular.

Authors' Introduction. The Mississippi River basin contains the largest and most intensively farmed region in the Nation. In order to increase yields from crops, large amounts of pesticides are used to protect against weeds, insects, and other pests. The major categories of pesticides are herbicides, insecticides, and fungicides. It is estimated that about two-thirds of all pesticides used for agriculture in the United States are applied to cropland and pasture land in the Mississippi River Basin (Gianessi and Puffer, 1990). The intense use of pesticides is of concern because of potential adverse effects on the quality and use of water resources. The most immediate concerns are for aquatic life and for the 18 million people in the basin who rely on surface-water sources for drinking water.

The report shows the leading pesticides transported by the Mississippi River are atrazine and its metabolites, cyanizine, metolachlor, and alachlor. This report shows levels and substances prior to widespread glyphosphate (Roundup) application and thus remains useful. https://pubs.usgs.gov/circ/circ1133/pesticides.html

Trends in Pesticide Concentrations and Use for Major Rivers of the United States, Karen Ryborg and Robert Gilliom, (2015), USGS, *Science of the Total Environment* 538:431-444.

Thorough study of pesticides including atrazine and its use with corn crops.

Authors' abstract: Trends in pesticide concentrations in 38 major rivers of the United States were evaluated in relation to use trends for 11 commonly occurring pesticide compounds. Pesticides monitored in water were analyzed for trends in concentration in three overlapping periods, 1992–2001, 1997–2006, and 2001–2010 to facilitate comparisons among sites with variable sample distributions over time and among pesticides with changes in use during different periods and durations. Concentration trends were analyzed using the SEAWAVE-Q model, which incorporates intra-annual variability in concentration and measures of long-term, mid-term, and short-term streamflow variability. Trends in agricultural use within each of the river basins were determined using interval-censored regression with high and low estimates of use. Pesticides strongly dominated by agricultural use (cyanazine, alachlor, atrazine and its degradate deethylatrazine, metolachlor, and carbofuran) had widespread agreement between concentration trends and use trends. Pesticides with substantial use in both agricultural and nonagricultural applications (simazine, chlorpyrifos, malathion, diazinon, and carbaryl) had concentration trends that were mostly explained by a combination of agricultural-use trends, regulatory changes, and urban use changes inferred from concentration trends in urban streams. When there were differences, concentration trends usually were greater than use trends (increased more or decreased less). These differences may occur because of such factors as unaccounted pesticide uses, delayed transport to the river through groundwater, greater uncertainty in the use data, or unquantified land use and management practice changes. https://water.usgs.gov/nawqa/pnsp/MajorRiverTrends.STOTEN.2015.pdf

Midwest Maize: How Corn Shaped the US Heartland, Cynthia Clampitt, (2015), University of Illinois Press.

Food historian Cynthia Clampitt describes the history of maize from when Mesoamerican farmers bred a nondescript grass into a staff of life so prolific, so protean, that it represents nothing less than one of humankind's greatest achievements. Blending history with expert reportage, she traces the disparate threads that have woven corn into the fabric of our diet, politics, economy, science, and cuisine.

Nature's Metropolis: Chicago and the Great West. William Cronon, (1992), W. W. Norton and Co.

This book examines key factors in the genesis of the widespread effects of a single city on millions of square miles of ecological, cultural, and economic frontier. Cronon combines archival accuracy, ecological evaluation, and a sweeping understanding of the impact of railroads, stockyards, catalog companies, and patterns of property on the design and development of the entire inland United States to this date. Cronon is considered the foremost environmental historian in the US and this book provides evidence of his mastery of the subject.

Endangered Rivers and the Conservation Movement, Tim Palmer, (2004), Rowman and Littlefield.

Rivers have played a major role in giving form to the American conservation movement, and perhaps the single most enduring virtue of Tim Palmer's book is that he documents this fact with greater clarity and detail than anyone before him has ever attempted; he has written what can only be described as the definitive work on the subject. A tremendously important addition to the literature of conservation. —*Orion*

First Along the River, Benjamin Kline, (2011 fourth edition), Rowman and Littlefield.

First Along the River provides a condensed historical perspective on the environmental movement in relation to major social and political events in US history, from the pre-colonial era to the present. The book highlights important people and events, places critical concepts in context, and shows the impact of government, industry, and population on the American landscape.

A Fierce Green Fire: The American Environmental Movement, Phillip Shabecoff, (2003), Island Press.

Even with present-day challenges for environmental preservation, restoration, regulation, and action, Shabecoff's history of the environmental movement remains important to understanding forces at work before the previous decade. The author traces the ecological transformation of North America as a result of the mass migration of Europeans to the New World, showing how the environmental impulse slowly formed among a growing number of Americans until, by the last third of the twentieth century, environmentalism emerged as a major social and cultural movement. The efforts of key environmental figures—among them Henry David Thoreau, George Perkins Marsh, Theodore Roosevelt, Gifford Pinchot, John Muir, Aldo Leopold, David Brower, Barry Commoner, and Rachel Carson—are examined. So, too, are the activities of non-governmental environmental groups as well as government agencies such as the EPA and Interior Department, along with grassroots efforts of Americans in communities across the country.

David Brower: The Making of the Environmental Movement, Tom Turner, (2015), University of California Press.

In this first comprehensive authorized biography of David Brower, a dynamic leader in the environmental movement over the last half of the twentieth century, Tom Turner explores Brower's impact on the movement from its beginnings until his death in 2000. Frequently compared to John Muir, David Brower was the first executive director of the Sierra Club, founded Friends of the Earth, and helped secure passage of the Wilderness Act, among other key achievements. Tapping his passion for wilderness and for the mountains he scaled in his youth, he was a central figure in the creation of the Point Reyes National Seashore and of the North Cascades and Redwood national parks. In addition, Brower worked tirelessly in successful efforts to keep dams from being built in Dinosaur National Monument and the Grand Canyon. Tom Turner began working with David Brower in 1968 and remained close to him until Brower's death. As an insider, Turner creates an intimate portrait of Brower the man and the decisive role he played in the development of the environmental movement. Culling material from Brower's diaries, notebooks, articles, books, and published interviews, and conducting his own interviews with many of Brower's admirers, opponents, and colleagues, Turner brings to life one of the movement's most controversial and complex figures.

Encounters with the Archdruid: Narratives about a Conservationist and Three of His Natural Enemies. John McPhee, (1980), Farrar, Straus, and Giroux.

"Brower was in the thick of battle when John McPhee profiled him for the *New Yorker* in a piece that would evolve into *Encounters with the Archdruid*. McPhee follows Brower into unusually close combat as Brower faces down a geologist who is, it seems, convinced that there is no sight quite so elevating as that of a fully operational mine; a developer who (successfully, it turned out) sought to convert an isolated stretch of the Carolina coast into a resort for the moneyed few—and who provided the title for McPhee's book, wryly opining that conservationists are at heart druids who 'sacrifice people and worship trees'; and, most formidable of all, former Interior Secretary Floyd Dominy, who oversaw the construction of a structure that for Brower stands as one of the most hated creations of our time, Glen Canyon Dam on the Colorado River. McPhee offers up an engaging portrait of Brower, a man unafraid of a good fight in the service of the earth, making *Encounters* an important contribution to the history of the modern environmental movement."—*Gregory McNamee*

The Sea Around Us, Rachel Carson, (2003, first published 1951), Oxford University Press.

Before *Silent Spring*, there were other popular books, *The Sea Around Us* perhaps the most well known. Her success as a science writer put her in a strong position for her work on the effects of pesticides presented in *Silent Spring.*

Braiding Sweet Grass: Indigenous Wisdom, Scientific Knowledge, and the Teachings of Plants. Robin Wall Kimmerer, (2013), Milkweed.

As a botanist, Robin Wall Kimmerer has been trained to ask questions of nature with the tools of science. As a member of the Citizen Potawatomi Nation, she embraces the notion that plants and animals are our oldest teachers. In *Braiding Sweetgrass*, Kimmerer brings these two lenses of knowledge together to take us on "a journey that is every bit as mythic as it is scientific, as sacred as it is historical, as clever as it is wise"—Elizabeth Gilbert.

Grass Soil Hope: A Journey Through Carbon Country, Courtney White, (2014), Chelsea Green Publishing.

Scientists maintain that a mere 2 percent increase in the carbon content of the planet's soils could offset *100 percent* of all greenhouse gas emissions going into the atmosphere. Author Courtney White says it is not only possible, but *essential* for the long-term health and sustainability of our environment and our economy. Right now, the only possibility of large-scale removal of greenhouse gases from the atmosphere is through plant photosynthesis and related land-based carbon sequestration activities. These include a range of already existing, low-tech, and proven practices: composting, no-till farming, climate-friendly livestock practices, conserving natural habitat, restoring degraded watersheds and rangelands, increasing biodiversity, and producing local food.

5 HUDSON RIVER: SALT FRONT OF THE RIVER THAT FLOWS BOTH WAYS

Running Silver: Restoring Atlantic Rivers and their Great Fish Migrations. John Waldman. (2013), Lyons Press.

John Waldman hears the cries of the fish as Thoreau once did. *"Running Silver* is a deeply important book that highlights the ancient exchange of biomass from land to sea and back again-through our finned creatures.... an impassioned plea, a call to action, a book that everyone should know about and read," writes James Prosek-artist and writer, author of *Eels: An Exploration from New Zealand to the Sargasso of the World's most Mysterious Fish.*

Heartbeats in the Muck: The History, Sea Life, and Environment of NY Harbor. John Waldman. (2012). Empire State Editions.

An intimate look at New York Harbor's incredible arc of history, from pristine animal abundances to the suffocation of marine life, and ultimately to an ongoing but surprisingly hopeful recovery.

The Cooperation Challenge of Economics and the Protection of Water Supplies: a Case Study of the NYC Watershed Collaboration. Joan Hoffman, (2010), Routledge.

Historical experience and lessons from other watershed collaborations informed the design of New York City's complex watershed collaboration which is shown to contain the elements of a "green milieu" that can foster sustainable economic development. The particular challenges to the collaboration's environmental and economic goals created by the watershed's rural economy, farming and forestry are described.

The unusual inclusion of the analysis of the economic aspects and effects of collaboration, of the relationship between collaboration and sustainable development, and of the processes of implementation and conflict make this book especially valuable to those interested in collaboration, regulation, environmental cooperation and conflict, watershed protection, economic development in general, and sustainable economic development in particular.

American Earth: Environmental Writing Since Thoreau, Bill McKibbon, Editor (2008), Library of America.

McKibben's selection of more than 100 writers includes some of the great early conservationists, such as Henry David Thoreau, John Muir and John Burroughs, and many other eloquent nature writers, including Donald Cultross Peattie, Edwin Way Teale and Henry Beston. The early exponents of national parks and wilderness areas have their say, as do writers who have borne witness to environmental degradation-John Steinbeck and

Caroline Henderson on the dust bowl, for example, and Berton Roueché and others who have reported on the effects of toxic pollution. Visionaries like Buckminster Fuller and Amory Lovins are represented, as are a wealth of contemporary activist/writers, among them Barry Lopez, Terry Tempest Williams, Barbara Kingsolver, Michael Pollan, Paul Hawken, and Calvin deWitt, cofounder of the Evangelical Environmental Network. McKibben's trenchant introductions to the pieces sum up each writer's thoughts and form a running commentary on the progress of the conservation movement.

A Fierce Green Fire: the American Environmental Movement. Phillip Shabecoff. (2003), Island Press, revised edition.

Shabecoff traces the ecological transformation of North America as a result of the mass migration of Europeans to the New World, showing how the environmental impulse slowly formed among a growing number of Americans until, by the last third of the twentieth century, environmentalism emerged as a major social and cultural movement. The efforts of key environmental figures—among them Henry David Thoreau, George Perkins Marsh, Theodore Roosevelt, Gifford Pinchot, John Muir, Aldo Leopold, David Brower, Barry Commoner, and Rachel Carson—are examined. So, too, are the activities of non-governmental environmental groups as well as government agencies such as the EPA and Interior Department, along with grassroots efforts of Americans in communities across the country.

Before Earth Day: The Origins of American Environmental Law 1945-1970. Karl Boyd Brooks (2009), University of Kansas Press.

While major strides in formal environmental law were made with the landmark Storm King settlement case from 1963 to 1981, there are earlier precedents that informed these laws. "Should be required reading in every environmental law class as an antidote to the belief that the subject began in 1969. It deftly demonstrates that all of the elements of environmental law evolved during the quarter century after the end of World War II."—Dale Goble, author of *Wildlife Law: A Primer*

The Riverkeepers: Two Activists Fight to Reclaim Our Environment as a Basic Human Right, John Cronin and Robert F. Kennedy, Jr. (1999), Scribner.

Cronin and Kennedy describe their dramatic confrontations with more than ninety environmental lawbreakers. *The Riverkeepers* remains timely call to action that resonates across America as the backlash spearheaded by congressional leaders and their major corporate allies threatens to reverse the hard-won victories in environmental law and policy.

The Hudson River: A Natural and Unnatural History. Robert Boyle, (1979), Norton.

Bob Boyle, who died in 2017 at age 88, was a living repository of knowledge of the Hudson, much of it not available in more recent books. Carl Carmer wrote in The New York Times Book Review: "It can safely be said that Mr. Boyle knows more about his subject—the wide stream by which he and his family live—than any other living man." His Fishermen's Association, founded in 1966, evolved in 1983 into Riverkeeper, inspired by the British concept of appointing guardians of private fishing grounds. Since then, the group has been a model for others around the world as part of the Waterkeeper Alliance, an umbrella group.

The Hudson: An Illustrated Guide to a Living River. Stephen P. Stanne et. al. (1996), Rutgers.

This richly illustrated volume covers the Hudson's natural history and human heritage. It introduces the Hudson's diversity of plants and wildlife, the geological forces that created the river, the people who explored and settled on its banks, and the river's place in American history and art.

Toms River: A Story of Science and Salvation. Dan Fagin, (2013), Bantam.

Toms River on coastal New Jersey, about 75 miles from N Y Harbor, sits in a different watershed than the Hudson. It became a chemical industry hotspot decades ago. This story is important to environmental epidemiology, a story repeated in so many places. It begins with a higher than expected number of childhood cancer cases identified in the 1990s that ignited a series of investigations into contamination of Toms River, New Jersey. Fagin's book, *Toms River,* unravels the destructive environmental practices that damaged a community. The book goes beyond the Toms River phenomenon itself to examine the many factors that came together in that one spot, from the birth of the synthetic chemical industry to the evolution of epidemiology and the physicians who fostered occupational and environmental medicine. Toms River is also a place so many marine animals feed and travel through on their way to the Hudson. "It's high time a book did for epidemiology what Jon Krakauer's best-selling *Into Thin Air* did for mountain climbing: transform a long sequence of painfully plodding steps and missteps into a narrative of such irresistible momentum that the reader not only understands what propels enthusiasts forward, but begins to strain forward as well, racing through the pages to get to the heady views at the end. . . . a sober story of probability and compromise, laid out with the care and precision that characterizes both good science and great journalism."—*The New York Times*

Changes in the Land: Indians, Colonists, and the Ecology of New England. William Cronon, (1983), Hill and Wang.

In this landmark work of environmental history, William Cronon offers an original and profound explanation of the effects European colonists' sense of property and their pursuit of capitalism had upon the ecosystems of New England.

Making Mountains: New York City and the Catskills. David Stradling, (2010), University of Washington Press.

"*Making Mountains* is the finest modern history yet written of the Catskills-a chain of mountains that looms far larger in the national consciousness than one might think possible given their limited extent and modest height. And yet, because of the Catskills special relationship to New York City, they became in the early nineteenth century the principal vehicle for helping Americans understand the meaning of the romantic sublime, and so shaped all subsequent American thinking about nature. David Stradling's book should interest anyone seeking to understand how rural and urban Americans have worked together to reinvent and reinterpret our national landscape." —William Cronon, University of Wisconsin-Madison

Gotham: A History of New York City to 1898. Edwin Burrows and Mike Wallace, (1998), Oxford University Press.

The authors have synthesized histories from various perspectives, cultural, economic, political, etc. into a novelistic narrative, providing the context for stories of the diverse denizens who shaped the city. Both New York academics (Brooklyn College and CUNY, respectively), Burrows and Wallace have produced a historical work that merits the term "definitive" yet still manages to entertain. Underneath reasoned academic prose lies a populist bent, unflinching in relating ugly events and describing the unsavory behavior of prominent figures; in its original sense, "Gotham" denotes a town of tricksters and fools, and this book is full of both.—Publisher's Weekly

Greater Gotham: A History of New York City from 1898 to 1919. Mike Wallace, (2017), Oxford University Press.

In this follow-up to *Gotham,* Mike Wallace captures the swings of prosperity and downturn, from the 1898 skyscraper-driven boom to the Bankers' Panic of 1907, the labor upheaval, and violent repression during and after the First World War. Here is New York on a whole new scale, moving from national to global prominence—an urban dynamo driven by restless ambition, boundless energy, immigrant dreams, and Wall Street greed.

The Island at the Center of the World: The Epic Story of Dutch Manhattan and the Forgotten Colony that Shaped America. Russell Shorto, (2005), Vintage.

When the British wrested New Amsterdam from the Dutch in 1664, the truth about its thriving, polyglot society began to disappear into myths about an island purchased for 24 dollars and a cartoonish peg-legged governor. But the story of the Dutch colony of New Netherland was rewritten by the victors but not entirely destroyed: 12,000 pages of its records are now being translated. Drawing on this remarkable archive, Russell Shorto has created a gripping narrative-a story of global sweep centered on a wilderness called Manhattan-that transforms our understanding of early America. The Dutch colony was cosmopolitan and multi-ethnic, valued free trade, individual rights, and religious freedom, although their record with Indigenous people was appalling. A progressive, young lawyer named Adriaen van der Donck, emerges in these pages as a forgotten thinker who learned from Native people and whose political vision brought him into conflict with Peter Stuyvesant, the autocratic director of the Dutch colony. The struggle between these two men laid the earliest foundation for New York City prior to British rule. —Publisher's summary.

Mannahatta: A Natural History of New York City. Eric Sanderson et. al. (2013), Abrams Books.

In this brilliantly illustrated volume, Sanderson and Boyer recreate the ecology of Manhattan as it was that 1609 September afternoon when Henry Hudson first saw it, "prodigious in its abundance, resplendent in its diversity." The project began as a simple thought exercise, when senior Bronx Zoo ecologist Sanderson (Human Footprint: Challenges for Wilderness and Biodiversity) tried visualizing pre-colonial Manhattan, but was promoted to full-blown science project after Sanderson discovered an "extraordinary" 1776 British Headquarters Map detailing the island's natural terrain. Developing a "georeference" system to coordinate the old map, Sanderson "relates its depiction of the old hills and valleys to their modern addresses." From there, he reconstructs data missing from the historical record using standard scientific tools-examining pollen layers, tree rings, archeological information, etc. Sanderson's text integrates political and sociological history; examines the culture of the original inhabitants, the Lenape (their word Mannahatta means "Island of Many Hills"); and covers a wealth of ecological data. —Publisher's Weekly

The Founding Fish. John McPhee, (2003 reprint edition), Farrar, Straus, and Giroux.

John McPhee's twenty-sixth book is a braid of personal history, natural history, and American history, in descending word count order. Each spring, American shad—*Alosa sapidissima*—leave the ocean in hundreds of thousands and run upriver to spawn. "The *Founding Fish* is . . . far more than a fishing book. It is a mini-encyclopedia, a highly informative and entertaining amalgam of natural and personal history, a work in a class by itself." —*Robert H. Boyle, The New York Times Book Review*

The Works: Anatomy of a City. Kate Ascher, (2007), Penguin, Reprint Edition.

Using New York City as its point of reference, *The Works* takes readers down manholes and behind the scenes to explain exactly how an urban infrastructure operates. Deftly weaving text and graphics, author Kate Ascher explores the systems that manage water, traffic, sewage and garbage, subways, electricity, mail, and much more. *The Works* gives readers a unique glimpse at what lies behind and beneath urban life in the twenty-first century.

Liquid Assets: A History of New York City's Water System, Expanded Edition. Diane Galusha, (2016), Purple Mountain Press.

Diane Galusha presents an extraordinary collection of facts with photos on the history of NYC's water system, especially in the Catskills. Many of the photos are of low quality but historically important and not included in other histories or public collections.

Water for Gotham: A History. Gerard Koeppel, (2000), Princeton University Press.

From its founding as New Amsterdam in 1624 until 1850, Manhattan was plagued by disasters related to water that killed thousands of residents in unrestrained outbreaks of infectious diseases, including small pox, yellow fever and cholera, and uncontrolled fires that destroyed blocks of stores and residences. Koeppel, relying on primary documents, diaries, personal histories and maps, charts the internecine schemes and failed business ventures to alleviate the island's water problems, from Christopher Colles' attempt to build a reservoir in 1774 to Aaron Burr's fraudulent 1789 Manhattan Company (which never delivered promised water but did become the hugely successful Chase Manhattan bank), to John Jevis's successful 1850 project to divert the waters of the Croton River into the rapidly growing city using a complex set of aqueducts and waterworks. The book centers on the rise of the Croton system.

Blessed Unrest: How the Largest Social Movement in History Is Restoring Grace, Justice, and Beauty to the World. Paul Hawken, (2007), Penguin Books.

Environmentalist Hawken believes that we are in the midst of a world-changing rise of activist groups, all "working toward ecological sustainability and social justice." Rather than an ideological or centralized movement, this coalescence is a spontaneous and organic response to the recognition that environmental problems are social-justice problems. Writing with zest, clarity, and a touch of wonder, Hawken compares this gathering of forces to the human immune system. Just as antibodies rally when the body is under threat, people are joining together to defend life on Earth. Hawken offers a fascinating history of our perception of nature and human rights and assesses the role indigenous cultures are playing in the quest for ecological responsibility and economic fairness. Hawken also presents an unprecedented map to this new "social landscape" that includes a classification system defining astonishingly diverse concerns, ranging from farming to child welfare, ocean preservation, and beyond. Fresh and informative, Hawken's inspired overview charts much that is right in the world.
—Donna Seaman, Booklist

Empire of Water: An Environmental and Political History of the New York City Water Supply. David Soll, (2013), Cornell University Press.

Almost as soon as New York City completed its first municipal water system in 1842, it began to expand the network, eventually reaching far into the Catskill Mountains, more than one hundred miles from the city. *Empire of Water* explores the history of New York City's water system from the late nineteenth century to the early twenty-first century, focusing on the geographical, environmental, and political repercussions of the city's search for more water. Soll reveals the tremendous shifts in environmental practices and consciousness that occurred during the twentieth century. Few episodes better capture the long-standing upstate-downstate divide in New York than the story of how mountain water came to flow from spigots in Brooklyn and Manhattan. Soll concludes by focusing on the landmark watershed protection agreement signed in 1997 between the city, watershed residents, environmental organizations, and the state and federal governments.

Behind the Scenes: The Inside Story of the Watershed Agreement. Nancy Burnett, (1997-2003), an oral history project partially funded by an Education Grant from the Catskills Watershed Corporation in partnership with the NYC DEP. Read transcripts and hear audio excerpts from all 12 interviews, conducted in the late 1990s and early 2000s by Nancy Burnett Productions, with assistance from Virginia Scheer. This series offers insights into the complicated negotiations, leaders in the agreement many of whom are underappreciated or not credited in public news stories, i.e. less Bobby Kennedy, Jr. and Al Appleton and more Marilyn Gelber. http://cwconline. org/a-history-of-the-moa/

New York's Piermont Marsh: A 7,000-year Archive of Climate Change, Human Impact, and Uncovered Mysteries. Dorothy Peteet. (2009), video Lamont-Doherty Observatory, Columbia University Earth Institute.

Digging deep into tidal marshes one discovers their important role as recorders of major environmental change in the Hudson Valley. Taking sediment cores and analyzing the peat, we count pollen grains, plant macrofossils, and charcoal —all of which document the dramatic and abrupt shifts in the Hudson Valley's regional climate such as the Medieval Warming drought that occurred between 800-1350 of the Common Era. Other studies show the impacts of human disturbance since the 1600s, such as the effects of regional forest clearance and the resulting spread of invasive species. https:// www.ldeo.columbia.edu/video/new-yorks-piermont-marsh

Late-glacial to early Holocene climate changes from a central Appalachian pollen and macrofossil record. M. Kneller and D. Peteet. *Quaternary Research,* (1999), 51:133-147.

A late-glacial to early Holocene record of pollen, plant macrofossils, and charcoal has been obtained from two cores from Browns Pond in the central Appalachians of Virginia. An AMS radiocarbon chronology defines the timing of moist and cold excursions, superimposed on the overall warming trend from 14,200 to 7500 C-14 yr B.P. This site had cold, moist conditions from ca. 14,200 to 12,700 C-14 yr B.P., with warming at 12,730, 11,280, and 10,050 C-14 yr B.P. A decrease in deciduous broadleaved tree taxa and Pinus strobus (haploxylon) pollen, simultaneous with a reexpansion of Abies, denotes a brief, cold reversal from 12,260 to 12,200 C-14 yr B.P. A second cold reversal, inferred from increases in montana conifers, is centered at 7500 C-14 yr B.P. The cold reversals at Browns Pond may be synchronous with climate change in Greenland and northwestern Europe. Warming at 11,280 C-14 yr B.P. shows the complexity of regional climate responses during the Younger Dryas chrono-zone.

Sensitivity and rapidity of vegetational response to abrupt climate change. Dorothy Peteet, (2000), *Proceedings of the National Academy of Sciences* 97:1359-1361.

Rapid climate change characterizes numerous terrestrial sediment records during and since the last glaciation. Vegetational response is best expressed in terrestrial records near ecotones where sensitivity to climate change is greatest, and response times are as short as decades.

Responding to Climate Change in New York. New York State Energy and Research and Development Authority (NYSERDA).

A final report in 2011 is available on the website along with updates, access to datasets, and other information. Also, NY Department of Environment Conservation (DEC) has an on-going program and web presence. https://www.nyserda.ny.gov/About/Publications/Research%20and%20 Development%20Technical%20Reports/Environmental%20Research%20 and%20Development%20Technical%20Reports/Response%20to%20 Climate%20Change%20in%20New%20York and http://www.dec.ny.gov/ energy/44992.html

Brilliant: The Evolution of Artificial Light. Jane Brox, (2010), Mariner Books.

Brox plumbs the class implications of light—who had it, who didn't—through the many centuries when crude lamps and tallow candles constricted waking hours. She convincingly portrays the hell-bent pursuit of whale oil as the first time the human desire for light thrust us toward an environmental tipping point. Only decades later, gas street lights opened up the evening hours to leisure, which changed the ways we live and sleep and the world's ecosystems. The first public application of the electric light bulb occurred in Menlo Park, NJ. Edison's "tiny strip of paper that a breath would blow away" produced a light that seemed to its users all but divorced from human effort or cost, and became integral to the rapid rise of NYC, the city that never sleeps. And yet, as Brox's informative portrait of our current grid system shows, the cost is ever with us.

The Last of the Handmade Dams: The Story of the Ashokan Reservoir. Bob Strueding, (1989), Purple Mountain Press.

The Last of the Handmade Dams tells the story of building New York City's first great Catskill Mountain Reservoir, largely built by pick-and-shovel work. It was a triumph of engineering but with profound consequences for more than 2,000 persons in the flooded Ashokan Valley. Eleven communities were razed for the mammoth project and graves were disinterred and relocated. The story is told in all aspects: political, social, engineering. It tells of immigrant laborers and their problems, of the dislocations and the lore of the drowned valley as the waters rose.

6 CHATTAHOOCHEE: THE RIVER OF PAINTED ROCKS

River Song: A Journey Down the Chattahoochee and Apalachicola Rivers.
Joe Cook and Monica Cook. (2000), University of Alabama Press.

In 1995 photographers Joe and Monica Cook explored the length of the Chattahoochee and the Apalachicola rivers in a source-to-sea journey. This book presents a photographic record of this trip, presenting an impassioned plea for the preservation of this waterway.

Living in the Woods in a Tree: Remembering Blaze Foley. Sybil Rosen, (2017 reprint edition), University of North Texas Press.

In a work that is part-memoir, part-biography, Rosen comes to terms with Foley's myth and her role in its creation. Her tracing of his impact on her life navigates a lovers' roadmap along the permeable boundary between life and death. A must-read for all Blaze Foley and Texas music fans, as well as romantics of all ages, *Living in the Woods in a Tree* is an honest and compassionate portrait of the troubled artist. Just as important as Blaze's story is that of Sybil who with clear introspection and courage takes steps away from Blaze to engage her own path as a writer and actor. She co-wrote the script and plays her own mother in Ethan Hawke's film, *Blaze.*

Waterborne outbreaks reported in the United States. Michael Craun et. al. (2006), *J. Water and Health.*

Authors' summary: Although the true incidence of waterborne illness is not reflected in the currently reported outbreak statistics, outbreak surveillance has provided information about the important waterborne pathogens, relative degrees of risk associated with water sources and treatment processes, and adequacy of regulations. Pathogens and water system deficiencies that are identified in outbreaks may also be important causes of endemic waterborne illness. In recent years, investigators have identified a large number of pathogens responsible for outbreaks, and research has focused on their sources, resistance to water disinfection, and removal from drinking water. Outbreaks in surface water systems have decreased in the recent decade, most likely due to recent regulations and improved treatment efficacy. Of increased importance, however, are outbreaks caused by the microbial contamination of water distribution systems. In order to better estimate waterborne risks in the United States, additional information is needed about the contribution of distribution system contaminants to endemic waterborne risks and undetected waterborne outbreaks, especially those associated with distribution system contaminants. http://courses.washington.edu/h2owaste/group1.pdf

Toxic Wastes and Race at Twenty 1987-2007. Robert Bullard et. al. (2007), Report prepared for the United Church of Christ and Justice and Witness Ministries. https://www.nrdc.org/sites/default/files/toxic-wastes-and-race-at-twenty-1987-2007.pdf

Dumping in Dixie: Race, Class, and Environmental Quality. Robert D. Bullard, (2000) Westview Press, (3rd Edition).

Starting with the premise that all Americans have a basic right to live in a healthy environment, *Dumping in Dixie* chronicles the efforts of five African American communities, empowered by the civil rights movement, to link environmentalism with issues of social justice. In the third edition, Bullard speaks to us from the front lines of the environmental justice movement about new developments in environmental racism, different organizing strategies, and success stories in the struggle for environmental equity.

The Quest for Environmental Justice: Human Rights and the Politics of Pollution. Robert Bullard and Maxine Waters, (2005), Counterpoint Press.

"Robert Bullard, whose scholarship created a whole field of study, continues to expand on our understanding of the environmental justice movement. In *The Quest for Environmental Justice*, Dr. Bullard has assembled a group of experts dedicated to eradicating the injustices suffered by people of color, indigenous peoples, and the poor. This volume presents more than 'the empirical evidence'; its focus is on the day-to-day struggles of those engaged in the environmental justice movement. It demonstrates our hopes and victories, our frustrations and defeats, our commitment to basic human rights and social justice." —David E. Camacho, Ph.D., Professor of Political Science and editor of *Environmental Injustices, Political Struggles: Race, Class, and the Environment*

The New Jim Crow: Mass Incarceration in the Age of Colorblindness. Michelle Alexander, (2012), The New Press.

Legal scholar Michelle Alexander argues that "we have not ended racial caste in America; we have merely redesigned it." By targeting black men through the War on Drugs and decimating communities of color, the US criminal justice system functions as a contemporary system of racial control—relegating millions to a permanent second-class status—even as it formally adheres to the principle of colorblindness. In the words of Benjamin Todd Jealous, president and CEO of the NAACP, this book is a "call to action." This especially applies now with a federal administration that does not even pretend to be colorblind but is openly racist.

Achievements in 1900-1999: Control of Infectious Diseases. Centers for Disease Control and Prevention (1999), *Morbidity and Mortality Weekly Report,* July 30, 1999, 48: 621-629

This report briefly summarizes major public health actions related to the decline in infectious diseases in the US including a graph of infectious disease mortality against major events such as municipal water supply chlorination, first use of penicillin, etc. It also graphs mortality by cause for 1900 and 1997 with data based on peer-reviewed papers. https://www.cdc.gov/mmwr/preview/mmwrhtml/mm4829a1.htm

Ecological Restoration and Management of Longleaf Pine Forests. L Katherine Kirkman and Steven Jackman, (2017), CRC Press.

Ecological Restoration and Management of Longleaf Pine Forests is a timely synthesis of the current understanding of the natural dynamics and processes in longleaf pine ecosystems. This book illustrates how incorporation of basic ecosystem knowledge and an understanding of socioeconomic realities shed new light on established paradigms and their application for restoration and management. Unique for its holistic ecological focus, rather than a more traditional silvicultural approach, the book highlights the importance of multi-faceted actions that robustly integrate forest and wildlife conservation at landscape scales, and merge ecological with socioeconomic objectives for effective conservation of the longleaf pine ecosystem. Recommended for graduate level text. The second hyperlink below is a more general description of the book and the participation of the Joseph W. Jones Ecological Center at Ichauway. https://www.crcpress.com/Ecological-Restoration-and-Management-of-Longleaf-Pine-Forests/Kirkman-Jack/p/book/9781498748186.

Book announcement and short review here: https://www.srs.fs.usda.gov/compass/2018/05/03/new-book-on-restoring-longleaf-pine-ecosystems/

Ecology of a Cracker Childhood (The World as Home). Janisse Ray. (2000), Milkwood Editions.

Janisse Ray grew up in a junkyard along US Highway 1, hidden from Florida-bound vacationers by the hedge at the edge of the road and by hulks of old cars and stacks of blown-out tires. Ecology of a Cracker Childhood tells how a childhood spent in rural isolation and steeped in religious fundamentalism grew into a passion to save the almost vanished longleaf pine ecosystem that once covered the South. In language at once colloquial, elegiac, and informative, Ray redeems two Souths. "Suffused with the same history-haunted sense of loss that imprints so much of the South and its literature. What sets *Ecology of a Cracker Childhood* apart is the ambitious and arresting mission implied in its title. . . . Heartfelt and refreshing." —The New York Times Book Review.

In Philadelphia thirty years ago, an eruption of illness and fear. Lawrence Altman, (2006), New York Times.

Altman, a former CDC EIS (epidemic intelligence service) and a news reporter, recounts the events of the officer Philadelphia Legionnaire's disease outbreak. https://www.nytimes.com/2006/08/01/health/01docs.html?_r=0

Epidemiology and Ecology of Opportunistic Premise Plumbing Pathogens: Legionella pneumophilia, Mycobacterium avium, and Psuedomonas aeruginosa. Joseph Falkinham et. al., (2015), *Environmental Health Perspectives* 123:749-758.

The objectives of this report are to alert professionals of the impact of OPPPs, the fact that 30% of the population may be exposed to OPPPs, and the need to develop means to reduce OPPP exposure. We herein present a review of the epidemiology and ecology of these three bacterial OPPPs, specifically to identify common and unique features. https://www.ncbi.nlm. nih.gov/pubmed/25793551

Legionnaire's Disease Outbreaks, list in Wikipedia—adequate list without combing through the extensive and growing world literature on outbreak investigations. https://en.wikipedia.org/wiki/List_of_ Legionnaires%27_disease_outbreaks—Worldwide_listings_by_year

The Global Challenge of Malaria: Past Lessons and Future Challenges. Frank Snowden and Richard Bucala—Editors, (2014), World Scientific Publications.

Malaria is one of the most important "emerging" or "resurgent" infectious diseases. According to the World Health Organization, this mosquito-borne infection is a leading cause of suffering, death, poverty, and underdevelopment in the world today. Every year 500 million people become severely ill from malaria and more than a million people die, the great majority of them women and children living in sub-Saharan Africa. In 2008, it was estimated a child would die of the disease every thirty seconds, making malaria—together with HIV/AIDS and tuberculosis—a global public health emergency. This is in stark contrast to the heady visions of the 1950s predicting complete global eradication of the ancient scourge. What went wrong? This question warrants a closer look at not just the disease itself, but its long history and the multitude of strategies to combat its spread. This book collects the many important milestones in malaria control. Importantly, it also traces the history of the disease from the 1920s to the present, and over several continents. It is the first multidisciplinary volume of its kind combining historical and scientific information that addresses the global challenge of malaria control.

Mosquito Empires: Ecology and War in the Greater Caribbean 1620-1914. J. R. McNeill, (2010), Cambridge University Press.

This book explores the links among ecology, disease, and international politics in the context of the Greater Caribbean—the landscapes lying between Surinam and the Chesapeake—in the seventeenth through early twentieth centuries. Ecological changes made these landscapes especially suitable for the vector mosquitoes of yellow fever and malaria, and these diseases wrought systematic havoc among armies and would-be settlers. Because yellow fever confers immunity on survivors of the disease, and because malaria confers resistance, these diseases played partisan roles in the struggles for empire and revolution, attacking some populations more severely than others. In particular, yellow fever and malaria attacked newcomers to the region, which helped keep the Spanish Empire Spanish in the face of predatory rivals in the seventeenth and early eighteenth centuries. In the late eighteenth and through the nineteenth century, these diseases helped revolutions to succeed by decimating forces sent out from Europe to prevent them.

Mosquito soldiers: Malaria, Yellow Fever, and the Course of the American Civil War. Andrew Bell, (2010), LSU Press.

Of the 620,000 soldiers who perished during the American Civil War, the overwhelming majority died not from gunshot wounds or saber cuts, but from disease. In this thorough medical history, Andrew McIlwaine Bell explores the impact of two primary mosquito-borne maladies—malaria and yellow fever—on the major political and military events of the 1860s, revealing how deadly microorganisms carried by a tiny insect were a major factor in the course of the Civil War.

House on Fire: *The Fight to Eradicate Smallpox.* William Foege, (2011), University of California Press.

A story of courage and risk-taking, *House on Fire* tells how smallpox, a disease that killed, blinded, and scarred millions over centuries of human history, was eradicated in human populations, although it still exists in laboratories, as a spectacular triumph of medicine and public health. Part autobiography, part mystery, the story is told by a man who was one of the architects of a radical vaccination scheme that became a key strategy in ending the disease when it was finally contained in India.

The Ghost Map: The Story of London's Most Terrifying Epidemic and How It Changed Science, Cities, and the Modern World. Steven Johnson. (2006), Riverhead Books.

John Snow and cholera are important to the history of epidemiology. *The Ghost Map* is a highly readable narrative centered on the work of Dr. John Snow. It's the summer of 1854, and London is just emerging as one of the first modern cities in the world. But lacking the infrastructure—garbage removal, clean water, sewers—necessary to support its rapidly expanding population, the city hosts a waterborne contagion although no one at the time understood its nature or its pathways of human infection. As the cholera outbreak takes hold, a physician and a local curate are spurred to action, ultimately solving the most pressing medical riddle of their time. In multidisciplinary thinking, Johnson illuminates the intertwined histories and interconnectedness of the spread of disease, contagion theory, the rise of cities, and elements of the basis of scientific inquiry.

How forest loss is leading to a rise in human disease. Jim Robbins (2016), Yale Environment 360.

Jim Robbins, author or *The Wonder of Birds*, reports on the growing body of scientific evidence showing that the felling of tropical and other forests creates optimal conditions for the spread of mosquito-borne scourges, including malaria and dengue. Primates and other animals are also spreading disease from cleared forests to people. https://e360.yale.edu/features/how_forest_loss_is_leading_to_a_rise_in_human_disease_malaria_zika_climate_change

Could Yellow Fever Return to the US, Peter Hotez and Kristy Murray, (2013), PLOS
Author's summary: We need to seriously evaluate the risks of the major southern cities of the US, including Houston, but also New Orleans, Tampa, and Miami for their vulnerability to *Aedes*-transmitted arbovirus infections, such as yellow fever. As we have pointed out, cities such as Houston have emerged as important endemic zones for neglected tropical diseases. While we are aware that US urban areas may not be as vulnerable to yellow fever as Memphis was more than a century ago, there is still an important risk that needs to be considered as part of our national emergency preparedness, particularly in light of an emerging dengue problem (i.e., another *Ae. Aegypti* mosquito transmitted virus infection) in Houston and other southern coastal US areas. http://blogs.plos.org/speakingofmedicine/2013/12/05/could-yellow-fever-return-to-the-united-states/

The American Plague: The Untold Story of Yellow Fever, the Epidemic that Shaped Our History. M C Crosby, (2006), Berkeley Books.
In a summer of panic and death in 1878, more than half the population of Memphis, Tenn., fled the raging yellow fever epidemic, which finally waned when cooler weather set in. The disease had been transmitted by the *Aedes aegypti* mosquito, which came in swarms on ships from the Caribbean or West Africa. This account has a narrower scope than James Dickerson's recent *Yellow Fever*, focusing on the Memphis tragedy, but journalist Crosby offers a forceful narrative of a disease's ravages and the quest to find its cause and cure. Crosby is particularly good at evoking the horrific conditions in Memphis, "a city of corpses" and rife with illness characterized by high fever, black vomit and hemorrhaging, treated by primitive methods. Crosby also relates arresting tales of heroism, such as how two nuns returned to the quarantined city from a vacation to nurse the victims. The author profiles scientists, some of whom died in their fight to identify the cause of this deadly disease. She also describes more recent outbreaks in Africa: yellow fever is making a frightening comeback despite the existence of a vaccine.

Yellow Fever: A Deadly Disease Poised to Kill Again. James Dickerson. (2006), Prometheus Books.
In a vividly told narrative, filled with poignant and graphic scenes culled from historical archives, Dickerson recounts the history of one of the most feared diseases in the United States. From the late eighteenth to the early twentieth century, yellow fever killed Americans by the tens of thousands in the Northeast and throughout the South. In Memphis alone, five thousand people died in 1878. Dickerson describes how public health officials gradually eliminated the disease from this country, so that by the mid 1950s it had ceased to be of much concern to the public at large. However, to this day no cure has been found. As a mosquito-borne viral infection, yellow fever is impervious to antibiotics, and it continues to wreak havoc in parts of South America and Africa. Focusing on the present, Dickerson discusses

the potential threat of yellow fever as a biological warfare agent. Also of concern to public health researchers is the effect of global warming on mosquito populations. Even a one-to-two degree warming enables disease-bearing mosquitoes to move into areas once protected by colder weather. He concludes with a discussion of current precautionary efforts based on interviews with experts and analysis of available studies.

Adult Mosquito Ecology in Southwestern Georgia. Eva Whitehead. (2009), University of Georgia thesis.

Author's summary: Understanding the ecology of mosquitoes is important for implementing control measures and explaining mosquito-borne disease prevalence. I compared mosquito population dynamics to selected weather variables and land use/ cover in a longleaf pine dominated landscape on the Gulf Coastal Plain of Georgia. Important factors for determining mosquito presence/ absence were precipitation, temperature, humidity, and drought index. *Aedes albopictus* and *Culex* spp. mosquitoes were associated with sites that had the most anthropogenic influence, while *Coquillettidia perturbans* and *Psorophora ferox* were associated with natural land cover such as wetlands and forested land. Arbovirus testing yielded one isolation of West Nile virus and three isolations of Potosi virus. This low arbovirus prevalence is likely due to the diversity of the wildlife in the area or factors related to the bird community, which typically serves as a reservoir for arboviruses. Examination of mosquito host-feeding patterns showed the mosquitoes collected predominantly fed on white-tailed deer. https://getd.libs.uga.edu/pdfs/whitehead_eva_a_200912_ms.pdf

History of domestication and spread of Aedes Egyptii—a review. Jeffrey Powell and Walter Tabachnick, (2013), *Mem. Insti. Oswaldo Cruz.*

The adaptation of insect vectors of human diseases to breed in human habitats (domestication) is one of the most important phenomena in medical entomology. Considerable data are available on the vector mosquito *Aedes aegypti* in this regard and here we integrate the available information including genetics, behaviour, morphology, ecology and biogeography of the mosquito, with human history. We emphasize the tremendous amount of variation possessed by *Ae. aegypti* for virtually all traits considered. Typological thinking needs to be abandoned to reach a realistic and comprehensive understanding of this important vector of yellow fever, dengue and Chikungunya. https://www.ncbi.nlm.nih.gov/pmc/articles/PMC4109175/

Global Risk Mapping for major diseases transmitted by Aedes egyptii and Aedes albopictus. Samson Leta et. al. (2018), *Int. J. Infectious Dis.*

Despite the fact that many arboviral diseases share the same vectors and often coexist, previous studies have focused on mapping the distribution of one or two diseases separately. In the present study, data from publicly available sources on the occurrence of major arboviral diseases (Zika, dengue fever, chikungunya, yellow fever, and Rift Valley fever) have been compiled and spatially mapped. The risk mapping indicated multiple occurrences of arboviral diseases, with 49% (123/250) of countries reporting two or more diseases in common. The maps include data on vector suitability and disease occurrence to provide decision-makers with a more complete picture when considering coordinated prevention and control programmes. Recognizing that arboviral diseases have common vectors and transmission features, the risk maps can be used to plan interventions in a cost-effective manner https://www.ijidonline.com/article/S1201-9712(17)30308-9/pdf

The Veterbrate Fauna at Ichauway, Baker County, GA. Lora Smith et. al. (2006), Southeastern Naturalist, 5:599-620.

Authors' summary: Less than 4% of the once extensive Pinus palustris (longleaf pine) ecosystem remains today. Although longleaf pine habitats are recognized for their high species diversity, few published accounts document the vertebrate faunas of remaining tracts. Here we report on the vertebrate species richness of Ichauway, an 11,300-ha property in Baker County, GA. The property includes ca. 7300 ha of longleaf pine with native ground cover, along with more than 30 seasonal wetlands and ca. 45 km of riparian habitat associated with Ichawaynochaway Creek, Big Cypress Creek, and the Flint River. The fauna includes 61 species of fish, 31 amphibians, 53 reptiles, 191 birds, and 41 mammals. Despite the relative isolation of the property from other natural ecosystems, the vertebrate fauna of Ichauway is remarkably diverse and may offer an example of reference conditions to guide restoration of longleaf pine forests, associated seasonal wetlands, and riparian areas elsewhere in the southeastern US. https://www.researchgate.net/publication/250069424_The_Vertebrate_Fauna_of_Ichauway_Baker_County_GA

The Invisible and Indeterminable Value of Ecology: from Malaria Control to Ecological Research in the American south. Albert Way. (2015), *Isis,* 106: 310-336.

Author's Abstract: This essay concerns the history of the Emory University Field Station, a malaria research station in southwest Georgia that operated from 1939 to 1958. Using the tools of environmental history and the history of science, it examines the station's founding, its fieldwork, and its place within the broader history of malaria control, eradication, and research. A joint effort of Emory University, the US Public Health Service, and the Communicable Disease Center (CDC), this station was closely aligned with a broader movement of ideas about tropical diseases across the globe, but it also offers a case study of how science in the field can veer from mainstream thinking and official policy. As the CDC and other disease-fighting organizations were moving toward a global strategy of malaria eradication through the use of DDT, the Emory Field Station developed a post-sanitarian approach to malaria. Drawing on resistance among American conservationists to environmental transformation in the name of malaria control, the station's staff embraced the science and worldview of ecology in an effort to lighten public health's hand on the land and to link human health to the environment in innovative, if sometimes opaque, ways. This essay, then, argues that the Emory Field Station represents an early confluence of ecology with the biomedical sciences, something very similar to what is now the important discipline of disease ecology.

Rats lice and history. Hans Zinsser. (1935, revised edition 2007), Transaction Publishers.

Zinsser's goal in *Rats, Lice and History* was to bring science, philosophy, and literature together to establish the importance of disease, and especially epidemic infectious disease, as a major force in human affairs. Zinsser cast his work as the «biography» of a disease. In his view, infectious disease simply represented an attempt of a living organism to survive. This classic work is devoted to a discussion of the biology of typhus and history of typhus fever in human affairs. This book opened up a whole new field of study, and many such works followed.

Spillover: Animal Infections and the Next Human Pandemic. David Quammam, (2012), WW Norton.

Science writer Quammen schools us zoonotic diseases, animal infections that sicken humans, such as rabies, Ebola, influenza, and West Nile. Zoonoses can escalate rapidly into global pandemics when human-to-human transmission occurs, and Quammen wants us to understand disease dynamics and exactly what's at stake. Drawing on the truly dramatic history of virology, he profiles brave and stubborn viral sleuths and recounts his own hair-raising field adventures, including helping capture large fruit bats in Bangladesh. Along the way, Quammen explains how devilishly difficult it is to trace the origins of a zoonosis and explicates the hidden process by which pathogens spill over from their respective reservoir hosts (water fowl, mosquitoes, pigs, bats, monkeys) and infect humans. Zoonotic diseases are now on the rise due to our increasing population, deforestation, fragmented ecosystems, and factory farming.

Geohydrology of the Lower Apalachicola-Chattahoochee-Flint River Basin, Southwestern Georgia, Northwestern Florida, and Southeastern Alabama. USGS *Scientific Investigations Report, 2006.* https://pubs.usgs.gov/sir/2006/5070/pdf/sir06-5070.pdf

Pinhook: Finding Wholeness in a Fragmented Land. Janisse Ray, (2005), Chelsea Green.

The author of *Ecology of a Cracker Childhood* celebrates South Georgia and Florida's humble Pinhook Swamp in an impassioned and poetic account of the area's environmental fragmentation and its subsequent restoration. The swamp, "170,000 acres of dreary dismal... too deep for a human to wade in, too shallow for a boat to draw," and populated by flies and mosquitoes, is the corridor connecting the Okefenokee Swamp with Osceola National Park. Most of its acres have now been purchased and protected, but environmentalists' work, Ray warns, is not finished yet. Ray meditates on the meaning of silence ("Silence is the ghost of the panther" that used to populate Pinhook), the animals of the area (black bears, bees, frogs) and the people dedicated to saving it. She also includes poems, a Native American blessing and italicized reflections on the land's fragmentation ("the separation of habitat in a landscape . . . chopping a wild place into pieces") by roads, logging, mining and developments. Her moving book is a tribute to a small but crucial wild place and a call for readers to help preserve it and others like it.

Cadillac Desert: the American West and its Disappearing Water. Marc Reisner. (1986), revised 1993. *Viking Press.*

Chapter Nine. *The Peanut Farmer and the Pork Barrel.* While most of *Cadillac Desert* is devoted to engineering water in the dry west, Reisner makes an exception for the southeast despite its relatively rain-rich climate. It too has massive water projects, and politicians typically form alliances with western governors and members of congress. Jimmy Carter, a politically naïve but trained engineer, wanted to chop environmentally questionable pork barrel water projects out of the federal budget. The term "pork barrel" is rooted in the south's racism as slave owners would roll out a barrel of salt pork on special occasions for the slaves in order to watch the nearly starved people scramble for it. Carter earmarked 18 projects to be cut, and later added others. Through massive outcry and political maneuvering by both parties, in the end none were cut. One dam project was proposed for the Little Tennessee, the last free flowing river in the east, home of the Cherokee and countless Native artifacts. It too was built, in spite of violations of NEPA and ESA, and its completion destroyed a beautiful valley, once again displacing the Cherokee. In the end none of Carters cuts were undertaken, despite his correct assessments of the projects as environmentally damaging and a waste of money.

7 THE RIO GRANDE NUCLEAR RIFT BETWEEN US

On the Mesa, John Nichols, (2005), Gibbs Smith.

To the average eye, the mesa (in northwestern New Mexico) is a wasteland, a sagebrush plain with little appeal. To Nichols, author of The Sterile Cuckoo and environmental activist, it is a place of refuge and renewal, a haven of tranquility in a hectic life. Seasonally, the mesa explodes with growth. The bone-dry stock pond of spring fills during summer rains, gradually receding in fall. Spadefoot toads, clam shrimp and other creatures hasten to complete their life cycles while there is water; birds (including a pair of bald eagles) are abundant. The author gives marvelous descriptions of a flash flood, of thunderstorms circling the mesa (only to drop rain on distant peaks), of brilliant starlit nights. On occasion, his solitude is punctured by surveyors, hunters, military aircraft and one kindred spirit. Nichols sides with a handful of sheepmen who want to improve pasturage, but opposes a faction that proposes to develop this fragile land. His book is a beautifully written appreciation of the wilderness.

Making of the Atomic Bomb, Richard Rhodes, (2012, reprint Edition), Simon and Schuster.

Twenty-five years after its initial publication, *The Making of the Atomic Bomb* remains the definitive history of nuclear weapons and the Manhattan Project. From the turn-of-the-century discovery of nuclear energy to the dropping of the first bombs on Japan, Richard Rhodes's Pulitzer Prize-winning book details the science, the people, and the socio-political realities that led to the development of the atomic bomb. The book introduces the players in this saga of physics, politics, and human psychology—from FDR and Einstein to the visionary scientists who pioneered quantum theory and the application of thermonuclear fission, including Planck, Szilard, Bohr, Oppenheimer, Fermi, Teller, Meitner, von Neumann, and Lawrence.

Which Countries Have Nuclear Weapons and How Big Are Their Arsenals, Kirstein Schmidt and Bill Marsh, (Dec 2016), *New York Times.*

On the eve of Donald Trump's losing the popular vote and winning the gerrymandered electoral college vote to take office as US President, the New York Times published maps and counts over time of nuclear weapons arsenals. The US and Russia with 7000 and 7,300 active weapons respectively vastly outnumber all other nuclear nations. In spite of this, Donald Trump aims to build up more weapons during his administration. https://www.nytimes.com/interactive/2016/12/23/world/nuclear-weapon-countries.html

Her, Infinite, Sawnie Morris, (2016), New Issues Poetry and Prose.

Sawnie Morris is a long-time leading light of Amigos Bravos and a celebrated poet of Taos, NM, now the poet laureate of Taos. Amigos Bravos website link: https://amigosbravos.org

Britt Runyon (Huggins) photography site with nature and rafting images. http://brittrunyon.com/nature-art/

A Near Disaster at a Federal Nuclear Weapons Laboratory Takes a Hidden Toll on America's Arsenal. Patrick Malone, (2017), The Center for Public Integrity, Six-Part Series on Nuclear Negligence. https://apps.publicintegrity.org/nuclear-negligence/near-disaster/

Hiroshima, John Hersey, (1945), *The New Yorker.* https://www.newyorker.com/magazine/1946/08/31/hiroshima

The Plutonium Files, Eileen Welsome, (2010), Delta.

From Publisher's Weekly: In a deeply shocking and important expose, Welsome takes the lid off the thousands of secret, government-sponsored radiation experiments performed on unsuspecting human "guinea pigs" at US hospitals, universities and military bases during the Cold War. This riveting report greatly expands on Welsome's Pulitzer Prize-winning 1994 articles in the Albuquerque Tribune, which told how 18 men, women and children scattered in hospital wards across the country were injected with plutonium by US Army and Manhattan Project doctors between 1945 and 1947. As Welsome demonstrates, the scope of the government's radiation experimentation program went much further. She documents how, between 1951 and 1962, the army, navy and air force used military troops in flights through radioactive clouds, "flashblindness" studies and tests to measure radioisotopes in their body fluids. Additionally, she reveals that cancer patients were subjected to total-body irradiation, and women, children, the poor, minorities, prisoners and the mentally disabled were targeted for radioisotope "tracer" studies, frequently without their consent and in some cases suffering excruciating side effects and premature deaths. In 1993, Energy Secretary Hazel O'Leary launched a campaign to make public all documents relating to the experiments, which had been kept secret. Welsome cogently argues that O'Leary's efforts resulted in a Republican vendetta that led to her ouster. Written with commendable restraint, this engrossing narrative draws liberally on declassified memos, briefings, phone calls, interviews and medical records to convey the enormity of the irradiation program and the bad science behind the flawed and dangerous tests and to document the government's systematic cover-up. Anyone who cares about America's history, moral health and future should read this book.

Background radiation and medical imaging radiation: http://www.fda.gov/radiationemittingproducts/radiationemittingproductsandprocedures/medicalimaging/medicalx-rays/ucm115329.htm

Background radiation: http://www.nrc.gov/about-nrc/radiation/around-us/sources/nat-bg-sources.html

Plutonium and the Rio Grande: Environmental change and contamination in the Nuclear Age*, William deGraf, (1994), Oxford.*
This book details an extensive study of plutonium in the Rio Grande watershed. See especially Ch 12, Lessons and Conclusions, pp 226-239.

Radiation Effects Research Foundation. Hiroshima and Nagasaki Atomic Bomb Survivors.
The principal focus of RERF's research program is to study radiation effects in the survivors of the atomic bombings of Hiroshima and Nagasaki. Several fixed cohorts and sub-cohorts have been established to provide epidemiological and clinical data on the health status and mortality of the survivors and their children. Laboratory-based research in the fields of radiobiology, immunology, genetics, and molecular epidemiology is conducted to interpret numerous findings and contribute to understanding of disease-induction mechanisms. https://www.rerf.or.jp/en/programs/general_research_e/

The Great Hiroshima Coverup, Greg Mitchell, (August 2011) The Nation. http://www.thenation.com/blog/162543/great-hiroshima-cover#

Atomic Coverup: Two US Soldiers, Hiroshima and Nagasaki, and the Greatest Movie Never Made, Greg Mitchell, (2011), Sinclair Books.

Mitchell, co-author of the classic *Hiroshima in America* and eleven other books, now reveals the full story, based on new research—from the Truman Library to Nagasaki. Along the way the book tells the story of our "nuclear entrapment"—from Hiroshima to Fukushima. How did this cover-up happen? Why? And what did the two military officers, Daniel McGovern and Herbert Sussan, try to do about it, for decades? *Atomic Cover-Up* opens this way: "This is the story of twenty hours of film footage, blazing with color, shot in Hiroshima and Nagasaki in early 1946 by a US military crew, that would change the lives of many people, including two American soldiers, and me. Its effect on us, and others, is deep and mysterious, because the film was hidden for decades and almost no one could see it, although that is also why its influence on each of us was so profound. While this unique and disturbing color film languished in obscurity, the atomic bombings fell into 'a hole in human history,' as the writer Mary McCarthy observed, and a costly nuclear arms race ensued. Nuclear threats of all kinds plague us to this day."

The Crazy Iris and Other Stories of the Atomic Aftermath, Kenzaburo Oe, Editor, (1994), Grove Press.

Edited by one of Japan's leading and internationally acclaimed writers, this collection of short stories was compiled to mark the fortieth anniversary of the August 1945 atomic bombings of Hiroshima and Nagasaki. Here some of Japan's best and most representative writers chronicle and re-create the impact of this tragedy on the daily lives of peasants, city professionals, artists, children, and families. From the "crazy" iris that grows out of season to the artist who no longer paints in color, the simple details described in these superbly crafted stories testify to the enormity of change in Japanese life, as well as in the future of our civilization. Included are "The Crazy Iris" by Masuji Ibuse, "Summer Flower" by Tamiki Hara, "The Land of Heart's Desire" by Tamiki Hara, "Human Ashes" by Katsuzo Oda, "Fireflies" by Yoka Ota, "The Colorless Paintings" by Ineko Sata, "The Empty Can" by Kyoko Hayashi, "The House of Hands" by Mitsuharu Inoue, and "The Rite" by Hiroko Takenishi.

Weapons of Mass Destruction, Brugge et. al., (2007), Am J Public Health 97:1595-1600.

Development of risk maps to minimize uranium exposures in the Navajo Churchrock mining district, deLemos J et. al., (2009) Environmental Health 8:29.

Yellow Dirt: an American Story of a Poisoned Land and a People Betrayed, Judith Pasternak,(2010), Free Press.

This book contains strong reporting and clear writing on contamination of indigenous especially Dineh people by an LA Times investigative journalist.

Uranium mining and lung cancer in Navajo men, Samet et. al., (1984) New England Journal of Medicine 310:1481-1484.

Navajo Uranium Workers and Effects of Occupational Illnesses, Susan Dawson (1992), Human Organization 51:381-287.

Author's Abstract: Fifty-five Navajo uranium workers and residents from the Navajo Reservation in Arizona and New Mexico were interviewed in a community study to determine the psychosocial effects of uncompensated occupational illnesses. Summary findings indicate that psychological trauma, resulting from long-term occupational illnesses and environmental degradation, was as serious a repercussion as physical trauma from work-related exposures. The perceptions of Navajo workers, their families, and residents are presented with regard to the uranium mining and milling processes which occurred on the reservation between the 1940s and the 1980s. Because the workers and residents were never informed about the dangers of radiation, they were not able to make rational decisions regarding their health and employment; consequently, they felt a sense of betrayal by both the government and their employers. A reduction in the incidence of occupational illnesses and death among the Navajo may have occurred had prevention and detection been provided. Moreover, unique Navajo cultural beliefs and economic factors also impacted whether or not workers and families accessed health, legal, and social services. http://sfaajournals.net/doi/abs/10.17730/humo.51.4.e02484g513501t35?code=apan-site

Uranium mining and lung cancer among Navajo men in New Mexico and Arizona, 1969-1996, Gilliland et. al., (2000), J Occup Env Med 42:278-83.

New Scientist http://www.newscientist.com/article/dn23665-nuclear-bomb-tests-reveal-brain-regeneration-in-humans.html#.Ub88wBbGXCE

Refuge, an Unnatural History of Family and Place, Terry Tempest Williams, (2015 Reprint Edition), Vintage.

In the spring of 1983 Terry Tempest Williams learned that her mother was dying of cancer. That same season, The Great Salt Lake began to rise to record heights, threatening the Bear River Migratory Bird Refuge and the herons, owls, and snowy egrets that Williams, a poet and naturalist, had come to gauge her life by. One event was nature at its most random, the other a by-product of rogue technology: Terry's mother, and Terry herself, had been exposed to the fallout of atomic bomb tests in the 1950s. As it interweaves these narratives of dying and accommodation, *Refuge* transforms tragedy into a document of renewal and spiritual grace, resulting in a work that has become a classic.

8 RIO GRANDE: THE GREAT RIVER DOES NOT DIVIDE

Thinking Like a Watershed, Voices from the West. Jack Loeffler and Celestia Loeffler, Editors, (2012), University of New Mexico Press.

Thinking Like a Watershed points our understanding of our relationship to the land in new directions. It is shaped by the bioregional visions of the great explorer John Wesley Powell, who articulated the notion that the arid

American West should be seen as a mosaic of watersheds, and the pioneering ecologist Aldo Leopold, who put forward the concept of bringing conscience to bear within the realm of "the land ethic." Produced in conjunction with the documentary radio series entitled *Watersheds as Commons*, this book comprises essays and interviews from a diverse group of south westerners including members of Tewa, Tohono O'odham, Hopi, Navajo, Hispano, and Anglo cultures. Their varied cultural perspectives are shaped by consciousness and resilience through having successfully endured the aridity and harshness of southwestern environments over time.

Sky Islands of North America, Matt Skroch, (2008) *Terrain,* winter-spring issue. https://www.terrain.org/articles/21/skroch.htm

The Southwest Environmental Center defends wildlife and places in the Southwest. The link below gives a summary of the work on recovery of the Lobo, the Mexican Wolf. http://www.wildmesquite.org/what-we-do/desert-lands-wildlife/mexican-wolves

A Sand County Almanac, Thinking Like a Mountain, Aldo Leopold, excerpt in link. http://www.eco-action.org/dt/thinking.html

Trophic cascade overview with examples: https://www.nature.com/scitable/knowledge/library/trophic-cascades-across-diverse-plant-ecosystems-80060347

Decade of the Wolf: Returning the Wild to Yellowstone, Douglas Smith and Gary Ferguson, (2012, updated revised edition), Lyons Press.

Co-authored by a leader of the Yellowstone Wolf Project, Doug Smith, this definitive book recounts the years since the wolves' return to Yellowstone. "Respectful and intriguing, this in an indispensable historical document on the West, all the more so for the elegance of the story and the clarity of writing." —Rick Bass, author of *The New Wolves* and *The Ninemile Wolves*

The Tenuous Fate of the Southwest's Last Jaguars, Richard Mahler, (2016), *High Country News* May 30. https://www.hcn.org/issues/48.9/the-tenuous-fate-of-the-southwests-last-jaguars

Otero mesa: Preseving America's Wildest Grassland. Gregory McNamee (text), Stephen Strom and Stephen Capra (photography), 2011, University of New Mexico Press.

Full-color images by renowned photographers Stephen Strom and Stephen Capra unite with text by nature and geography writer Gregory McNamee to document the subtle landscape of 1.2 million acres of remote Chihuahuan Desert grassland in southern New Mexico. Home to many species of wildlife and native plants, Otero Mesa is a place of extraordinary beauty and ecological significance faced with the increasing threat of oil and gas development that has plagued the Rocky Mountain West.

Tainted Earth: Smelters, Public Health, and the Environment, Marianne Sullivan, (2014), Rutgers University Press.

Thoroughly grounded in extensive archival research, *Tainted Earth* traces the rise of public health concerns about nonferrous smelting in the western United States, focusing on three major facilities: Tacoma, Washington; El Paso, Texas; and Bunker Hill, Idaho. Marianne Sullivan documents the response from community residents, public health scientists, the industry, and the government to pollution from smelters as well as the long road to protecting public health and the environment. Placing the environmental and public health aspects of smelting in historical context, the book connects local incidents to national stories on the regulation of airborne toxic metals.

Their Mines. Our Stories. Work, Environment, and Justice in ASARCO Impacted Communities. Lin Nelson and Anne Fischel. Evergreen State College.
　　This website contains case studies of ASARCOs effect on communities. It carries stories unknown or untold along with summaries of actions, lawsuits, and health studies. http://www.theirminesourstories.org/?cat=18

Epidemic Lead Absorption Near an Ore Smelter: the Role of Particulate Lead. Phillip Landrigan et. al., (1975), *New Engl J Med.*

Neuropsychological Dysfunction in Children with Chronic Low-level Lead Absorption. Phillip Landrigan, (1975), *Lancet.*
　　Earth Justice attorneys for plaintiffs Sierra Club, Amigos Bravos, Great Basin Resource, and Idaho Conservation League lawsuit against ASARCO filed by Mariana Chew. The 2008 document contains a history of the problems and actions against ASARCO up to that point. https://www.findforms.com/pdf_files/cand/201328/73.pdf

Formal Request for a Congressional Inquiry, posting by Annunciation House, El Paso. https://annunciationhouse.org/2009/10/22/gustavo-hickerson-congressional-inquiry/

The River Has Never Divided Us: A Border History of La Junta de los Rios. Jefferson Morgenthaler, (2004), University of Texas Press.
　　La Junta de los Rios straddles the border between Texas and Chihuahua, occupying the basin formed by the conjunction of the Rio Grande and the Rio Conchos. It is one of the oldest continuously inhabited settlements in the Chihuahuan Desert, ranking in age and dignity with the Anasazi pueblos of New Mexico. In the first comprehensive history of the region, Jefferson Morgenthaler traces the history of La Junta de los Rios from the formation of the Mexico-Texas border in the mid-19th century to the 1997 ambush shooting of teenage goatherd Esquiel Hernandez by US Marines performing drug interdiction in El Polvo, Texas. "Though it is scores of miles from a major highway, I found natives, soldiers, rebels, bandidos, heroes, scoundrels, drug lords, scalp hunters, medal winners, and mystics," writes Morgenthaler. "I found love, tragedy, struggle, and stories that have never been told." In telling the turbulent history of this remote valley oasis, he examines the consequences of a national border running through a community older than the invisible line that divides it.

War of a Thousand Deserts: Indian Raids and the US-Mexican War. Brian DeLay, (2009), Yale University Press.

In the early 1830s, after decades of relative peace, northern Mexicans and the Indigenous Nations whom they called "the barbarians" descended into a terrifying cycle of violence. For the next fifteen years, owing in part to changes unleashed by American expansion, warriors launched devastating attacks across ten Mexican states. Raids and counter-raids claimed thousands of lives, ruined much of northern Mexico's economy, depopulated its countryside, and left man-made "deserts" in place of thriving settlements. Just as important, this vast interethnic war informed and emboldened US arguments in favor of seizing Mexican territory while leaving northern Mexicans too divided, exhausted, and distracted to resist the US invasion and subsequent occupation. Exploring Mexican, US citizen (diaries and captive narratives), and Indigenous (usually oral or pictorial) history plus diplomatic correspondence and congressional debates, *War of a Thousand Deserts* recovers the surprising and previously unrecognized ways in which economic, cultural, and political developments within native communities affected nineteenth-century nation-states. In the process this ambitious book offers a rich and often harrowing new narrative of the era when the United States seized half of Mexico's national territory.

Empire of the Summer Moon: Quanah Parker and the Rise and Fall of the Comanches. S. C. Gwynne, (2010), Schribner.

The war with the Comanche Nation (Numunuu) lasted four decades, in effect blocking the development of major areas of the new US nation west of the Mississippi. Gwynne's account delivers a narrative that encompasses Spanish colonialism, the Civil War, the destruction of the buffalo herds, and the arrival of the railroads. Against this backdrop Gwynne presents the compelling drama of Cynthia Ann Parker, a nine-year-old girl who was kidnapped by Comanches from the far Texas frontier in 1836. She grew to love her captors and became infamous as the "White Squaw" who refused to return until her tragic capture by Texas Rangers in 1860. More famous still was her son Quanah, a warrior who was never defeated and whose guerrilla wars in the Texas Panhandle made him a legend. One of the important points of the Treaty of Guadelupe Hidalgo establishing the border between Mexico and the US was control of the Indigenous people, primarily the Comanche and Apache Nations.

Will Mexico Get Half of Its Territory Back?, Enrique Krauze, (2017), *New York Times Op-Ed.*

The treaty of Guadalupe Hidalgo signed in 1848 to establish the border between Mexico and the US is examined in this well-informed Op-ed piece, including the issues surrounding its signing and a move to overturn it. https://www.nytimes.com/2017/04/06/opinion/will-mexico-get-half-of-its-territory-back.html?action=click&pgtype=Homepage&clickSource=

story-heading&module=opinion-c-col-right-region&region=opinion-c-col-right-region&WT.nav=opinion-c-col-right-region

Rights of Nature: A Legal Revolution That Could Save the World, David Boyd, (2017), ECW Press.

Lawyers from California to New York are fighting to gain legal rights for chimpanzees and killer whales, and lawmakers are ending the era of keeping these intelligent animals in captivity. In Hawaii and India, judges have recognized that endangered species—from birds to lions—have the legal right to exist. Around the world, more and more laws are being passed recognizing that ecosystems—rivers, forests, mountains, and more—have legally enforceable rights.

Reining in the Rio Grande: People, Land, and Water. Fred Phillips et. al. (2011), University of New Mexico Press.

This study examines human interactions with the Rio Grande from prehistoric time to the present day and explores what possibilities remain for the desert river.

A Great Aridness, Climate Change and the Future of the American Southwest. William Debuys, (2013 reprint edition), Oxford University Press.

"DeBuys's research takes place in the field, one of the real strengths of this book. In lyrical prose rich in place and politics, his stories take us from the Navajo reservation to research labs. . . . A Great Aridness is both fascinating and frightening." —Orion

The Goldsboro NC Broken Arrow Incident, East Carolina University presentation by Jack Revelle, weapons disposal expert during the incident. http://www.ecu.edu/cs-admin/news/brokenarrow.cfm

Murder City: Ciudad Juarez and the Global Economy's New Killing Fields, Charles Bouden. (2011), Nation Books.

In *Murder City*, Charles Bowden-one of the few journalists who spent extended periods of time in Juarez-has written an extraordinary account of what happens when a city disintegrates. Interweaving stories of its inhabitants-a beauty queen who was raped, a repentant hitman, a journalist fleeing for his life-with a broader meditation on the town's descent into anarchy, Bowden believed Juarez's culture of violence will not only worsen, but inevitably spread north. The inhabitants of Ciudad Juarez and El Paso, once a single city, hope he was not right.

Great river: The Rio Grande in North American History, Paul Horgan, (1991 two-volume set), Wesleyan.

Winner of both the Pulitzer Prize and Bancroft Prize for History, *Great River* was hailed as a literary masterpiece and enduring classic when it first appeared in 1954. It is an epic history of four civilizations—Native American, Spanish, Mexican, and Anglo-American—that people the Southwest through ten centuries or more in the case of Indigenous people. With the skill of a novelist, the veracity of a scholar, and the love of a long-time resident, Paul Horgan describes the Rio Grande, its role in human history, and the overlapping cultures that have grown up alongside it or entered into conflict over the land it traverses. Now in its fourth revised edition, *Great River* remains a monumental part of American historical writing.

Continental Crossroads: Remapping US—Mexico Borderlands, Samuel Truett and Elliot Young Editors, (2004), Duke University Press.

"Using new approaches and demonstrating the results of extensive research into the archives of both Mexico and the United States, this path breaking book provides a new perspective on our common frontier legacies as well as surprising borderland stories involving Chinese immigrants and African American colonizers, transnational identities, and borderland 'body politics.' These highly readable original essays comprise a new history of the US-Mexico borderlands, one that is enhanced by poignant human stories. This seminal volume should stimulate new studies of US-Mexico border relations in the years to come. Editors Samuel Truett and Elliott Young are to be congratulated on their accomplishment."—Howard R. Lamar, Sterling Professor Emeritus of History, Yale University

Enduring Acequias, Wisdom of the Land, Knowledge of Water, Juan Estevan Arellano, (2014), University of New Mexico Press.

While this book begins with northern New Mexico ancient irrigation methods, it applies to all arid regions. For generations the Río Embudo watershed in northern New Mexico has been the home of Juan Estevan Arellano and his ancestors. From this unique perspective Arellano explores the ways people use water in dry places around the world. Touching on the Middle East, Europe, Mexico, and South America before circling back to New Mexico, Arellano makes a case for preserving the *acequia* irrigation system and calls for a future that respects the ecological limitations of the land.

Rivers of Empire: Water, Aridity, and the Growth of the American West, Donald Worster, (1992 reprint edition), Oxford.

Now a classic work on western water, Wallace Stegner writes: "Worster is an eloquent, often passionate historian. . . . This important book, sure to be furiously debated, is a history of the West in terms of its most essential resource, water. . . . It examines how manipulation of water has combined with frontier myths, expectations, and illusions, some of them carefully cultivated by interested parties, to create the ambiguous modern West."

Tecate Journals, Seventy Days on the Rio Grande, Keith Bowden, (2007), Mountaineers Books.

The Rio Grande is a national border, a water source, a dangerous rapid with house-sized boulders, a nature refuge, a garbage dump, and a playground, depending on where you are on its 1885-mile course. Journalist Keith Bowden decided to become the first person to travel the entire length of the Rio as it forms the border between America and Mexico. This is his fascinating account of the journey by bike, canoe, and raft along one of North America's most overlooked resources. From illegal immigrants and drug runners trying to make it into America to the border patrol working to stop them; from human coyotes—smugglers who help people navigate their way into the United States—to encounters with real coyotes, mountain lions, and other flora and fauna, Bowden reveals a side of America that few of us ever see. The border between the US and Mexico is, in many ways, a country unto itself, where inhabitants share more in common with fellow riverside dwellers than they do with the rest of their countrymen.

9 WE CONTINUE

The Beautiful Bronx 1920-1950, Lloyd Ultan, (1988), Crown Publishing.

In this photo history book Gerry Segal can be seen as a young boy holding his cowboy hat and standing by the Bronx River. Later Gerry Segal wrote the Bronx River Song about the restoration of the Bronx River. https://www.reverbnation.com/gerrysegal/playlist (link may not directly work).

He and Linda Cox, retired head of the Bronx River Alliance, appear in this news video. https://www.youtube.com/watch?v=6cM0_txkC7A

Behind the Scenes: The Inside Story of the Watershed Agreement. Nancy Burnett, (1997-2003), an oral history project partially funded by an Education Grant from the Catskills Watershed Corporation in partnership with the NYC DEP. Read transcripts and hear audio excerpts from all 12 interviews, conducted in the late 1990s and early 2000s by Nancy Burnett Productions, with assistance from Virginia Scheer. This series offers insights into the complicated negotiations, leaders in the agreement many of whom are underappreciated or not credited in public news stories, i.e. less Bobby Kennedy, Jr. and Al Appleton and more Marilyn Gelber. http://cwconline.org/a-history-of-the-moa/

ABOUT THE AUTHOR

After living and working in New York City for many years, Diana Hartel took up a somewhat nomadic life, traveling to write on ecosystem health and to paint in wild places throughout the United States and British Columbia, Canada. She graduated from Columbia University with a doctorate in epidemiology and concentrations in infectious diseases and environment-related chronic diseases. She has held faculty positions at Columbia University and Einstein College of Medicine in New York City, and has published widely for biomedical journals, including, as a co-author, in The New England Journal of Medicine. Additionally, she served at the National Institutes of Health in Bethesda, Maryland for three years, chairing inter-agency projects with the Centers for Disease Control and Prevention. She created two non-profit organizations, Bronx Community Works in New York in 1993 and Madrona Arts in Oregon in 2006. Both organizations addressed issues of social and environmental justice. The Oregon-based Madrona Arts primarily employed arts to raise awareness of ecosystems and efforts to restore lives within them, human and non-human.

Made in the USA
Lexington, KY
07 September 2019